DEVELOPMENTS IN
HYDRAULIC ENGINEERING—3

CONTENTS OF VOLUMES 1 AND 2

Volume 1

Volume 2

DEVELOPMENTS IN HYDRAULIC ENGINEERING—3

Edited by

P. NOVAK

Emeritus Professor of Civil and Hydraulic Engineering, University of Newcastle upon Tyne, UK

ELSEVIER APPLIED SCIENCE PUBLISHERS
LONDON and NEW YORK

ELSEVIER APPLIED SCIENCE PUBLISHERS LTD
Crown House, Linton Road, Barking, Essex IG11 8JU, England

Sole Distributor in the USA and Canada
ELSEVIER SCIENCE PUBLISHING CO., INC.
52 Vanderbilt Avenue, New York, NY 10017, USA

British Library Cataloguing in Publication Data

Developments in hydraulic engineering.—3
1. Hydraulic engineering
627   TC145

ISBN 0-85334-375-6

WITH 5 TABLES AND 141 ILLUSTRATIONS

© ELSEVIER APPLIED SCIENCE PUBLISHERS LTD 1985

$$D$$
$$627$$
$$DEV$$

Photoset in Malta by Interprint Limited
Printed in Great Britain by Page Bros. (Norwich) Limited

PREFACE

In preparing this, the third volume of *Developments in Hydraulic Engineering* the editor has followed the previously stated aim of providing an outlet where individual chapters are an authoritative, comprehensive and up-to-date review of the state-of-the-art of an area, treated by authors who are themselves active in the subject and have significantly contributed to it.

It is further intended that these statements should be considerably longer than papers in technical and scientific journals, yet shorter than books or monographs. The first two volumes of the series dealt with ten subjects loosely or closely related to the design of hydraulic structures — starting with the role and some applications of computational hydraulics, developments in the design of irrigation structures and related sediment transport problems and continuing with vibrations of structures in general and gates in particular, aeration phenomena and developments in the design of spillways and energy dissipation at high dams.

There are, of course, a great many other types and aspects of hydraulic structures. Some of these are treated together with *some* selected topics in the broad context of river and coastal engineering which is the main theme of this third volume.

The increasing emphasis on the need to understand and deal with contaminant transport in rivers and estuaries prompted the editor to seek a comprehensive statement of dispersion in rivers in coastal waters. The first chapter thus deals in some detail with the physical principles involved in the process and the resulting dispersion equations. This is followed by a closely related chapter on the methods available for the numerical solution and computation of dispersion including perspectives in dispersion research and modelling. The third chapter deals with new developments in the design and operation of one type of structure closely associated with contaminant transport — the sea outfall. Although the coverage of this subject in the chapter is fairly broad, the emphasis is on new advances made in the analysis and handling of the important problem of sea water intrusion into the outfalls. The fourth chapter has as its topic flood routing in rivers. As the methods of flood routing based on the complete dynamic wave equations as well as those based on kinematic wave, storage, diffusion analogy and empirical methods have in the past been fairly extensively discussed elsewhere, the author, although touching on these aspects, concentrates on the development and application of a complete diffusion wave model of flood routing based on strict hydraulic principles.

The last three chapters of this volume turn to some other aspects of river and coastal engineering and related structures. Chapter 5 gives an overview of ice engineering in the context of river engineering, reviewing ice properties, ice formation on rivers, its observation and forecasting and its effect on river flow and structures. Chapter 6 looks at inland waterways, reviewing the reasons for their renaissance and the present state of integration of the European waterway network and problems associated with the modern concepts of multipurpose utilisation of inland waterways. This is followed by a review of some new developments in design of locks and high head navigation structures and the design of inland ports. The last chapter is a logical continuation of the navigation topic to the design of sea ports and harbours. After referring fairly briefly to the wave climate the chapter deals mainly with the sea harbour layout as influenced by hydraulic parameters and its physical and mathematical modelling and with new findings in breakwater design; navigation and sediment aspects are also dealt with.

The editor is aware that complete uniformity in style and presentation by individual authors has not been achieved — indeed this was not the objective. He is also aware that some 'chapters' offer a fairly complete coverage of the subject whereas others place an emphasis on the authors' own main contribution — even in this case, however, the text and the references provided should give a broader coverage. It is thus hoped that this volume presents an up-to-date state-of-the-art treatment of chosen areas and forms a further contribution towards progress in hydraulic engineering.

P. Novak

CONTENTS

LIST OF CONTRIBUTORS

J. ČÁBELKA
  Professor, Czechoslovak Academy of Sciences, Na Kocínce 8, 16000 Praha 6, Dejvice, Czechoslovakia

J. A. CHARLTON
  Senior Lecturer, Department of Civil Engineering, University of Dundee, Dundee DD1 4HN, UK

P. GABRIEL
  Professor. Technical University of Prague, Thákurova 7, 16629 Praha 6, Czechoslovakia

FORREST M. HOLLY JR
  Associate Professor, Iowa Institute of Hydraulic Research, University of Iowa, Iowa City, Iowa 52242, USA

M. W. OWEN
  Head of Coastal Engineering, Hydraulics Research Limited, Wallingford, Oxfordshire OX10 8BA, UK

ROLAND K. PRICE
  Department of Computational Drainage, Hydraulics Research Limited, Wallingford, Oxfordshire OX10 8BA, UK

PATRICK SAUVAGET.
   *SOGREAH Consulting Engineers, 6 Rue de Lorraine, Grenoble,
   38130 Echirolles, France*

Ö. STAROSOLSZKY
   *Head of Institute of Hydraulic Engineering, Research Centre for
   Water Resources Development, H-1453, Budapest Pf. 27, Hungary*

Chapter 1

DISPERSION IN RIVERS AND COASTAL WATERS — 1. PHYSICAL PRINCIPLES AND DISPERSION EQUATIONS

FORREST M. HOLLY JR

Iowa Institute of Hydraulic Research,
University of Iowa, Iowa City, USA

NOTATION

(M = mass; T = time; L = length)

a	distance separating parallel plates (L)
a_z	calibration coefficient for transverse mixing coefficient
A	cross-sectional area (L^2)
b	local width of stream tube (L)
B	channel width (L)
C	contaminant concentration
$\hat{C}$	cross-sectional average concentration
$\tilde{C}'''$	local deviation of depth-averaged concentration from $\hat{C}$
$\tilde{C}$	average concentration over the depth, or between plates
$\bar{C}$	short-time average concentration
C'	concentration deviation from short-time average
C_e	concentration of continuous point source
C''	deviation of local concentration from $\tilde{C}$
D	diffusion factor in cumulative discharge equation (L^5/T_2)
E_a	transverse advective mixing coefficient (L^2/T)
E_z	depth-averaged transverse mixing coefficient (L^2/T)
f_s	standardised normal probability distribution function

1

F_a cross-sectional average longitudinal mixing coefficient (L^2/T)

g acceleration due to gravity (L/T^2)

h flow depth (L)

i summation index

K_a effective longitudinal advective dispersion coefficient (L^2/T)

K_0 modified Bessel function of the second kind, order zero

K_x effective longitudinal dispersion coefficient (L^2/T)

l length scale for transverse mixing (L)

L x coordinate of solid boundary in a canal (L); length scale of contaminant cloud (L)

L_x, L_z curvilinear distances in x and z directions (L)

L_{tx} Lagrangian integral time scale of turbulence (T)

m intensity of distributed contaminant source $(M/L^3/T)$

m_1, m_2, m_3 metric coefficients in x, y, z directions

M_1 intensity of instantaneous plane contaminant source (M/L^2)

M_2 intensity of instantaneous line source (M/L)

M_3 intensity of instantaneous point source (M)

n summation index for superposition solution

N number of particles released

p dimensionless cumulative discharge coordinate

q_c cumulative discharge (L^3/T)

q_e volumetric discharge rate of continuous point source (L^3/T)

q_0 cumulative discharge coordinate of continuous vertical line source (L^3/T)

Q total water discharge (L^3/T)

R radius of curvature in river bend (L)

$R_{u'}$ Lagrangian correlation coefficient

t time (T)

t_1 dummy variable of integration

T time period for averaging of turbulent fluctuations (T)

T_i elapsed time before gradient diffusion process is valid (T)

T_0 time beyond which successive particle displacements are uncorrelated (T)

u, v, w velocities in x, y, z directions (L/T)

$\mathbf{u}$ instantaneous velocity vector (L/T)

u_i' velocity of the ith particle with respect to mean cloud position (L/T)

$\bar{u}, \bar{v}, \bar{w}$ short-time average velocities (L/T)

u', v', w' velocity deviations from short-time average (L/T)

u''	deviation of local velocity from $U(L/T)$
$\tilde{u}'''$	local deviation of depth-averaged velocity from cross-section average (L/T)
u_*	shear velocity (L/T)
U	x direction velocity for plug flow; depth-averaged velocity (L/T)
W	depth-averaged velocity in z direction (L/T)
x, y, z	spatial coordinates (L)
x_1	dummy variable of integration
X_i	displacement of ith particle from group mean position (L)
y'	dummy variable of integration
z_L, z_R	transverse coordinates of left and right banks (M)
Γ	velocity gradient $(1/T)$
Δ	indicates incremental quantity
∇	vector gradient operator $(1/L)$
∇^2	Laplacian scalar operator $(1/L^2)$
ε	diffusion coefficient (L^2/T)
ε_m	molecular diffusion coefficient (L^2/T)
ε_t	turbulent diffusivity for momentum transfer (L^2/T)
$\varepsilon_x, \varepsilon_y, \varepsilon_z$	turbulent diffusivities (L^2/T)
$\varepsilon_{11}, \varepsilon_{12}, \varepsilon_{22}$	elements of diffusion tensor (L^2/T)
$\tilde{\varepsilon}_x, \tilde{\varepsilon}_y$	depth-averaged longitudinal and transverse turbulent diffusivities (L^2/T)
ζ	line-source injection location relative to channel centreline (L)
η	dimensionless distance above bed; axis perpendicular to local flow direction (L)
θ	angle between local flow direction and x-axis
κ	Von Karman's constant
ξ	longitudinal coordinate in moving reference frame (L); axis of local flow direction (L)
ρ	water density (M/L^3)
σ_x^2	x direction variance of tracer distribution (L^2)
Σ	indicates summation
τ	dummy variable of integration; time separation (T); shear stress (M/LT^2)
τ_0	bed shear stress (M/LT^2)
ϕ	skew parameter in solution for uniform shear flow $(1/T^2)$

1 INTRODUCTION

An increasing amount of effort in computational hydraulics is being
devoted to the simulation of contaminant dispersion in rivers and coastal
waters. The objective of this and the following chapter is to review both
the theory of dispersion and numerical solution of the resulting equations, as a basis for identifying the strengths and weaknesses of existing
knowledge and techniques.

Although the emphasis of these chapters is on numerical models and
their theoretical bases, it should be recognised that reduced scale physical models offer an alternative means of investigation under certain
circumstances. The primary restriction to their use is that, as shown by
Fischer and Holley,[12] scale distortion cannot legitimately be used. The
consequence is that the sheer horizontal extent of physical scale models
limits their use to the study of local, three-dimensional dispersion in
particular geometries. Numerical models cannot feasibly simulate local
geometrical details, but they have no inherent limitation on spatial
extent. The natural domain of numerical models is the simulation of
contaminant dispersion over extended river reaches or coastal waters,
usually where complete depth-averaged mixing can be assumed.

The remainder of this chapter is devoted to a review of basic dispersion theory and its implications for practical analysis. The following
chapter deals with numerical techniques for an approximate solution of
the dispersion equations. The overall context is assumed to be one in
which the engineer seeks to obtain the time-variation of contaminant
concentration anywhere in a natural water body, as a result of any specified contaminant spill or initial condition.

2   DERIVATION OF TURBULENT DIFFUSION EQUATION

The various theories and derivations of contaminant dispersion equations in natural waterways have a common theme which appears in
various forms. This theme is a progressive averaging process over time
and space, one of whose most important consequences is the representation of mixing due to differential advection as a gradient diffusion
process. The averaging processes reduce the detail with which the input
time- and space-variations of the flow hydrodynamics must be known,
and often reduce the dimensionality of the problem to be solved. The
price to be paid is considerable uncertainty as to the justification for, and

quantification of, the supposedly equivalent diffusion process. These ideas are developed in more detail in the sequel.

2.1 Instantaneous Mass Conservation

The most general statement of conservation of contaminant mass in a control volume subject to advective and diffusive flux across its boundaries is the following:[31]

$$\frac{\partial C}{\partial t} + \mathbf{u} \cdot \nabla C = \varepsilon_m \nabla^2 C \qquad (1)$$

where $C(x, y, z, t) =$ contaminant concentration by weight (dimensionless), $\mathbf{u}(x, y, z, t) =$ three-dimensional, instantaneous vector velocity at a point, and $\varepsilon_m =$ molecular diffusivity, having dimensions of length squared per unit time. Equation (1) incorporates an assumption of incompressible ambient fluid, and adopts Fick's law of simple proportionality between diffusive contaminant flux and the concentration gradient. ε_m is taken to be a property only of the contaminant and ambient fluids, and not of the flow dynamics. Thus it is a known quantity.

2.2 Taylor's Theory of Diffusion by Continuous Movements

Although eqn (1) is a rigorously correct and complete description of turbulent mixing in rivers, it is of little use for hydraulic engineering purposes. The main reason for this is that the velocity vector $\mathbf{u}(x, y, z, t)$ must be known with sufficient precision in time and space to resolve the details of random turbulent fluctuations. Such detailed information, not to speak of the computer memory needed to store and manipulate it, is simply not available. Turbulence measurements and numerical modelling of the Navier–Stokes equations are able to furnish certain statistics, or average quantities, of the turbulent fluctuations at a point, but this is invariably for special geometries and flow situations. Therefore eqn (1) must be replaced by some mean, or average, description of the dispersion process before engineering use of it can be envisaged.

The fundamental insight into, and theoretical support for, the time-average description of turbulent dispersion was published by Taylor in his classic paper entitled 'Diffusion by Continuous Movements'.[32] The framework for Taylor's analysis is a homogeneous (turbulence properties the same throughout the flow field), stationary (properties at a point do not change with time), one-dimensional turbulent flow, into which a group of particles is instantaneously released at a point. Taylor tackled the problem of relating the spread (dispersion) of the *group* of particles to the correlation between successive displacements of *individual* particles. The purely kinematic analysis begins with adoption of the variance (mean-square displacement) of the group of N particles about their mean position as a measure of the spread

$$\sigma_x^2(t) = \frac{1}{N} \sum_{i=1}^{N} [X_i(t)]^2 \equiv \overline{\overline{[X(t)]^2}} \tag{2}$$

in which $\sigma_x^2(t)$ = variance in the x direction, $X_i(t)$ = displacement of the ith particle from the mean position of the group, and the double overbar denotes an ensemble average over the particles.

Expressing the growth of the 'cloud' of particles as the time derivative of its variance, and recognising that

$$X_i(t) = \int_0^t u_i'(\tau) d\tau \tag{3}$$

in which $u_i'(\tau)$ = velocity of the ith particle with respect to the mean displacement of the cloud, Taylor differentiated eqn (2) with respect to time to obtain

$$\frac{d}{dt}(\sigma_x^2(t)) = 2\overline{\overline{u'^2}} \int_0^t R_{u'}(\tau) d\tau \tag{4}$$

in which $\overline{\overline{u'^2}}$ = mean-square velocity fluctuation, and $R_{u'}(\tau)$ = Lagrangian correlation coefficient for successive particle displacements, defined as

$$R_{u'}(\tau) = \frac{\overline{\overline{u'(t)u'(t+\tau)}}}{\overline{\overline{u'^2}}} \tag{5}$$

The final step of the analysis is integration of eqn (4) by parts, invoking $R_{u'}(0) = 1$, to obtain the 'Lagrangian Equation of Turbulent Diffusion':

$$\sigma_x^2(t) = 2\overline{\overline{u'^2}} \int_0^t (t-\tau) R_{u'}(\tau) d\tau \tag{6}$$

Now eqn (6) is still of little direct use, since the Lagrangian correlation coefficient for turbulent flow fields is seldom known. The power of eqn (6) is in what it reveals about the rate of cloud growth as time increases. Shown in Fig. 1 is the general shape of the Lagrangian autocorrelation function. Now consider eqn (4) for three limiting cases:

(a) *Very small time, $t \to 0$*
  $R_{u'}(\tau)$ tends to unity as τ tends to zero, and $0 \le \tau \le t$. Thus eqn (4)

can be integrated to yield

$$\sigma_x^2(t) \approx \overline{u'^2} t^2 \tag{7}$$

(b) *Moderately large time, $t > T_0$*

$R_{u'}(\tau)$ tends to zero as t tends to infinity, representing the fact that particle displacements become totally uncorrelated at large separations in time. Thus eqn (6) can be written

$$\sigma_x^2(t) = 2\overline{u'^2} t L_{tx} - 2\overline{u'^2} \int_0^t \tau R_{u'}(\tau) d\tau \tag{8}$$

in which L_{tx}, the Lagrangian integral time scale of turbulence, is defined as

$$L_{tx} = \int_0^\infty R_{u'}(\tau) d\tau \tag{9}$$

(c) *Very large time, $t \to \infty$*

Since the second term of eqn (8) is bounded while the first term increases with t, the variance growth can be written

$$\sigma_x^2(t) \approx 2\overline{u'^2} t L_{tx} \tag{10}$$

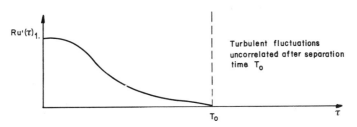

FIG. 1. Lagrangian autocorrelation function.

Equation (10) is the most important result of Taylor's theory. It says that if one waits long enough, the variance of the particle cloud will increase linearly with time at a rate given by $2\overline{u'^2} L_{tx}$; this rate is a property of the turbulent flow field and not the fluid. Now, a characteristic feature of any gradient diffusion process is that the variance of the distribution in question (heat, contaminant, particles, etc.) increases linearly with time.[11] Therefore Taylor's theory provides formal justification for attempting to model mixing due to turbulent fluctuations as a gradient diffusion process for reasonably large times after release, obviating the need to deal with the local details of turbulent motions.

To see how this concept is put into practice, we now consider the problem from a different point of view. In an approach quite equivalent to that used to obtain the Reynolds equations of motion from the Navier–Stokes equations, one can apply Reynolds' averaging principles to eqn (1) and thereby isolate contaminant transport due to turbulent advection.[37] The concentrations and velocities appearing in eqn (1) are instantaneous values; they can be written as

$$C = \bar{C} + C' \tag{11}$$

$$u = \bar{u} + u' \tag{12}$$

etc., in which the overbar represents an average over a time period T which is short compared to the time scale of interest, yet long with respect to turbulent fluctuations. The fluctuating components designated by primes are the instantaneous, local deviations from the means over T. When the definitions such as eqns (11) and (12) are substituted into eqn (1), and then the resulting expression is averaged over time T and simplified using Reynolds' Rules of Averaging,[37] the following modified contaminant conservation equation results

$$\frac{\partial \bar{C}}{\partial t} + \bar{u}\frac{\partial \bar{C}}{\partial x} + \bar{v}\frac{\partial \bar{C}}{\partial y} + \bar{w}\frac{\partial \bar{C}}{\partial z} = \varepsilon_{\mathrm{m}}\left(\frac{\partial^2 \bar{C}}{\partial x^2} + \frac{\partial^2 \bar{C}}{\partial y^2} + \frac{\partial^2 \bar{C}}{\partial z^2}\right)$$

$$- \frac{\partial}{\partial x}(\overline{u'C'}) - \frac{\partial}{\partial y}(\overline{v'C'}) - \frac{\partial}{\partial z}(\overline{w'C'}) \tag{13}$$

in which the last three terms represent the aforementioned isolation of contaminant transport due to turbulent advection (turbulent fluctuations have been averaged out of the terms on the left-hand side of eqn (13)). Taylor's theory tells us that this transport can be represented as a gradient diffusion process, for example:

$$\varepsilon \frac{\partial \bar{C}}{\partial x} = -(\overline{u'C'}) \tag{14}$$

in which ε is a diffusion coefficient. If in addition one accepts the common assumption that molecular diffusion is much smaller than, and occurs independently of, turbulent motion, then the molecular and turbulent terms on the right-hand side of eqn (13) can be combined to give

$$\frac{\partial \bar{C}}{\partial t} + \bar{u}\frac{\partial \bar{C}}{\partial x} + \bar{v}\frac{\partial \bar{C}}{\partial y} + \bar{w}\frac{\partial \bar{C}}{\partial z} = \frac{\partial}{\partial x}\left(\varepsilon_x \frac{\partial \bar{C}}{\partial x}\right)$$

$$+ \frac{\partial}{\partial y}\left(\varepsilon_y \frac{\partial \bar{C}}{\partial y}\right) + \frac{\partial}{\partial z}\left(\varepsilon_z \frac{\partial \bar{C}}{\partial z}\right) \tag{15}$$

in which the diffusivities ε_x, ε_y and ε_z can be written

$$\varepsilon_x = \varepsilon_m - \frac{\overline{u'C'}}{\partial \bar{C}/\partial x} \tag{16}$$

It must be recognised that some liberty has been taken in writing eqn (15); the possible spatial variation of diffusivities has been anticipated by moving ε_x, ε_y and ε_z inside their respective first differentiations. This anticipation, along with possible time variations implied in the unsteady form of eqn (15), formally violate Taylor's restrictions of homogeneous and stationary turbulence. Nonetheless the existence of a gradient diffusion process has been verified experimentally in many flow fields which do not strictly respect Taylor's restrictions.

Taylor's asymptotic result, eqn (10), is valid only for times which are large compared to the time over which turbulent motions are correlated. Expressed spatially, this means that eqn (15) can be considered to be valid only for contaminant clouds whose spatial extent substantially exceeds the distance over which turbulent motions are correlated. In confined natural water bodies this distance is the order of the depth of flow.

Nothing has been said thus far about the numerical values of the diffusion coefficients ε_x, ε_y and ε_z. They are in fact quite difficult to evaluate; the previously mentioned problem of needing detailed knowledge of turbulent velocity fluctuations has been replaced by a new problem of evaluating these diffusivities. We shall see further on that it is only in the context of dispersion in specific shear flows that the diffusivities can be estimated *a priori*.

2.3 Review of Analytical Solutions

It is in general not possible to obtain analytical solutions to eqn (15) for dispersion in natural waterways with arbitrary boundary conditions. On the other hand, a variety of exact solutions exists for idealised situations, and these can be useful in obtaining order-of-magnitude estimates and verifying numerical methods designed for natural water bodies. The purpose of this section is briefly to present the more prominent of the exact solutions and associated references.

The simplest situation for which an analytical solution exists is that of one-dimensional mixing in an infinitely long domain, represented by the contaminant conservation equations:

$$\frac{\partial C}{\partial t} + u\frac{\partial C}{\partial x} = \varepsilon_x \frac{\partial^2 C}{\partial x^2} \tag{17}$$

in which the overbars have been dropped and the diffusivity ε_x is taken to be constant. The solution to eqn (17) for an instantaneous plane source of intensity M_1 units of mass per unit area is

$$C(x,t) = \frac{M_1}{\sqrt{4\pi\varepsilon_x t}} \exp\{-(x-ut)^2/4\varepsilon_x t\} \tag{18}$$

An important property of this solution is that the variance of the concentration distribution increases linearly with time, according to

$$\frac{d}{dt}(\sigma_x^2(t)) = 2\varepsilon_x \tag{19}$$

which is entirely consistent with Taylor's theory.

The linearity of eqn (15) makes it possible to construct solutions for more complex initial and boundary conditions through superposition, in time and/or space, of eqn (19). For example if a one-dimensional distributed source in time and space is defined by the function $m(x,t)$, having units of contaminant mass per unit volume per unit time, then the concentration distribution in an unbounded domain with constant diffusivity is

$$C(x,t) = \int_{-\infty}^{t} \int_{-\infty}^{\infty} \frac{m(x_1,t_1)}{\sqrt{4\pi\varepsilon_x(t-t_1)}} \exp\left\{\frac{-(x-ut-x_1)^2}{4\varepsilon_x(t-t_1)}\right\} dx_1\, dt_1 \tag{20}$$

The effects of confining boundaries are taken into account by introducing 'image sources', the effect of which is to nullify any mixing across solid boundaries. For mixing of an instantaneous plane source in a one-dimensional canal with solid boundaries at $x = \pm L$, and $u \equiv 0$, the solution is

$$C(x,t) = \sum_{n=-\infty}^{\infty} \frac{1}{\sqrt{4\pi\varepsilon_x t}} \exp\left\{-\frac{(x+2nL)^2}{4\varepsilon_x t}\right\} \tag{21}$$

Extensions to two and three dimensions follow the same general pattern. For example the two- and three-dimensional equivalents of eqn (18) are

$$C(x,y,t) = \frac{M_2}{4\pi t\sqrt{\varepsilon_x \varepsilon_y}} \exp - \left\{ \frac{(x-ut)^2}{4\varepsilon_x t} + \frac{(y-vt)^2}{4\varepsilon_y t} \right\} \tag{22a}$$

and

$$C(x,y,z,t) = \frac{M_3}{\sqrt{(4\pi t)^3 \varepsilon_x \varepsilon_y \varepsilon_z}} \exp - \left\{ \frac{(x-ut)^2}{4\varepsilon_x t} + \frac{(y-vt)^2}{4\varepsilon_y t} + \frac{(z-wt)^2}{4\varepsilon_z t} \right\} \tag{22b}$$

in which M_2 has units of mass per unit length and M_3 has units of mass.

Several analytical solutions have been obtained for a so-called 'plug flow' in which the constant flow field is described by $u = U$, $v = w = 0$. For a continuous point source having a volumetric discharge q_e and concentration C_e in three-dimensional, unbounded plug flow, the superposition solution is

$$C(x,y,z,t) = \int_0^t \frac{C_e q_e}{\sqrt{(4\pi \tau)^3 \varepsilon_x \varepsilon_y \varepsilon_z}} \exp - \left\{ \frac{(x-Ut)^2}{4\varepsilon_x \tau} + \frac{y^2}{4\varepsilon_y \tau} + \frac{z^2}{4\varepsilon_z \tau} \right\} dt_1 \tag{23}$$

with $\tau = t - t_1$. When $\varepsilon_x \ll \varepsilon_y$ and $\varepsilon_x \ll \varepsilon_z$, i.e. when the x direction diffusion is weak, Frenkiel[13] obtained an asymptotic steady state limit of eqn (23):

$$C(x,y,z) = \frac{C_e q_e}{4\pi x\sqrt{\varepsilon_y \varepsilon_z}} \exp - \left\{ \frac{Uy^2}{4\varepsilon_y x} + \frac{Uz^2}{4\varepsilon_z x} \right\} \tag{24}$$

Sayre[30] integrated eqn (23) over a finite extent h in the y direction (such as over the depth of a river) to obtain a solution for the case of complete mixing in the y direction under steady state conditions:

$$C(x,z) = \frac{q_e C_e}{2\pi h\sqrt{\varepsilon_x \varepsilon_z}} \exp \left\{ \frac{Ux}{2\varepsilon_x} \right\} K_0 \left[\frac{U}{2\varepsilon_x} \sqrt{x^2 + \frac{\varepsilon_x}{\varepsilon_z} z^2} \right] \tag{25}$$

in which $K_0 =$ modified Bessel function of the second kind, order zero. When $\varepsilon_x \ll \varepsilon_z$, eqn (25) converges to

$$C(x,z) = \frac{q_e C_e}{2hU\sqrt{\frac{\pi x}{U}\varepsilon_z}} \exp - \left\{ \frac{Uz^2}{4\varepsilon_z x} \right\} \tag{26}$$

Sayre[30] introduced the effects of confining boundaries (such as the banks of a channel) through superposition of solutions such as eqn (25) or eqn (26):

$$C(x, z) = C_0(x, z, -\zeta) + \sum_{n=1}^{\infty} \{C_0(x, nB - \zeta + (-1)^n z)$$
$$+ C_0(x, nB + \zeta - (-1)^n z)\} \qquad (27)$$

in which $C_0(x, z)$ is the appropriate unbounded solution, ζ is the line source injection location relative to the channel centreline, and B is the channel width.

Other, more specialised, exact solutions have also been developed (see for example refs 1, 5, 11, 28, 38). Virtually all such analytical solutions are limited to cases of constant velocities and diffusion coefficients, severely limiting their use in natural water bodies, where the numerical methods described in the following chapter must be employed.

2.4 Dispersion in Unbounded Domains

In large water bodies and at large distances from confining boundaries (e.g. lakes and oceans), there may be no natural limit to the distance over which turbulent motions are correlated, that is to say, there may be no upper limit to the size of 'eddies' which may form. In practical terms, this means that the asymptotic linear variance growth of eqn (10) may never be achieved, and thus that a gradient-diffusion description of the mixing process is not justified, invalidating eqn (15). The so-called 'two particle' theory described by Csnady,[6] Fischer et al.[11] and others deals with this situation. The most important result is that as the contaminant cloud grows in size and is thus subjected to differential advection by larger and larger eddies, the effective 'diffusivity' depends not only on the turbulence properties, but also on the size of the cloud itself. This behavior is formalised in the well known '4/3 law':

$$\varepsilon(L) \propto L^{4/3} \qquad (28)$$

in which L is some measure of the spatial extent of the contaminant cloud.

In rivers and coastal waters, the eddy size is essentially bounded by the depth of flow, obviating the need to introduce the effects of the 4/3 law.

3   DISPERSION IN SHEAR FLOWS

3.1   Introduction

We have seen in Section 2 that Taylor's Theory of Diffusion by Continuous Movements, combined with the Reynolds' averaging of the three-dimensional instantaneous contaminant conservation equation, has the important result of allowing us to express mixing due to temporal velocity fluctuations as an equivalent gradient diffusion process. Thus the entire arsenal of exact and approximate numerical solutions to linear advection-diffusion and heat flow problems is available for turbulent mixing stituations. However, eqn (15) is still too general for most riverine and coastal mixing situations, in which the depth-average, or possibly cross-sectional average, concentration is of primary interest. The second major contribution of Taylor in dispersion theory was to show that when eqn (15) is averaged over one or more spatial dimensions, the mixing due to *spatial velocity variations* can also be expressed as an equivalent gradient diffusion process. This is of fundamental importance, as it allows the continuing use of a simple advection-diffusion model for spatially-averaged processes in natural waters under certain conditions. In this section we shall briefly outline Taylor's contribution, and then focus on its significance for mixing in natural waterways.

3.2   Taylor's Pipe Flow Analysis

Taylor first considered the problem of mixing in laminar flow in a tube.[33] The ideas are perhaps more clearly illustrated by considering laminar, steady flow between parallel plates.[11] Figure 2 shows a parabolic velocity distribution between plates separated by a distance a. If a particle is released somewhere along the line $x = 0$ as shown, molecular diffusion will cause it to wander around the flow field as it is swept downstream. Taylor hypothesised that after enough time has elapsed, any particle will have wandered over the entire space between the plates, thereby having 'sampled', or felt the effects of, the entire range of velocities existing between the plates. At some point, the particle's velocity can be said to be independent of its initial velocity. Viewed from a coordinate system moving at the mean velocity, the particle will have appeared to undergo random displacements forward or backward. Thus, one could view the particle's longitudinal velocity as a stationary, random function of time, which puts us squarely in the framework of Taylor's earlier Theory of Diffusion by Continuous Movements. The important implication is that

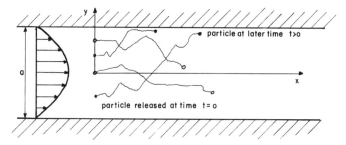

Fɪɢ. 2. Dispersion in flow between parallel plates.

by analogy with eqn (10), the longitudinal spread of a group of particles initially distributed between the plates at $x=0$ as shown will behave like a gradient diffusion process, after sufficient time has elapsed.

Taylor followed this insight with an analysis to determine the effective longitudinal diffusion coefficient for the cross-sectional average concentration in a pipe. For the analogous parallel plate problem, the local concentration and longitudinal velocities are written as the sums of average values between the plates and local deviations from the averages, in much the same way as eqns (11) and (12). These sums are substituted into the two-dimensional form of eqn (1) written for plug flow, longitudinal molecular diffusion is neglected as being small, and the resulting equation is then averaged over the width a between the plates. Rather tedious simplication of the equation, with extensive use of Leibniz's theorem and invocation of boundary conditions of no transport normal to the plates, set the stage for another of Taylor's fundamental injections of insight and intuition. The working equation at this point is

$$\frac{\partial C''}{\partial t}+u''\frac{\partial \tilde{C}}{\partial \xi}+u''\frac{\partial C''}{\partial \xi}-\overline{u''\frac{\partial C''}{\partial \xi}}=\varepsilon_{\mathrm{m}}\frac{\partial^2 C''}{\partial y^2} \qquad (29)$$

in which the double prime denotes deviations from the average value between the plates (denoted by wavy overbars), and $\xi=$ longitudinal coordinate with respect to a system moving at the mean flow velocity. Taylor first hypothesised that if C'' and $\tilde{C}$ are slowly varying functions,

$$u''\frac{\partial C''}{\partial \xi}\approx\overline{u''\frac{\partial C''}{\partial \xi}} \qquad (30)$$

Then eqn (29) simplifies to

$$\frac{\partial C''}{\partial t} = \varepsilon_m \frac{\partial^2 C''}{\partial y^2} - u'' \frac{\partial \tilde{C}}{\partial \xi} \tag{31}$$

Taylor recognised this as a simple one-dimensional diffusion equation with a source term $-u''(\partial \tilde{C}/\partial \xi)$ whose net contribution between the plates must be zero (since $\widetilde{u''} \equiv 0$). If there is no net source contribution, then a steady state (in the moving coordinate system) must exist after sufficient time. Thus the time derivative in eqn (31) disappears, and the final result is

$$u'' \frac{\partial \tilde{C}}{\partial \xi} = \varepsilon_m \frac{\partial^2 C''}{\partial y^2} \tag{32}$$

Equation (32) can be integrated to obtain an expression for $C''(y)$. The total contaminant mass transport can be obtained by integrating the product $u''(y) \cdot C''(y)$ between the plates. When this is done, it is seen that the total contaminant mass transport per unit area is proportional to the longitudinal gradient of average concentration — which is precisely the definition of a gradient diffusion process, as foreseen in the analogy with the Theory of Diffusion by Continuous Movements. Consequently, we are justified in writing

$$\frac{\partial \tilde{C}}{\partial t} + U \frac{\partial \tilde{C}}{\partial x} = K_x \frac{\partial^2 \tilde{C}}{\partial x^2} \tag{33}$$

with the constant of proportionality, or 'diffusivity', given by

$$K_x = -\frac{1}{a\varepsilon_m} \int_0^a u'' \int_0^y \int_0^y u'' \, dy' \, dy' \, dy' \tag{34}$$

and U is the depth-averaged velocity. If the velocity distribution $u(y)$ is known, then the integrations of eqn (34) can be accomplished in any appropriate manner.

Both the analogy with the Theory of Diffusion by Continuous Movements and the specific simplifications of eqn (29) are restricted to a rather vague 'large time after release'. Through dimensional analysis and empirical tests, Chatwin[4] identified the 'diffusive period', in which eqns (33) and (34) would be valid, as beginning about $0 \cdot 4a^2/\varepsilon_m$ time units after release of the contaminant cloud.

Taylor's actual analysis[33] was based on laminar flow in a pipe, but follows the same general lines outlined here. An extension to rectangular and elliptical pipes is described by Fukushima and Hayakawa.[14] A year after his laminar publication, Taylor published an extension of his analysis to turbulent flow in a pipe.[34] The basic mechanics of the analysis differed from those of the laminar case only in the use of an empirical logarithmic velocity distribution and a spatially variable transverse turbulent diffusivity $\varepsilon_y(y)$. The significance of the work for subsequent riverine dispersion analysis is in its quantification of $\varepsilon_y(y)$ in terms of bulk flow parameters, using the Reynolds analogy of equivalent mass and momentum transfer, as follows.

If we neglect molecular diffusion as being small compared to turbulent mixing, the y direction equivalent of eqn (16) can be written

$$\overline{v'C'} = -\varepsilon_y \frac{\partial \bar{C}}{\partial y} \tag{35}$$

Analyses similar to those of Section 2 can be performed to show that turbulent transport of momentum can also be expressed as a gradient diffusion process,

$$\overline{u'v'} = -\varepsilon_t \partial \bar{u}/\partial y \tag{36}$$

in which ε_t is the turbulent diffusivity. The Reynolds analogy states simply that $\varepsilon_y = \varepsilon_t$; the problem of evaluating ε_y then becomes one of evaluating ε_t. Since turbulent momentum transport can also be written in terms of the shear stress τ, and density ρ,

$$\overline{u'v'} = -(\tau/\rho) \tag{37}$$

the analogy tells us:

$$\varepsilon_y = \varepsilon_t = \frac{\tau/\rho}{\partial \bar{u}/\partial y} \tag{38}$$

Thus if the velocity distribution and the shear stress are known, ε_y can in principle be evaluated. Taylor did so for flow in a pipe, but the most pertinent application of the concept to free surface flows was performed by Elder.[7]

3.3 Elder's Analysis of Two-Dimensional Turbulent Flow Down a Plane

Elder assumed an infinitely wide channel in which the vertical distribution of longitudinal velocity is taken to be Von Karman's velocity defect profile. Integration of the profile over the depth yields

$U = u_{max} - u_*/\kappa$; the velocity deviation from the mean, $u''(\eta) = u(\eta) - U$, can be written

$$u''(\eta) = \left(\frac{u_*}{\kappa}\right)(\ln \eta + 1) \qquad (39)$$

with the dimensionless distance above the bed being denoted by $\eta = y/h$; h = depth of flow, κ = Von Karman's constant, and u_* = bed shear velocity. Now, a force balance for this simple flow shows that the shear stress τ must vary linearly between zero at the surface and τ_0 at the bed:

$$\tau = \tau_0(1 - \eta) \qquad (40)$$

Using eqns (39) and (40) in eqn (38), noting also that $u_* = \sqrt{\tau_0/\rho}$ by definition, leads to Elder's parabolic expression for ε_y:

$$\varepsilon_y(\eta) = h u_* \kappa \eta (1 - \eta) \qquad (41)$$

Equation (41) is useful from two points of view. First, its integration over the depth yields

$$\tilde{\varepsilon}_y = \frac{\kappa}{6} u_* h \qquad (42)$$

A rough order-of-magnitude check for typical open channel flow shows $\tilde{\varepsilon}_y$ to be of the order of $0.02 \, \mathrm{m^2/s}$. By comparison, molecular diffusivity is of the order of $10^{-7} \, \mathrm{m^2/s}$. Secondly, the more general form of eqn (34), allowing for variable diffusivity, is

$$K_a = -\frac{1}{h}\int_0^h u'' \int_0^y \frac{1}{\varepsilon_y} \int_0^y u'' \, dy' \, dy' \, dy' \qquad (43)$$

Elder substituted eqns (39) and (41) into eqn (43) and performed the integration to obtain

$$K_a = \frac{0.404}{\kappa^3} h u_* \approx 5.86 u_* h \qquad (44)$$

when κ is taken as 0.4.

The significance of Taylor's and Elder's work for channel flow is that the longitudinal spread of depth-averaged concentration can be described by a one-dimensional advection-diffusion equation,

$$\frac{\partial \tilde{C}}{\partial t} + U\frac{\partial \tilde{C}}{\partial x} = K_a \frac{\partial^2 \tilde{C}}{\partial x^2} \qquad (45)$$

with K_a given by eqn (44), as long as 'enough' time has elapsed since the contaminant injection for the conditions of Taylor's theory to apply.

It should be remarked that the advective diffusivity given by eqn (44) incorporates only the longitudinal spread due to the interaction between differential advection and vertical turbulent diffusion. Additional longitudinal spread is caused by pure longitudinal turbulent diffusion. Taylor considered this (small) additional mixing as one which could be simply added to the advective portion. Thus the K_a in eqn (45) should really be replaced by

$$K_x = K_a + \tilde{\varepsilon}_x \qquad (46)$$

Elder[7] found that

$$\tilde{\varepsilon}_x \approx \tilde{\varepsilon}_y = \frac{\kappa}{6} u_* h \qquad (47)$$

It is interesting to note that $K_a/\tilde{\varepsilon}_x = 5\cdot86/(\kappa/6) \approx 90$, so that the longitudinal turbulent diffusion is indeed small compared to the differential advection. Using $\kappa = 0\cdot4$,

$$K_x = 5\cdot93 u_* h \qquad (48)$$

By direct analogy with Chatwin's[4] result for molecular diffusion, the time which must elapse after injection before the gradient longitudinal diffusion process would be valid is

$$T_i = 0\cdot4 h^2 / \tilde{\varepsilon}_y \qquad (49)$$

In a channel 5 m deep with a shear velocity of $0\cdot05$ m/s, eqn (49) suggests that about 10 min must elapse before the longitudinal mixing of released contaminant can be described by eqns (44) and (45).

While Elder's analysis strictly applies only to longitudinal dispersion of depth-averaged concentration in infinitely wide, uniform flow, the mixing coefficient of eqn (48) is widely used for the longitudinal component of depth-averaged/mixing in two-dimensional (plan view) dispersion models.

3.4 Fischer's Analysis of One-Dimensional Dispersion in Streams

The history of dispersion analysis has involved, as we have seen, a succession of averaging processes of eqn (1). The time-averaging of Taylor's theory[32] shifted mixing due to differential advection by turbulent fluctuations to an equivalent diffusion process. The cross-sectional averaging of Taylor's analysis[33] shifted mixing due to differential advection within the cross-section to another equivalent diffusion process. Similarly, Elder's depth-averaging of turbulent flow down a plane shifted mixing due to differential advection over the depth to an equivalent diffusion process. In all of these analyses, the magnitude of the equivalent, differential advection generated diffusion process completely overshadows the inherent physical diffusion process appearing before the averaging process is performed.

The need for a final step in the chain of averaging processes was brought out by physical observations that Elder's longitudinal mixing coefficient of eqn (48) grossly underestimated the apparent longitudinal diffusion of cross-sectional average concentration in natural channels. Fischer[9] hypothesised that in a natural channel, the longitudinal dispersion of cross-sectional average concentration is caused primarily by transverse, rather than vertical, deviations of velocity from the cross-sectional mean velocity. This intuitive hypothesis suggests that a cross-sectional averaging of eqn (1) should yield an equivalent diffusive mixing coefficient whose value would be far greater than Elder's prediction, eqn (48). This is precisely the nature of Fischer's analysis and theory, whose details can be found in refs 9 and 11.

Fischer's analysis can be presented through the detailed averaging of the mass conservation equation, closely following the intuitive simplifications first performed by Taylor. But the essential result of the analysis, as we saw earlier in the derivation of eqn (32), is a sort of equilibrium between longitudinal differential advection and transverse depth-averaged diffusion. This equilibrium can be written, for a control volume between the left bank at $z = z_L$ and any transverse position z,

$$\int_{z_L}^{z} \tilde{u}'''(z)h(z)\,\frac{\partial \hat{C}}{\partial x}\mathrm{d}z = hE_z\frac{\partial \tilde{C}'''}{\partial z} \tag{50}$$

in which $\tilde{u}'''(z) = $ local deviation of the depth-averaged velocity from the cross-sectional average, $\hat{C}(x) = $ cross-sectional average concentration, $\tilde{C}'''(z) = $ local deviation of the depth-averaged concentration from $\hat{C}$, and E_z is an appropriate depth-averaged transverse mixing coefficient (to be discussed later). When eqn (50) is integrated over the entire channel width, an expression is obtained for $\tilde{C}'''(z)$. Finally, the total contaminant flux through a cross-section moving at the mean flow velocity is computed by integrating the product $\tilde{u}''' \cdot \tilde{C}'''$ over the entire cross-section, leading to recognition of an equivalent overall diffusion coefficient,

$$F_a = -\frac{1}{A} \int_{z_L}^{z_R} h\tilde{u}''' \int_{z_L}^{z} \frac{1}{hE_z} \int_{z_L}^{z} (\tilde{u}'''h)dz' dz' dz' \tag{51}$$

If the cross-sectional shape and velocity distribution are known, then F_a can be calculated by numerically performing the integrations of eqn (51).

Just as we added the physical diffusion $\tilde{\varepsilon}_x$ to K_a in eqn (46) to obtain a total coefficient K_x, we now write

$$F_x = F_a + \hat{K}_x \tag{52}$$

where $\hat{K}_x$ denotes the cross-sectional average of eqn (48).

To the extent that F_x is valid, Fischer's one-dimensional equation can be written

$$\frac{\partial \hat{C}}{\partial t} + \hat{U}\frac{\partial \hat{C}}{\partial x} = \frac{1}{A}\frac{\partial}{\partial x}\left(AF_x \frac{\partial \hat{C}}{\partial x} \right) \tag{53}$$

where A = cross-sectional area of flow and $\hat{U}$ = cross-sectional average velocity. Once again, if A and F_x do not change with x (uniform flow), then the analytical solutions of Section 2 are available for use in predicting concentration distributions. In general neither A nor F_x are constant, so that the numerical methods of the following chapter must be employed.

The common element in Taylor's, Elder's and Fischer's analysis is the hypothesis of the existence of a gradient diffusion description of mixing due to random velocity deviations (in space or time) from some mean value. Associated with each analysis is the elapsed time of the 'initial' or 'advective' period before which the gradient diffusion hypothesis is valid, as we have already seen for the work of Taylor and Elder. The evaluation of the initial period for Fischer's one-dimensional analysis in streams is based on the notion that *transverse* mixing is the predominant factor. By simple dimensional reasoning supplemented with experimental observations, Fischer found the duration of the initial period to be about

$$T_i = \frac{0.4l^2}{\hat{E}_z} \tag{54}$$

in which l is taken as the distance from the thread of maximum velocity to the farthest bank, and $\hat{E}_z$ is the corss-sectional value of the transverse mixing coefficient. In a straight channel with no secondary currents, Elder[7] found

$$\tilde{E}_z = \tilde{\varepsilon}_z = 0.23u_*h \tag{55}$$

It is interesting to note that while eqn (54) might have been deduced directly from eqn (49), Fischer obtained it as a by-product of an attempt to evaluate F_a without having to do the detailed integration of eqn (51). His alternative estimator is written

$$F_a = 0.3\widehat{\tilde{u}'''^2} \frac{l^2}{\widehat{u_*\hat{h}}} \tag{56}$$

in which $\tilde{u}'''^2$ is the mean square velocity deviation from the cross-sectional average and $\hat{h}$ is the cross-sectional average depth.

Other investigators have attempted to obtain simplified predictors of F_x, obviating the need to perform the integration of eqn (51) by relating F_a directly to easily-obtainable bulk flow parameters (see e.g. ref. 19). However, the availability of such simplified methods belies the fact that in many engineering investigations the period of interest is of shorter duration than T_i, and in addition most dispersion events of engineering interest result from localised injection at one bank or from a point-source outfall. In such cases, one is simply not interested in the cross-sectional average concentration. For example, in a large river such as the Missouri, eqn (54) gives $T_i \approx 13\,\text{h}$, corresponding to a longitudinal distance of some 50 miles. In other words, mixing across the width occurs much more slowly than mixing over the depth. This fact is responsible for the widespread use of two-dimensional (depth-averaged) models in engineering practice.

Several authors have documented the fact that even in a nominally straight, uniform channel, the longitudinal variance of the cross-sectional average concentration does not grow linearly with time, even in the diffusive period.[25] This is contrary to what would be expected for the one-dimensional eqn (53), one of the properties of whose analytical solution is a strictly linear time-rate of variance growth. It has been generally agreed that this behaviour implies the existence of so-called 'dead zones', i.e. small-scale bed and bank irregularities which trap contaminant and subsequently re-release it into the flow. Conceptual models which attempt to incorporate this phenomenon have been developed and applied with some success.[27,35]

3.5 Summary
The theoretical analyses of Taylor, Elder and Fischer do not, in general, produce quantitative results which are directly usable in engineering

modelling. Their great significance is, rather, in providing solid theoretical support for the description of mixing due to differential advection as an equivalent gradient diffusion process, and in defining the limits of applicability of this hypothesis. In the following sections we develop working depth-averaged dispersion equations which implicitly incorporate the gradient diffusion assumption; then we discuss the available knowledge of, and techniques for evaluating, the various mixing coefficients we have been using.

4 DISPERSION EQUATIONS FOR NATURAL WATERWAYS

4.1 General Curvilinear Coordinate System

The various contaminant mass conservation equations we have discussed thus far are not suitable for application to dispersion problems in natural waterways. In the first place, the relative rapidity with which mixing over the depth occurs, and the relative slowness of mixing over the channel width, justify the use of a two-dimensional, depth-averaged dispersion equation. In the second place, the longitudinal curvature of most natural channels must be taken into account through use of a curvilinear coordinate system. Therefore we begin by writing the three-dimensional turbulent equation in a general curvilinear system, then averaging the equation over the depth, following Yotsukura and Sayre.[41]

Figure 3 shows a reach of natural river with curvilinear bank alignment. The surface $z = 0$ is taken to be a vertical plane, generally (but not necessarily) aligned such that it is parallel to a depth-averaged velocity

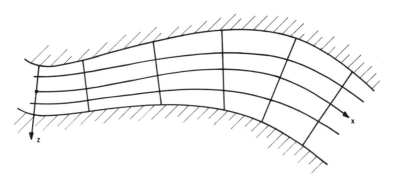

FIG. 3. Definition sketch for curvilinear coordinate system.

vector. The surface $x = 0$ is another curved vertical plane, orthogonal to planes $z = $ constant. The surface $y = 0$ is a horizontal datum.

Due to curvature and/or changes in width, the horizontal distances along different coordinate surfaces, from one coordinate surface to another, are generally not equal. Therefore scaling factors, or 'metric coefficients', are introduced to relate distances measured along arbitrary curvilinear coordinate surfaces to distances measured along the axes. Thus if ΔL_x is the distance measured along the coordinate surface from point A to point B, and Δx is the corresponding change in the x coordinate, the metric coefficient m_1 is defined as

$$m_1(x, z) = \Delta L_x / \Delta x \tag{57}$$

and similarly

$$m_3(x, z) = \Delta L_z / \Delta z \tag{58}$$

Thus along the x-axis, $m_1 \equiv 1$, and along the z-axis, $m_3 \equiv 1$. Since no curvature is introduced in the vertical coordinate surfaces, $m_2 \equiv 1$ everywhere. In a perfectly straight channel, $m_1 = m_2 = m_3 = 1$ everywhere. Even in highly curved channels, the metric coefficients generally remain between 0·8 and 1·2.

When the time-averaged water and contaminant mass conservation equations are re-derived for a control volume bounded by curvilinear surfaces, one obtains

$$\frac{\partial}{\partial x}(m_3 u) + m_1 m_3 \frac{\partial v}{\partial y} + \frac{\partial}{\partial z}(m_1 w) = 0 \tag{59}$$

and

$$m_1 m_3 \frac{\partial C}{\partial t} + \frac{\partial}{\partial x}(m_3 uC) + m_1 m_3 \frac{\partial}{\partial y}(vc) + \frac{\partial}{\partial z}(m_1 wC)$$
$$= \frac{\partial}{\partial x}\left(\frac{m_3}{m_1}\varepsilon_x \frac{\partial C}{\partial x}\right) + m_1 m_3 \frac{\partial}{\partial y}\left(\varepsilon_y \frac{\partial C}{\partial y}\right) + \frac{\partial}{\partial z}\left(\frac{m_1}{m_3}\varepsilon_z \frac{\partial C}{\partial z}\right) \tag{60}$$

in which the time-average overbars have been dropped.

4.2 Generalised Depth-Averaged Dispersion Equation

The depth-averaged equations are obtained by integration of eqns (59) and (60) over the depth (h) with use of the Leibniz theorem and imposition of a boundary condition of no water or contaminant transfer across solid boundaries or the water surface. The resulting expression for water continuity is

$$m_1 m_3 \frac{\partial h}{\partial t} + \frac{\partial}{\partial x}(m_3 h \tilde{u}) + \frac{\partial}{\partial z}(m_1 h \tilde{w}) = 0 \tag{61}$$

As for the contaminant conservation equation, we introduce the usual expressions

$$C(x, y, z, t) = \tilde{C}(x, z, t) + \tilde{C}''(x, y, z, t) \tag{62}$$

and similarly for u, v and w. Depth integration and imposition of the boundary conditions leads to

$$\frac{\partial \tilde{C}}{\partial t} + \frac{U}{m_1} \frac{\partial \tilde{C}}{\partial x} + \frac{W}{m_3} \frac{\partial \tilde{C}}{\partial z} = \frac{1}{hm_1 m_3} \frac{\partial}{\partial x}\left(\frac{m_3}{m_1} h \tilde{\varepsilon}_x \frac{\partial \tilde{C}}{\partial x}\right)$$

$$+ \frac{1}{hm_1 m_3} \frac{\partial}{\partial z}\left(\frac{m_1}{m_3} h \tilde{\varepsilon}_z \frac{\partial \tilde{C}}{\partial z}\right) - \frac{1}{hm_1 m_3} \frac{\partial}{\partial x}(m_3 \overline{hu'' C''})$$

$$- \frac{1}{hm_1 m_3} \frac{\partial}{\partial z}(m_1 \overline{hw'' C''}) \tag{63}$$

in which $U = \tilde{u}$ and $W = \tilde{w}$.

In eqn (63) we recognise $\overline{u'' C''}$ as being the longitudinal transport of contaminant per unit area due to differential advection, in a frame of reference moving at the mean velocity U. Taylor's theory then tells us once again that if we are in the diffusive period:

$$\overline{u'' C''} = -\frac{K_a}{m_1} \frac{\partial \tilde{C}}{\partial x} \tag{64}$$

in which m_1 appears to transform the differential coordinate distance ∂x into a local differential length. Similarly, the term $\overline{w'' C''}$ represents the transverse transport due to differential advection associated with any secondary flow. It is commonly assumed, though with little theoretical justification, that Taylor's theory can also be applied in the transverse direction, so that we write

$$\overline{w'' C''} = -\frac{E_a}{m_3} \frac{\partial \tilde{C}}{\partial z} \tag{65}$$

in which E_a is a transverse advective mixing coefficient. (The implications of this assumption are discussed in the next section.)

If eqns (64) and (65) are accepted as valid, then eqn (63) can be written in its final working form:

$$\frac{\partial \tilde{C}}{\partial t} + \frac{U}{m_1}\frac{\partial \tilde{C}}{\partial x} + \frac{W}{m_3}\frac{\partial \tilde{C}}{\partial z} = \frac{1}{hm_1m_3}\frac{\partial}{\partial x}\left(\frac{m_3}{m_1}hK_x\frac{\partial \tilde{C}}{\partial x}\right)$$

$$+\frac{1}{hm_1m_3}\frac{\partial}{\partial z}\left(\frac{m_1}{m_3}hE_z\frac{\partial \tilde{C}}{\partial z}\right) \tag{66}$$

with $K_x = K_a + \tilde{\varepsilon}_x$ (as in eqns (46) and (48)), and $E_z = E_a + \tilde{\varepsilon}_z$.

It is perhaps useful to summarise the applicability of eqn (66), which:

— assumes that longitudinal and transverse mixing due to differential advection can be described as a gradient diffusion process;
— allows for unsteady, non-uniform, curvilinear flow;
— ignores any tensorial cross-diffusion behaviour caused by local non-alignment of the x, z coordinate surfaces with the flow direction.

In many coastal models it is not possible to align the coordinate system with the time-varying velocity vectors. In this case it is necessary to work with a diffusion tensor, whose introduction into eqn (66) written for a Cartesian system yields:

$$\frac{\partial \tilde{C}}{\partial t} + U\frac{\partial \tilde{C}}{\partial x} + W\frac{\partial \tilde{C}}{\partial z} = \frac{1}{h}\frac{\partial}{\partial x}\left(h\tilde{\varepsilon}_{11}\frac{\partial \tilde{C}}{\partial x}\right)$$

$$+\frac{1}{h}\frac{\partial}{\partial x}\left(h\tilde{\varepsilon}_{12}\frac{\partial \tilde{C}}{\partial z}\right) + \frac{1}{h}\frac{\partial}{\partial z}\left(h\tilde{\varepsilon}_{12}\frac{\partial \tilde{C}}{\partial x}\right) + \frac{1}{h}\frac{\partial}{\partial z}\left(h\tilde{\varepsilon}_{22}\frac{\partial \tilde{C}}{\partial z}\right) \tag{67}$$

With reference to Fig. 4, if θ is the (space- and time-varying) angle between the local flow direction ξ and the x-axis, then a coordinate transform yields:[16]

$$\tilde{\varepsilon}_{11} = K_\xi \cos^2\theta + E_\eta \sin^2\theta \tag{67a}$$

$$\tilde{\varepsilon}_{22} = K_\xi \sin^2\theta + E_\eta \cos^2\theta \tag{67b}$$

$$\tilde{\varepsilon}_{12} = (K_\xi - E_\eta)\sin\theta\cos\theta \tag{67c}$$

in which K_ξ and E_η are understood to be the appropriate mixing coefficients in the directions parallel and perpendicular, respectively, to the local velocity vector.

4.3 Cumulative Discharge (Steady Flow) Transformation

The practical use of eqn (67) in rivers is severely hampered by the

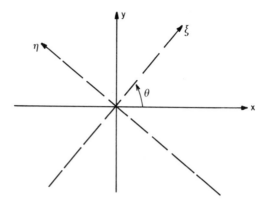

FIG. 4. Definition sketch for diffusion tensor.

difficulty of quantifying the depth-average transverse velocity $\tilde{w}$ and the transverse mixing coefficient E_z. Yotsukura and Cobb[39] transformed the equation to a new form which obviates the need to know $\tilde{w}$ explicitly and has analytical solutions for some mixing situations in natural waters. The physical justification for the transformation is the observation that the concentration distributions downstream from a continuous vertical line source in a river tend to resemble a Gaussian distribution not with respect to the transverse coordinate z, but with respect to the so-called cumulative discharge q_c:

$$q_c(x, z) = \int_0^z \tilde{u}(x, z')h(x, z')m_3 \, dz' \qquad (68)$$

Thus $q_c(x, z_L) = 0$, and $q_c(x, z_R) = Q$, where $Q =$ total discharge, and z_L and z_R are the transverse coordinates of the left and right banks, respectively. Implicit in the cumulative discharge transformation is the requirement of *steady water flow*, limiting its use to dispersion problems in which the time scale of significant concentration changes is much smaller than the time scale of significant changes in water flow.

Formal transformation of the water continuity eqn (61), invoking the orthogonality of the x, z coordinates, and zero tangential and normal flow at the banks, leads to

$$\frac{\partial q_c}{\partial x} + m_1 h\tilde{w} = 0 \qquad (69)$$

Using this continuity equation to replace $\tilde{w}$ in eqn (66) ($\tilde{w} = W$) and performing the formal transformation from the (x, z) system to (x, q_c), one obtains the transformed contaminant mass conservation equation:

$$\frac{\partial \tilde{C}}{\partial t} + \frac{U}{m_1}\frac{\partial \tilde{C}}{\partial x} = \frac{1}{hm_1 m_3}\frac{\partial}{\partial x}\left(\frac{m_3}{m_1}hK_x\frac{\partial \tilde{C}}{\partial x}\right) + \frac{U}{m_1}\frac{\partial}{\partial q_c}\left(m_1 h^2 UE_z\frac{\partial \tilde{C}}{\partial q_c}\right) \quad (70)$$

The significant feature of eqn (70) is that the transverse depth-averaged advection term has been eliminated through the continuity equation.

The cumulative discharge model has been most often used to obtain steady state concentration distributions resulting from continuous vertical line source injection. For such cases the time derivative disappears, and moreover it can be shown that the longitudinal diffusion plays a minor role in such cases. Therefore eqn (70) reduces to a simple one-dimensional diffusion equation (x playing the role of time):

$$\frac{\partial \tilde{C}}{\partial x} = \frac{\partial}{\partial q_c}\left(m_1 h^2 UE_z\frac{\partial \tilde{C}}{\partial q_c}\right) \quad (71)$$

Yotsukura and Cobb identified a 'diffusion factor' D in eqn (71):[39]

$$D = m_1 h^2 UE_z \quad (72)$$

and observed that D tends to be fairly constant in steady flow in a natural river. When this is the case, there exists an analytical solution to eqn (71), analogous to eqn (18), for continuous vertical line source injection in an unbounded fluid:

$$\tilde{C}(x, q_c) = \frac{q_e C_e}{\sqrt{4\pi Dx}}\exp\left\{\frac{-(q_c - q_0)^2}{4Dx}\right\} \quad (73)$$

in which q_0 is the cumulative discharge coordinate of the continuous vertical line source. Sayre[30] then defined a dimensionless coordinate,

$$p = q_c/Q \quad (74)$$

and applied the superposition principle to develop continuous-injection solutions taking into account the effects of bank reflection in natural channels. For a continuous vertical line source at dimensionless coordinate p_0, with $D' = D/Q^2$

$$\tilde{C}(x, p) = \frac{q_e C_e}{Q\sqrt{2D'x}}\left\{f_s\left(\frac{p - p_0}{\sqrt{2D'x}}\right) + f_s\left(\frac{p + p_0}{\sqrt{2D'x}}\right) + \sum_{n=1}^{\infty}\left[f_s\left(\frac{2n - p - p_0}{\sqrt{2D'x}}\right)\right.\right.$$
$$\left.\left. + f_s\left(\frac{2n + p - p_0}{\sqrt{2D'x}}\right) + f_s\left(\frac{2n - p - p_0}{\sqrt{2D'x}}\right) + f_s\left(\frac{2n + p + p_0}{\sqrt{2D'x}}\right)\right]\right\} \quad (75)$$

in which f_s is the standardised normal probability distribution function, and the summation need be carried to only $n = 4$ or 5. Sayre obtained a similar result for a distributed continuous vertical source, as well as a general expression capable, in principle, of treating any continuous source configuration.

A particular implementation of the cumulative discharge equation is the so-called 'stream tube' model, first used by Fischer[9] and Yotsukura et al.[40] and subsequently further generalised by Holly[17] and others. The idea, as shown in Fig. 5, is to discretise a river into stream tubes whose

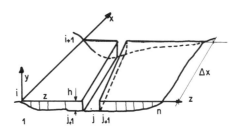

FIG. 5. Discretisation of a river into stream tubes.

boundaries are lines $q_c = $ constant. Thus the discharge in a given tube is everywhere the same. There are various ways to obtain an equation equivalent to eqn (70) in which the variables become stream tube average quantities; all involve one form or another of integrating eqn (70) across the width of a stream tube with liberal applications of Leibniz's rule and judicious neglect of some higher-order residual terms which occur when averages of products are replaced by products of averages. The resulting equation, written for a particular stream tube, is

$$(m_1 A)^s \frac{\partial C^s}{\partial t} + (uA)^s \frac{\partial C^s}{\partial x} = \frac{\partial}{\partial x} \left[\left(\frac{A}{m_1} K_x \right)^s \frac{\partial C^s}{\partial x} \right] + \left[\frac{m_1}{m_3} h E_z \frac{\partial C}{\partial z} \right]_{z-b/2}^{z+b/2} \quad (76)$$

in which the superscript s denotes a stream tube average, and b is the local width of the stream tube in question. In practical terms, the utility of the stream tube equation is as the basis for numerical models of mixing from sources which are arbitrarily distributed in time and/or space.

In summary, the significant feature of the cumulative discharge transformation is that it shifts the problem of evaluating the transverse depth-averaged velocity from the dispersion equation onto the coordinate system, whose configuration is constrained by the requirement that the water continuity equation be satisfied. Numerical methods for solution of eqns (70) and (76) are presented in the following chapter.

4.4   Analytical Solution for Uniform Shear Flow

There is a special case of dispersion in shear flow for which an analytical solution exists. Consider an unbounded parallel shear flow as sketched in Fig. 6. Assuming constant turbulent diffusion coefficients and depth, eqn (66) simplifies to

$$\frac{\partial \tilde{C}}{\partial t} + \Gamma z \frac{\partial \tilde{C}}{\partial x} = \tilde{\varepsilon}_x \frac{\partial^2 \tilde{C}}{\partial x^2} + \tilde{\varepsilon}_z \frac{\partial^2 \tilde{C}}{\partial z^2} \tag{77}$$

in which Γ is the velocity gradient, $\Gamma = d\tilde{u}/dz$, there is assumed to be no equivalent diffusion due to differential advection in the y direction, and $U_0 = 0$. Monin and Yaglom[23] developed an exact solution to eqn (77) for the case of instantaneous vertical line source injection in an unbounded fluid. It is illustrative to develop the solution through consideration of the various mixing mechanisms involved.

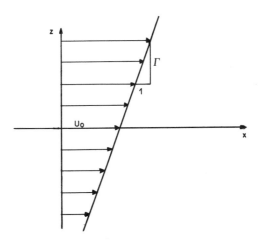

FIG. 6.   Unbounded parallel shear flow.

If the longitudinal and transverse mixing are independent, then the transverse (z direction) cloud growth should proceed as pure diffusion (recall eqn (19)):

$$\sigma_z^2 = 2\tilde{\varepsilon}_z t \tag{78}$$

(ignoring the short initial period before Taylor's diffusive period begins in purely turbulent mixing).

Now the longitudinal cloud growth should be described by the differential form of Taylor's result in eqn (10):

$$\frac{d\sigma_x^2}{dt} = 2\overline{u''^2 L_{tx}} \qquad (79)$$

At any given instant, the velocity deviation 'seen' by the cloud over its width σ_z is $\Gamma\sigma_z$, so one might say

$$u''^2 \propto \Gamma^2 \sigma_z^2 \qquad (80)$$

Also, by dimensional arguments,

$$L_{tx} \propto \frac{\sigma_z^2}{\tilde{\varepsilon}_z} \qquad (81)$$

Monin and Yaglom[23] established the constants of proportionality through statistical arguments, then added the pure longitudinal diffusion, to obtain

$$\sigma_x^2 = \frac{1}{6}\Gamma^2 \tilde{\varepsilon}_z t^3 + 2\tilde{\varepsilon}_x t \qquad (82)$$

Using the transverse and longitudinal variances of eqns (78) and (82), Monin and Yaglom[23] simply wrote a jointly Gaussian solution with appropriate constants:

$$\tilde{C}(x, z, t) = \frac{M}{2\pi h\sigma_x\sigma_y} \exp\left\{ -\frac{(x-x_0)^2}{2\sigma_x^2} - \frac{z^2}{2\sigma_z^2} \right\} \qquad (83)$$

with $x_0 = \Gamma zt/2$. It is illuminating to rewrite eqn (82) as

$$\sigma_x^2 = 2\tilde{\varepsilon}_x t(1 + \phi^2 t^2) \qquad (84)$$

with $\phi^2 = (\Gamma^2/12)(\tilde{\varepsilon}_z/\tilde{\varepsilon}_x)$. The term $\phi^2 t^2$ represents the additional longitudinal cloud growth due to differential advection, which becomes important only as time increases. In fact, it is clear that for large times, the longitudinal variance grows at t^3, i.e. the unboundedness of the flow precludes any Taylor diffusive period for longitudinal spread due to differential advection. It is of some interest to note that eqn (84) can be manipulated into a form which is seen to be a special case of the 4/3 law, eqn (28).

5   EVALUATION OF MIXING COEFFICIENTS

5.1   Existing Knowledge

Our discussions up to this point have been primarily interested in formal mathematical manipulation of the contaminant mass dispersion equation. In so doing, we have been tacitly assuming that the ubiquitous mixing coefficients we so casually manipulate can be quantified for use in actual engineering studies. In fact, while some of the coefficients can be evaluated with some confidence, others cannot. The major current research need in riverine and coastal dispersion modelling is directed towards a more reliable quantification of mixing coefficients.

Table 1 summarises the state of knowledge of the various mixing coefficients we have been using. Several points should be noted:

— In case (2), we see that in the absence of either Reynolds analogy for equivalence of mass and momentum transfer in a shear layer, or of a differential advection dominated equivalent diffusion process, there is no theoretical basis for evaluating the turbulent diffusion coefficients short of turbulence simulation and/or measurements.

— In case (5), there is considerable uncertainty as to how to quantify the role of secondary currents in transverse mixing. This problem is discussed in more detail in Section 5.2.

— In case (7), the values of K_x reported in the literature vary over several orders of magnitude from one river to another. Experience has shown that field measurements of transverse velocity distributions, combined if possible with actual tracer studies, are essential for evaluation of K_x (see ref. 11 for field measurement techniques). The strong dependence of K_x on flow conditions renders the one-dimensional technique of little value for predictive simulations.

5.2   Difficulties in Evaluating the Transverse Mixing Coefficient in Natural Channels

Unfortunately there is little theoretical or practical justification for representing the transverse mixing due to transverse differential advection as a gradient diffusion process as in eqn (65), then combining this with transverse turbulent diffusion in an overall coefficient E_z (see eqn (66)). To do so would require that the secondary flow profile appearing in $\widetilde{w''C''}$ be established long enough for an initial or advective period to be surpassed. Yet such secondary flow profiles develop due to flow curvature, be it in bends or in the vicinity of local bed and bank

TABLE 1
SUMMARY OF EXISTING KNOWLEDGE ON MIXING COEFFICIENTS

Dispersion situation	Mixing coefficients	Commonly adopted values	Theoretical basis (Reference No.)	Remarks
(1) Molecular diffusion	ε_m	$\sim 10^{-7}\, m^2/s$	—	Value depends on type of contaminant and solute
(2) 3-D turbulent diffusion, unbounded	ε_x ε_y ε_z			Must be measured or estimated by turbulence modeling
(3) 3-D turbulent diffusion, shear flow	ε_x ε_y ε_z	$\kappa/6 u_* h$ $\kappa/6 u_* h$ $0.23 u_* h$	34 7 7	Reynolds analogy; Elder assumed $\varepsilon_y = \varepsilon_x$; Elder measurements
(4) 2-D depth-averaged dispersion, plane flow	K_x $\tilde{\varepsilon}_z$	$5.93 u_* h$ $0.23 u_* h$	7 7	Assumes log velocity profile (coefficient 0.23 subject to debate)
(5) 2-D depth-averaged dispersion, confined channel	K_x E_z	$5.93 u_* h$ $\tilde{\varepsilon}_z + ?$	7	Role of secondary currents in E_z difficult to quantify
(6) 1-D cross-sectional average dispersion, turbulent pipe flow	K_x	$10.1 u_* r$	34	
(7) 1-D cross-sectional average dispersion, turbulent river flow	F_a	eqn (51)	9 11	F_a strongly dependent on channel geometry and flow patterns

irregularities. Such curvature is by nature constantly changing (in a spatial sense), developing and decaying as stream alignment and irregularities vary longitudinally. Thus Taylor's 'diffusive' period for transverse differential advection is never attained, formally disallowing the use of an overall gradient representation such as eqn (65).

This theoretical obstacle has not obviated the engineer's need to incorporate transverse mixing in numerical models of contaminant mixing in rivers. Consequently many investigators have adopted eqn (65) despite its theoretical weakness, often, if not always, invoking a supposed analogy with longitudinal mixing in writing

$$E_z = a_z u_* h \qquad (85)$$

in which a_z is taken as a coefficient to be calibrated.

In the absence of secondary circulation perpendicular to the mean flow direction, w'' is everywhere zero, and eqn (85) should be a sound formulation in view of obtaining an extrapolatable calibration. The original work of Elder[7] yielded $a_z = 0.23$ for uniform flow in a straight, wide, open channel. Subsequent work by many investigators has led to a consensus that a_z should be from 0·1 to 0·2 in uniform flow where lateral mixing is due only to bed-generated turbulence, as fully described by the parameter $u_* h$.[21] But in natural channels, when the gradient diffusion mixing of eqn (65) is assumed and the diffusivity is presumed to follow eqn (85), a wide range of values of a_z has been reported, from 0·2–0·3 in irrigation canals[39] to 0·5–5 or more in natural rivers.[22] Recognising that some of this variation is undoubtably due to advective effects which were not separated from diffusive ones in the analysis of data, several researchers have attempted to explain the variation by correlating a_z with overall channel characteristics such as width-to-depth ratio, sinuosity, meander amplitude-to-wavelength ratio, bed friction factor, etc., and even to propose alternative formulations of eqn (85).[20,21,22,26,36] These analyses have met with varying degrees of success in reducing the range of uncertainty in the variation of E_z. Another research approach has been directed towards finding how E_z varies within the cross-section. Holley[15] proposed several possible alternative formulations of eqn (85) for local evaluation of E_z. These and other proposals were investigated by Holly[17] and Krishnappan and Lau.[20,22] Although the results are not conclusive, it would appear that if an E_z exists, its variation across a section is unimportant compared to its variation from one section to another.

When secondary circulation exists, as in bends or near local channel irregularities, there is no reason to expect $\overline{w''C''}/(\partial\tilde{C}/\partial z)$ to be simply proportional to u_*h, which cannot provide a complete description of secondary flows. For example, in an analysis similar to Elder's derivation for E_x, Fischer[10] used Rozovskii's[29] secondary flow profile in the central portion of a wide stream to obtain

$$a_z \sim \frac{U^2 h^2}{R^2 u_*^2} \qquad (86)$$

where U is the longitudinal velocity in the bend and R is the radius of curvature. In a dimensional analysis of the problem, Krishnappan and Lau[20] found that a_z should depend on the bed friction factor, width-to-depth ratio, width-to-radius of curvature ratio, and position. Therefore when secondary circulation exists in bends, a_z is a property of the flow itself, and its calibration in eqn (85) for one flow condition would have no general applicability. The implication is that, when secondary circulation exists, no attempt should be made to group the diffusive and advective transverse transport in a single gradient-diffusion process. Instead, the separate contribution of advection must be explicitly taken into account, using a specific, physically based formulation.

These uncertainties as to the value and existence of E_z, and indeed as to the validity of eqns (65) and (85) in natural channels, are preventing the full development of mathematical dispersion models as reliable engineering tools. Model results can always be brought into close agreement with field experiments using appropriate values of E_z and/or a_z; but do the calibrated values have any generality for flow conditions other than those for which calibration was performed? The large variability of a_z discussed above, plus the lack of a clear physical interpretation of a_z, suggests that the answer to the above question is no. In a study of dispersion in a short, fairly straight reach of the Isère River in France, Holly and Nerat[18] found that in order to reproduce results from a field study of dye dispersion, a mathematical model based on the stream tube eqn (76) had to have a_z values ranging from 0·5 to 2·5, in a single 4 km reach! Because there is no quantifiable physical explanation for this range of values, the authors concluded that use of the calibrated model to simulate conditions after dam construction was at best very tenuous. Yet the study had been commissioned for just such a purpose. In a similar study on several Canadian rivers, Beltaos[2] concluded that, given the two distinct components of transverse mixing in a stream tube model — turbulent diffusion and transverse advection — it is difficult to see how a single mixing coefficient like E_z can be simply correlated with bulk hydraulic parameters.

It is obvious that a new approach to the transverse mixing problem in the context of a calibratable depth-averaged models is needed. Past theoretical and experimental support for treating *local longitudinal* mixing as a simple gradient diffusion process with diffusivity proportional to u_*h has been adopted for *reach-averaged transverse* mixing. Yet theoretical support is lacking and experimental evidence is proving difficult to interpret.

The remedy for the difficulties described above would appear to lie in obtaining a new formulation of transverse mixing. This formulation would explicitly recognise the three processes which produce transverse mixing: (1) turbulent and molecular diffusion; (2) differential advection due to bend-generated secondary currents, if present; and (3) differential advection due to local secondary circulation generated by local bed non-uniformities.

The mathematical description of each of these processes would still require calibration of a parameter *particular to that process*, and related to the river geometry but not to the flow. In item (1) above, the parameter would be the constant of proportionality with u_*h, with a value presumably close to the 0·1–0·2 observed in straight, wide canals. In item (2) the parameter would be related to the secondary-flow formulation adopted, be it Fischer's formulation as in eqn (86) or one based on more recent investigations, such as those of Nakato et al.[24] or Falcon-Ascanio and Kennedy.[8] In item (3), the parameter would result from a new, physically based representation of the mechanisms of local secondary current generation in straight river reaches whose development is one of the principal objects of research currently underway at the Iowa Institute of Hydraulic Research.

The problem at hand is one of evaluating the additional transverse mixing caused by differential advection when local bed or bank non-uniformities generate local secondary flow. Such secondary flow would seldom become fully established, in the sense that an observer moving downstream with the depth-averaged flow would see a constantly changing transverse velocity profile. This fact precludes an analysis such as Taylor's,[34] in which a sort of equilibrium between vertical diffusion and longitudinal differential advection is hypothesised to exist during the 'diffusive' period. Indeed, a fully developed, stable secondary flow profile would have to be maintained over a streamwise length of the order of one hundred depths for Taylor's asymptotic results to apply, whereas the length scale of local non-uniformities (dunes, bars, etc.) is of the order of only several depths. Therefore the transverse transport represented symbolically by $\widetilde{w''C''}$ must be evaluated without recourse to Taylor's asymptotic results, i.e. without assuming a constant coefficient gradient diffusion process. This is the problem at hand.

REFERENCES

1. BATU, V. Two-dimensional dispersion from strip sources. *J. Hydraul. Eng. ASCE*, **109** (6) (1983), 827–41.
2. BELTAOS, S. Transverse mixing tests in natural streams. *J. Hydraul. Div. ASCE*, **106** (HY10) (1980), 1607–25.
3. CARNAHAN, B., LUTHER, H. A. and WILKES, J. O. *Applied Numerical Methods*, John Wiley, New York, 1969.
4. CHATWIN, P. C. The approach to normality of the concentration distribution of a solute in a solvent flowing along a straight pipe. *J. Fluid Mech.*, **43** (1970), 321–52.
5. CLEARY, R. W. and ADRIAN, D. D. New analytic solutions for dye diffusion equations. *J. Environ. Eng. Div. ASCE*, **99** (EE3) (1973), 213–27.
6. CSNADY, G. T. *Turbulent Diffusion in the Environment*, D. Reidel, Boston, 1973.
7. ELDER, J. W. The dispersion of marked fluid in turbulent shear flow. *J. Fluid Mech.*, **5** (1959), 544–60.
8. FALCON-ASCANIO, M. and KENNEDY, J. F. Flow in alluvial-river curves. *J. Fluid Mech.*, **133** (1983), 1–16.
9. FISCHER, H. B. The mechanics of dispersion in natural streams. *J. Hydraul. Div. ASCE*, **93** (1967), 187–216.
10. FISCHER, H. B. The effect of bends on dispersion in streams. *Water Resources Res.*, **5** (1969), 496–506.
11. FISCHER, H. B., LIST, E. J., KOH, R. C. Y., IMBERGER, J. and BROOKS, N. H. *Mixing in Inland and Coastal Waters*, Academic Press, New York, 1979.
12. FISCHER, H. B. and HOLLEY, E. R. Analysis of the use of distorted hydraulic models for dispersion studies. *Water Resources Res.*, **7**(1), (1971), 46–51.
13. FRENKIEL, F. N. Turbulent diffusion. *Adv. Appl. Mech.*, **3** (1953), 61–107.
14. FUKUSHIMA, Y. and HAYAKAWA, N. Laminar dispersion in an elliptical pipe and a rectangular pipe. *J. Hydrosci. Hydraul. Eng.*, **1**(1) (1983), 65–73.
15. HOLLEY, E. R. Transverse mixing in rivers. Report No. S-132, Delft Hydraulics Laboratory, Delft, The Netherlands, 1971.
16. HOLLY, F. M. JR and USSEGLIO-POLATERA, J. M. Dispersion simulation in two-dimensional tidal flow. *J. Hydraul. Eng. ASCE*, **110**(7) (1984), 905–26.
17. HOLLY, F. M. JR. Two dimensional mass dispersion in rivers. Hydrology Paper No. 78, Colorado State University, Fort Collins, 1975.
18. HOLLY, F. M. JR. and NERAT, G. Field calibration of a stream tube dispersion model. *J. Hydraul. Eng. ASCE*, **109**(11) (1983), 1145–470.
19. JAIN, S. C. Longitudinal dispersion coefficients for streams. *J. Environ. Eng. Div. ASCE*, **102** (EE2) (1976), 465–74.
20. KRISHNAPPAN, B. G. and LAU, Y. L. Transverse mixing in meandering

channels with varying bottom topography. *J. Hydraul. Res.* **15**(4) (1977), 351–71.

21. LAU, Y. L. and KRISHNAPPAN, B. G. Transverse dispersion in rectangular channels. *J. Hydraul. Div. ASCE*, **103** (1977), 1173–89.

22. LAU, Y. L. and KRISHNAPPAN, B. G. Modeling transverse mixing in natural streams. *J. Hydraul. Div. ASCE*, **107** (HY2) (1981), 209–26.

23. MONIN, A. S. and YAGLOM, A. M. *Statistical Fluid Mechanics*, MIT Press, Cambridge, Mass., 1971.

24. NAKATO, T., KENNEDY, J. F. and VADNAL, J. A numerical model for flow and sediment transport in alluvial-river bends. IIHR Report No. 271, Iowa Institute of Hydraulic Research, University of Iowa, Iowa City, Dec. 1983.

25. NORDIN, C. F. and SABOL, G. V. Empirical data on longitudinal dispersion in rivers. USGS Water Resource Investigation 20–24, August, 1974.

26. OKOYE, J. K. Characteristics of transverse mixing in open channel flows. Report KH-R-23, California Institute of Technology, Pasadena, 1970.

27. PETERSEN, F. B. Prediction of longitudinal dispersion in natural streams. Series Paper 14, Institute of Hydrodynamics and Hydraulic Engineering, Technical University of Denmark, Lyngby, 1977.

28. PRAKASH, A. Convective dispersion in perennial streams. *J. Environ. Eng. Div. ASCE*, **103** (EE2) (1977), 321–40.

29. ROZOVSKII, I. L. *Flow of Water in Bends of Open Channels*. Translation No. OTS 60-51133, Office of Technical Services, US Dept. of Commerce, Washington, DC, 1957.

30. SAYRE, W. W. Environmental dispersion processes. Unpublished class notes, Iowa Institute of Hydraulic Research, University of Iowa, Iowa City, 1977.

31. SAYRE, W. W. Dispersion of mass in open channel flow. Hydraulic Paper No. 3, Colorado State University, Fort Collins, Feb. 1968.

32. TAYLOR, G. I. Diffusion by continuous movements. *Proc. London Math. Soc. Ser. A*, **20** (1921), 196–211.

33. TAYLOR, G. I. Dispersion of soluble matter in solvent flowing slowly through a tube. *Proc. R. Soc. London Ser. A*, **219** (1953), 186–203.

34. TAYLOR, G. I. The dispersion of matter in turbulent flow through a pipe. *Proc. R. Soc. London Ser. A*, **223** (1954), 446–68.

35. VALENTINE, E. M. and WOOD, I. R. Longitudinal dispersion with dead zones. *J. Hydraul. Div. ASCE*, **103**(HY9) (1977), 975–90.

36. WEBEL, G. and SCHATZMANN, M. The role of bed roughness in turbulent diffusion and dispersion. Theme D, International Symposium River Engineering and its Interaction with Hydrological and Hydraulic Research, IAHR, Belgrade, May, 1980.

37. WHITE, F. M. *Viscous Fluid Flow*, McGraw-Hill, New York, 1974.

38. YEH, G.-T. and TSAI, Y.-J. Analytical three-dimensional transient modeling of effluent discharges. *Water Resources Res.*, **12**(3) (1976), 533–40.

39. YOTSUKURA, N. and COBB, E. D. Transverse diffusion of solutes in natural streams. USGS Professional Paper 582-C, 1972.

40. YOTSUKURA, N., FISCHER, H. B. and SAYRE, W. W. Measurement of mixing characteristics of the Missouri river between Sioux City, Iowa and Platts-mouth, Nebraska. USGS Water Supply Paper 1899-G, 1970.

41. YOTSUKURA, N. and SAYRE, W. W. Transverse mixing in natural channels. *Water Resources Res.*, **12**(4) (1976), 695–704.

Chapter 2

DISPERSION IN RIVERS AND COASTAL WATERS — 2. NUMERICAL COMPUTATION OF DISPERSION

Patrick Sauvaget

SOGREAH Consulting Engineers, Grenoble, France

NOTATION

(M = mass; T = time; L = length; K = temperature)

a_i, b_i, a_i', b_i' $(i = 1, 4)$	coefficients of the Hermitian interpolation polynomial in the one-dimensional Holly–Preissmann scheme; coefficients of the discretised one-dimensional diffusion equation
a_k, b_k, d_k, e_k $(k = 1, 4)$	coefficients of the Hermitian interpolation polynomial in the two-dimensional Holly–Preissmann scheme
a_x, a_z	calibration coefficients for longitudinal and transverse mixing coefficients $(L^2 T^{-1})$
A	cross-sectional area (L^2)
C_d	dissolved oxygen concentration
C_n	heat capacity of water $(L^2 T^{-2} K^{-1})$
C_s	saturation dissolved oxygen concentration
$\hat{C}$	cross-sectional average concentration
$\hat{C}_i^n$	cross-sectional average concentration at the calculation point i, at time n
$\tilde{C}$	average concentration over the depth
Cr	Courant-like number
$\hat{C}X$	x derivative of the cross-sectional average concentration
$\hat{C}X_i^n$	x derivative of the cross-sectional average concentration at the calculation point i, at time n

$\hat{C}T$ t derivative of the cross-sectional average concentration

$\tilde{C}X$ x derivative of the average concentration over the depth

$\tilde{C}Z$ z derivative of the average concentration over the depth

$\tilde{C}XZ$ 2nd order derivative of the average concentration over the depth with respect to x and z

E_z depth-average transverse mixing coefficient $(L^2 T^{-1})$

f_i^n value of the function f at the calculation point i, at time n

F_x cross-sectional average longitudinal mixing coefficient $(L^2 T^{-1})$

g acceleration due to gravity $(L^2 T^{-1})$

h cross-sectional average depth (L)

k_1, k_2 decay coefficients of Streeter–Phelps model (T^{-1})

K_1, K_2 interdependence constants for non-conservative processes

K_n coefficient of longitudinal numerical diffusion in the Bella and Dobbins scheme $(L^2 T^{-1})$

K_x effective longitudinal diffusion coefficient $(L^2 T^{-1})$

L wavelength of one component in the Von-Neumann stability analysis of the one-dimensional Holly–Preissmann scheme; biological oxygen demand concentration

S slope of the energy line

t time (T)

T temperature of the water (K)

T_e equilibrium water temperature (K)

u, v x and z direction velocities (LT^{-1})

u_{10} wind velocity 10 m above water surface (LT^{-1})

u_z z derivative of the x direction velocity (LT^{-1})

u_* cross-sectional average shear stress velocity (LT^{-1})

$\hat{U}$ cross-sectional average velocity (LT^{-1})

x, y, z spatial coordinates (L)

α, β coefficients indicating the position of the foot of the characteristic in the Dobbins and Bella, as well as in the Holly and Preissmann schemes

β thermal exchange coefficient $(MT^{-3} K^{-1})$

Δ is used to indicate a small increment of one quantity

ε_{ij} turbulent diffusivities tensor $(L^2 T^{-1})$

θ coefficient of implication

λ eigenvalue in the stability analysis of the one-dimensional Holly–Preissmann scheme

Σ indicates summation

1 INTRODUCTION

The previous chapter reviewed the theory and basic equations of dispersion. Engineering analysis of dispersion requires that this theory furnish a means of predicting contaminant concentration as a function of time anywhere in the flow field of interest, as a result of a specific contaminant spill. The use of the analytical solutions presented in Sections 2.3 and 4.4 of the previous chapter is restricted to rather idealised flow geometries and spill configurations; solution of the equations for arbitrary flows and spills requires the use of approximate numerical techniques.

The purpose of this chapter is to present and analyse a few of the many numerical techniques available. Since space limitations preclude an extensive, objective appraisal of the many methodologies available, the author takes the admittedly subjective route of describing only the methods he has found to be most effective in his investigatory and consulting activity with SOGREAH Consulting Engineers. However, reference is made to other work where appropriate.

An essential input to numerical contaminant dispersion models is detailed depth and current data, varying in both space and time. It is precisely because such information can now be so readily furnished by numerical hydrodynamic models that dispersion models have come into their own. In fact the primary purpose of many hydrodynamic modelling efforts is to furnish the required input for a dispersion model. If hydrodynamic data are taken from field observations or physical scale model measurements, then it is extremely important to ensure that water depths and velocities are mutually consistent in satisfying the water continuity equation in the form it is implicitly or explicitly used in a dispersion model. This is because the assumption of water continuity is made throughout the dispersion equation derivation.

2 NUMERICAL SOLUTION OF THE DISPERSION EQUATION

To simplify presentation of the numerical problems posed by solution of the dispersion equation, this equation is considered here in its general one-dimensional form, which is

$$\frac{\partial(A\hat{C})}{\partial t} + \frac{\partial(A\hat{U}\hat{C})}{\partial x} = \frac{\partial}{\partial x}\left(AF_x \frac{\partial \hat{C}}{\partial x}\right) \tag{1}$$

with $A(x,t)$ = wetted cross-section; $\hat{U}(x,t)$ = mean longitudinal flow velocity in the section; $\hat{C}(x,t)$ = mean concentration in the section and $F_x(x,t)$ = coefficient of longitudinal diffusivity mixing.

If the values of U and A satisfy at all points the continuity equation

$$\frac{\partial A}{\partial t} + \frac{\partial(A\hat{U})}{\partial x} = 0 \tag{2}$$

then eqn (1) can be written in the form presented as eqn (53) of the previous chapter

$$A\frac{\partial \hat{C}}{\partial t} + A\hat{U}\frac{\partial \hat{C}}{\partial x} = \frac{\partial}{\partial x}\left(AF_x\frac{\partial \hat{C}}{\partial x}\right) \tag{3}$$

2.1 Physical and Mathematical Distinction between Advection and Diffusion

Each of the terms of eqn (3) represents a particular physical phenomenon: $A(\partial\hat{C}/\partial t)$ is the variation of pollutant contained in an elementary fluid volume per unit time; $A\hat{U}(\partial\hat{C}/\partial x)$ represents the bulk transport of the pollutant due to the displacement of the fluid volume which conveys it; this is the advective term and $(\partial/\partial x)(AF_x(\partial\hat{C}/\partial x))$ incorporates various mixing processes: molecular diffusion, turbulent diffusion and differential advection, the last two terms coming from integration of the three-dimensional transport equations as described in Section 3 of the previous chapter.

If the diffusive term is ignored, eqn (3) is reduced to the following

$$\frac{\partial \hat{C}}{\partial t} + \hat{U}\frac{\partial \hat{C}}{\partial x} = 0 \tag{4}$$

Since the velocity $\hat{U}$ is independent of the concentration $\hat{C}$, this is an equation of linear partial derivatives of the first order. It can also take the form

$$\frac{d\hat{C}}{dt} = 0 \tag{5}$$

$d\hat{C}/dt$ being the total, or substantial, derivative of the concentration $\hat{C}(x,t)$. This means that the value of $\hat{C}$ attached to a fluid volume remains constant during the movement of this volume along its course. Each course is defined by the characteristic equation of (4):

$$\frac{dx}{dt} = \hat{U}(x,t) \tag{6}$$

To solve eqn (4), it is necessary to know an upstream boundary condition and an initial state. A large number of schemes of finite differences and of finite elements have been used to solve eqn (4), but most are affected by a numerical error equivalent to an artificial diffusion. This error is of varying importance according to the solution scheme adopted, and may dominate the physical diffusion completely when eqn (3) is considered in full. The nature of eqn (4) justifies the use of schemes based on the method of characteristics, applications of which are considered later on in this chapter. These schemes allow natural processing of the boundary conditions, and certain of them give a high degree of precision.

Now consider a flow in which transport takes place by longitudinal diffusion only, so that eqn (3) reduces to

$$A\frac{\partial \hat{C}}{\partial t}=\frac{\partial}{\partial x}\left(AF_x\frac{\partial \hat{C}}{\partial x}\right) \qquad (7)$$

A and F_x vary with the longitudinal distance x and time t, but are independent of the concentration $\hat{C}$. Mathematically, this is an equation of linear partial derivatives of the second order, of the parabolic type. It can be solved numerically by a large number of schemes of finite differences and finite elements, and requires knowledge of two boundary conditions (upstream and downstream) and of an initial state. There are few numerical problems in solving this equation, the main difficulty being definition of the boundary conditions.

The overall solution of eqn (3) has been tackled in numerous ways. Gray and Pinder[7] describe a certain number of these in their analysis. However, the different mathematical nature of the advection eqn (4) and the diffusion eqn (7) justifies the adoption of different solution methods, bearing in mind that diffusion poses much fewer numerical problems than advection. Thus the solution of eqn (3) may be separated into two stages: for each time step, eqn (4) and then eqn (7) are solved successively by computational schemes that are appropriate to each of them.

The following paragraphs set out the difficulties involved in this split-operator solution of eqn (3). Subsequently, a general approach for solution of eqn (3) is proposed in Section 3.

2.2 Difficulties in Computing Advection

It may seem straightforward to solve eqn (4), which expresses the following fact: at constant speed $\hat{U}$, if a particle is at x at time t, it will be at $x+\hat{U}\Delta t$ at time $t+\Delta t$. The pollutant distribution will thus satisfy the following

$$\hat{C}(x, t + \Delta t) = \hat{C}(x - \hat{U}\Delta t, t) \qquad (8)$$

The method of characteristics is based on this reasoning, and is the most natural way of tackling eqn (4). This method is adopted herein to highlight the different types of numerical error encountered.

An Eulerian solution of eqn (3) requires definition of a computational network, i.e. the time step Δt and spatial interval Δx_i, both of which may be varied if necessary (see Fig. 1).

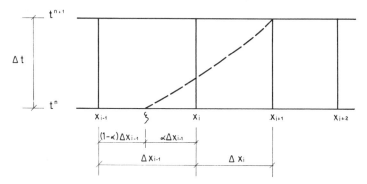

FIG. 1. Computational grid and characteristic trajectory for numerical solution of 1-D dispersion equation.

The flow velocity $\hat{U}(x, t)$ must also be known at each point of the network. With $\hat{U}_i^n$ denoting the velocity at the calculation point x_i at time t_n, application of eqn (8) gives

$$\hat{C}_{i+1}^{n+1} = \hat{C}_\xi^n \qquad (9)$$

ξ being the foot of the trajectory leading to the point (x_{i+1}, t_{n+1}). If $\hat{U}$ is a constant throughout between time t_n and time t_{n+1}, this trajectory is a straight line of slope $\hat{U}$. If at the same time Δx_i and Δt are such that the Courant-like number $Cr = U\Delta t/\Delta x_i = 1$, then

$$\hat{C}_{i+1}^{n+1} = \hat{C}_i^n \qquad (9a)$$

However, generally speaking the following conditions apply.

On the one hand, the velocity $\hat{U}$ is variable over the time interval $\Delta t = t_{n+1} - t_n$, so that a reverse trajectory calculation has to be made from point (x_{i+1}, t_{n+1}).

On the other hand, the condition $Cr = 1$ is not respected everywhere. The value of C_ξ^n therefore has to be interpolated between the values for known points close to ξ. The first type of interpolation which comes to mind is linear interpolation between two points in the immediate vicinity of ξ, leading to the scheme proposed by Bella and Dobbins.[2]

In this case, eqn (9) is written as follows

$$\hat{C}_{i+1}^{n+1} = (1-\alpha)\hat{C}_i^n + \alpha\,\hat{C}_{i-1}^n \tag{10}$$

α being defined as shown on Fig. 1.

Taking $\hat{U}$ as constant over time interval Δt, and assuming $\Delta x_{i-1} = \Delta x_i = \Delta x$, the present approach is to identify the consistency of such a scheme with the initial equation. Taylor's series developments of $\hat{C}_{i+1}^{n+1}$, $\hat{C}_i^n$ and $\hat{C}_{i-1}^n$ in the vicinity of point (x_{i+1}, t_n), considering only terms of the 2nd order, are as follows

$$\hat{C}_{i+1}^{n+1} \doteq \hat{C}_{i+1}^n + \frac{\partial \hat{C}}{\partial t}\Delta t + \frac{\partial^2 \hat{C}}{\partial t^2}\frac{\Delta t^2}{2}$$

$$\hat{C}_i^n \doteq \hat{C}_{i+1}^n - \frac{\partial \hat{C}}{\partial x}\Delta x + \frac{\partial^2 \hat{C}}{\partial x^2}\frac{\Delta x^2}{2}$$

$$\hat{C}_{i-1}^n \doteq \hat{C}_{i+1}^n - 2\frac{\partial \hat{C}}{\partial x}\Delta x + 2\frac{\partial^2 \hat{C}}{\partial x^2}\Delta x^2$$

Substituting these in eqn (10), the following is obtained

$$\frac{\partial \hat{C}}{\partial t}\Delta t + (1+\alpha)\frac{\partial \hat{C}}{\partial x}\Delta x = \frac{(1+3\alpha)}{2}\frac{\partial^2 \hat{C}}{\partial x^2}\Delta x^2 - \frac{1}{2}\frac{\partial^2 \hat{C}}{\partial t^2}\Delta t^2$$

Thus, applying the equations $(\alpha + 1)\Delta x = \hat{U}\Delta t$ and $\partial^2 \hat{C}/\partial t^2 = \hat{U}^2(\partial^2 \hat{C}/\partial x^2)$,

$$\frac{\partial \hat{C}}{\partial t} + \hat{U}\frac{\partial \hat{C}}{\partial x} = \frac{\alpha(1-\alpha)}{2}\frac{\Delta x^2}{\Delta t}\frac{\partial^2 \hat{C}}{\partial x^2} \tag{11}$$

The Bella and Dobbins[2] scheme is therefore consistent with eqn (4) to the first order in the general case. If $\alpha = 0$ or $\alpha = 1$, then consistency is ensured to the 2nd order. In this case, the trajectory reaching point (x_{i+1}, t_{n+1}) originates from one of the points (x_{i-1}, t_n) or (x_i, t_n) of the computational grid. The parasitic term

$$\frac{\alpha(1-\alpha)}{2}\frac{\Delta x^2}{\Delta t}\frac{\partial^2 \hat{C}}{\partial x^2}$$

may be considered as a numerical diffusion, for which the coefficient of diffusivity is as follows:

$$K_n = \frac{\alpha(1-\alpha)}{2}\frac{\Delta x^2}{\Delta t} \qquad (12)$$

Similarly, for ξ situated between the abscissa points x_i and x_{i+1} (see Fig. 1), the same analysis would give:

$$\frac{\partial \hat{C}}{\partial t} + \hat{U}\frac{\partial \hat{C}}{\partial x} = K_n\frac{\partial^2 \hat{C}}{\partial x^2} \qquad (13)$$

with

$$K_n = \frac{\beta(1-\beta)}{2}\frac{\Delta x^2}{\Delta t} \qquad (14)$$

β being such that $x_\xi = (1-\beta)\, x_{i+1} + \beta x_i$. The maximum value of K_n is reached in the middle of each spatial interval Δx_i and amounts to $K_n = \frac{1}{8}(\Delta x^2/\Delta t)$. Numerically, K_n may be significantly greater than the physical diffusivity coefficient and may thus completely conceal this phenomenon. For application of the Bella and Dobbins[2] scheme, the following general recommendations must therefore be followed:[19] (a) take Δx as short as possible; (b) take Δt as long as possible, while still representing the transport process in detail; and (c) choose Δx and Δt so that $\Delta x \simeq (\hat{U}\Delta t/n)$, n being a positive integer.

In the same way as for the scheme just described, any scheme consistent with eqn (4) to the first order will be affected by numerical diffusion. To eliminate this error, it is possible to use schemes of a higher order, for example using, with the characteristics method, an interpolating function of a higher degree. The amplitude of the profiles of transported concentrations will be more precise, but there will remain an error resulting in non-symmetry of an initially symmetrical concentration, as remarked by Abbott.[1] Moreover, such schemes give rise to numerical oscillations, since they involve the introduction of data remote from the computation point. A typical example is provided by Martin's[15] schemes to the 2nd, 3rd and 4th orders on advection of a Gaussian profile. In a Martin's scheme to the nth order, the data for $n+1$ points surrounding the computation point are used. Figure 2 shows that the numerical oscillations increase with the degree of consistency of the scheme (curves 3 and 4). Moreover, when the number of computation points involved in the scheme is large, the boundary conditions are difficult to impose, thus

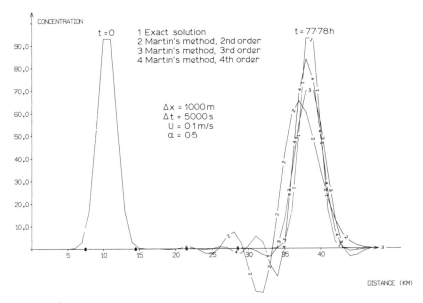

FIG. 2. Martin's[15] schemes for pure advection of a Gaussian.

requiring approximations at the boundaries which have the effect of reducing the formal order of accuracy. The Leendertse[14] scheme (Fig. 3) also produces numerical oscillations. This scheme highlights another type of error: the maximum on the computed concentration profile is not situated on the same abscissa as the maximum on the analytical profile. This is called numerical phase error.

The main property of all the schemes described above is conservation of the initial pollutant mass, that is

$$\sum \hat{C}_i^n = \sum \hat{C}_i^0 \qquad (15)$$

at any time t_n. Care must be taken not to destroy this property, for example by fixing at zero the negative concentrations obtained by calculation. Physically, of course, such results have no meaning, but their elimination would have the effect of artificially creating a pollutant mass in the middle of the calculation.

2.3 Difficulties in Computing Diffusion
In most real situations, longitudinal diffusion plays a secondary role by comparison with advection. It is only in elongated reservoirs, where flow

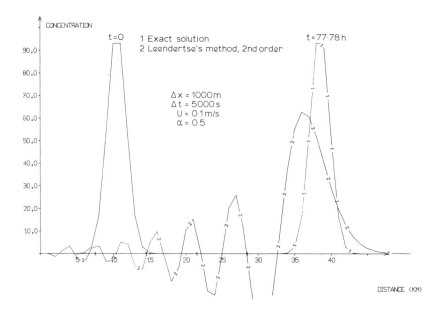

FIG. 3. Leendertse's[14] scheme for pure advection of a Gaussian.

velocities are low, and in tidal estuaries, with their periodic currents, that diffusion is preponderant. Among the finite difference schemes commonly used, preference will be given herein to an unconditionally stable scheme.

2.3.1 Imposed Boundary Conditions

Physically, if diffusion is considered independently of any other phenomenon, there are two typical situations as regards boundary conditions. (a) The concentration $\hat{C}(x_0, t)$ is imposed at x_0. This is a boundary condition of the Dirichlet type, involving, for example, injection of a pollutant of imposed concentration at a boundary of the simulated network, or a reservoir with constant concentration. (b) The derivative of concentration $(\partial \hat{C}/\partial x)(x_0, t)$ is imposed at x_0. This is a boundary condition of the Neuman type, involving for example reflection at an impermeable boundary of the model, which imposes $(\partial \hat{C}/\partial x) = 0$. Other situations, such as a permeable boundary, depend on information remote from the boundary point, and can only be represented with difficulty and imprecisely.

In any event, if the advection eqn (4) and diffusion eqn (7) are solved successively for each time step, it is necessary to impose conditions at each of the model boundaries for each stage of the process. This is in contradiction with real conditions, under which advection and diffusion take place simultaneously. For the reasons given above, it is preferable to adopt for the diffusion stage boundary conditions that are compatible with the advection stage, even if this means not following strictly the physics of the diffusion phenomenon.

3 CALCULATION OF ONE-DIMENSIONAL DISPERSION

3.1 Detailed Description of the One-Dimensional Holly–Preissmann Method

The characteristics method consists in replacing solution of the partial differential derivatives eqn (4) by the successive solution of the two ordinary differential eqns (5) and (6) on a grid (x, t) similar to that shown in Fig. 4. For a given time step, three operations are performed for each computational point: the position of point A is calculated by integration of eqn (6); the concentration at point A is computed by some interpolation scheme; and this concentration is assigned directly to point B (integration of eqn (5)).

The precision obtained for the integration of eqn (6) depends on the data available on velocity in the vicinity of A. Generally, $\hat{U}$ is known for each point of the grid, $\hat{U}_i^n$ for each x_i and for each t_n. Supposing that variations of $\hat{U}$ are linear on each of the lines of the grid, it is possible to calculate the position of A with a precision of 2nd order, since the velocity is the derivative of the position of the point. This integration may be effected by the following iterative method:

$$\hat{U}_A^{(0)} = \hat{U}_B$$

$$x_A = x_i - \frac{\hat{U}_A^{(j-1)} + \hat{U}_B}{2} \Delta t \tag{16}$$

$$\hat{U}_A^{(j)} = [(x_A^{(j)} - x_{i-1})\hat{U}_i + (x_i - x_A^{(j)})\hat{U}_{i-1}]/(x_i - x_{i-1})$$

$x_A^{(j)}$ and $\hat{U}_A^{(j)}$ being the abscissa of point A and its velocity at iteration j. The calculation is stopped when the precision of the non-dimensional number $(\hat{U}^{(j)} \Delta t)/(x_i - x_A^{(j)})$ (Courant-like number) is sufficient. This procedure is applicable regardless of the position of point A on one of the segments PQ, QR, RS or ST.

Once the location of the foot of the characteristic A has been determined, it is necessary to calculate by interpolation the value of

PATRICK SAUVAGET

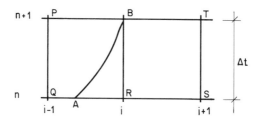

FIG. 4. Computational grid for the Holly–Preissmann method.

concentration at this point. Where velocities are concerned, linear interpolation is sufficient, since the velocity varies only slowly with x. On
the other hand, the pollutant concentration in a flow may present sudden
variations, since the equalising diffusion process only gradually makes
itself felt. Consequently, it will be preferable to interpolate the concentration by a higher order method. To calculate the concentration $\hat{C}_A$,
the data given for points $i-1$, i, $i+1$, etc., at time n have to be used. If
information remote from point A is used, the scheme produces numerical
oscillations and the boundary conditions are difficult to impose, as was
shown in Section 2.2. Holly and Preissmann[8] propose interpolation of
$\hat{C}_A$ using information at points $i-1$ and i only, thanks to a Hermite
cubic function which gives a precision of the 4th order. This function
takes the following form

$$\hat{C}_A = a_1 \hat{C}_{i-1} + a_2 \hat{C}_i^n + a_3 \hat{C}X_{i-1}^n + a_4 \hat{C}X_i^n \tag{17}$$

with $\hat{C}_i^n$ = concentration at point i and at time n, $\hat{C}X_i^n$ = derivative with
respect to x of the concentration at point i and at time n, and a_1, a_2, a_3,
a_4 are coefficients of the Hermite function depending on the position of
point A. The information on the form of distribution of the pollutant $\hat{C}$
in the section $i-1$, i originates from the spatial derivatives $\hat{C}X_{i-1}^n$ and
$\hat{C}X_i^n$, as is shown by Fig. 5. In order to respect the values $\hat{C}_{i-1}^n$, $\hat{C}_i^n$,
$\hat{C}X_{i-1}^n$ and $\hat{C}X_i^n$, the coefficients a_1, a_2, a_3 and a_4 are expressed as
follows

$$a_1 = \alpha^2(3 - 2\alpha) \qquad a_3 = \alpha^2(1 - \alpha)(x_i - x_{i-1})$$

$$a_2 = 1' - a_1 \qquad a_4 = -\alpha(1 - \alpha)^2(x_i - x_{i-1})$$

with $\alpha = (x_i - x_A)/(x_i - x_{i-1})$ indicating the position of point A. This
interpolation presupposes that the values $\hat{C}X_{i-1}^n$ and $\hat{C}X_i^n$ are known.
These could be calculated by finite differences from the concentrations at

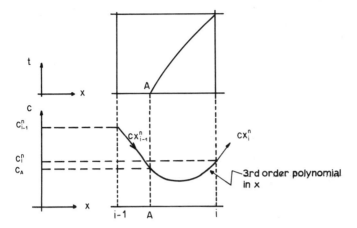

FIG. 5. Hermite interpolating polynomial for concentration.

neighbouring points, but this method reduces the precision obtained by interpolation of the 4th order, especially where the grid is irregular.[9] To keep the high degree of precision, the spatial derivatives $\hat{C}X$ must be advected at the same time as the concentrations $\hat{C}$. Differentiation of eqn (4) with respect to x leads to

$$\frac{\partial \hat{C}X}{\partial t} + \hat{U}\frac{\partial \hat{C}X}{\partial x} = -\hat{C}X\frac{\partial \hat{U}}{\partial x} \tag{18}$$

and this equation may be solved in three steps, in the same way as for concentration: calculation of the characteristic, already effected for $\hat{C}$; interpolation of $\hat{C}X$ at the foot of the characteristic A by the Hermite function and integration along the characteristic of

$$\frac{d\hat{C}X}{dt} = -\hat{C}X\frac{\partial \hat{U}}{\partial x} \tag{19}$$

The interpolating function for $\hat{C}X$ takes the following form

$$\hat{C}X_A = b_1\hat{C}_{i-1}^n + b_2\hat{C}_i^n + b_3\hat{C}X_{i-1}^n + b_4\hat{C}X_i^n \tag{20}$$

with

$$b_1 = 6\alpha(\alpha-1)/(x_i - x_{i-1}) \qquad b_3 = \alpha(3\alpha-2)$$

$$b_2 = -b_1 \qquad b_4 = (\alpha-1)(3\alpha-1)$$

and $\alpha = (x_i - x_A)/(x_i - x_{i-1})$, as for the concentrations. The integration of eqn (19) can be effected simply by the trapezium method

$$\hat{C}X_i^{n+1} = \hat{C}X_A \left[1 - \frac{\Delta t}{2} \frac{\partial \hat{U}}{\partial x} \Big|_A \right] \bigg/ \left[1 + \frac{\Delta t}{2} \frac{\partial \hat{U}}{\partial x} \Big|_B \right] \tag{21}$$

Since it is supposed that $\hat{U}$ varies linearly over the interval $(i-1, i)$, $\partial \hat{U}/\partial x$ is constant over this same interval.

One of the main advantages of this scheme is its compactness. It is based on only two calculation points, thus facilitating processing of the boundary conditions. However, when the grid and the current field are such that $\alpha = ((\hat{U}_A + \hat{U}_B)\Delta t)/(2\Delta t) > 1$ for a given mesh, then point A is situated on the PQ segment of the mesh (see Fig. 4). Calculation of the characteristic could be continued from point A until time n is reached, but this would extend the calculation beyond the limits of the mesh $(i-1, i)$. It is preferable to stop calculation of the characteristic at A and to interpolate the values of $\hat{C}_A$ and $\hat{C}T_A$ from the values $\hat{C}_{i-1}^n$, $\hat{C}_{i-1}^{n+1}$, $\hat{C}T_{i-1}^n$, $\hat{C}T_{i-1}^{n+1}$ ($\hat{C}T_i^n$ being the derivative of the concentration vs t, at point i and at time n). The calculation is identical to that effected previously. $\hat{C}X_A$ is again determined by using eqn (4), that is

$$\hat{C}T_A + U_A \hat{C}X_A = 0 \tag{22}$$

taking care to ensure that $U_A \neq 0$. This interpolation gives

$$\hat{C}_A = a_1' \hat{C}_{i-1}^n + a_2' \hat{C}_{i-1}^{n+1} + a_3' \hat{C}X_{i-1}^n + a_4' \hat{C}X_{i-1}^{n+1} \tag{23}$$

and

$$\hat{C}X_A = -\frac{1}{\hat{U}_A} [b_1' \hat{C}_{i-1}^n + b_2' \hat{C}_{i-1}^{n+1} + b_3' \hat{C}X_{i-1}^n + b_4' \hat{C}X_{i-1}^{n+1}] \tag{24}$$

a_1', a_2', a_3', a_4', b_1', b_2', b_3', b_4' being 3rd order polynomials of the position of point A on the segment PQ, identified by

$$\beta = \frac{t^{n+1} - t_A}{t^{n+1} - t^n} = \frac{1}{\alpha} < 1$$

To conclude, the values C^{n+1} and CX^{n+1} are obtained by integration of eqns (5) and (19).

This interpolation procedure used for $\alpha > 1$ requires knowledge of $\hat{C}_{i-1}^{n+1}$ and $\hat{C}X_{i-1}^{n+1}$ before calculation of $\hat{C}_i^{n+1}$ and $\hat{C}X_i^{n+1}$. This is possible if the calculation is effected following the direction of flow from upstream to downstream. Cases of reversal of the characteristic curves may be processed by an iterative procedure over the whole network. For example, for rivers subjected to tides, it will be found advantageous to be able to calculate the pollutant transport for a value of α either well above or well below 1, without losing too much precision. Moreover, in this type of situation, reversal of the characteristics occurs twice per tidal cycle.

Figure 6 shows application of the numerical scheme just described to the transport by advection of a Gaussian distribution of pollutant in a uniform flow, for different values of the Courant number. Since this method is based on integration along the characteristic curves, the calculated solution closest to the analytical solution is obtained for α = 1. The precision obtained for α = 2 (i.e. for β = 1/α = 0·5) is not quite as good as for α = 0·5.

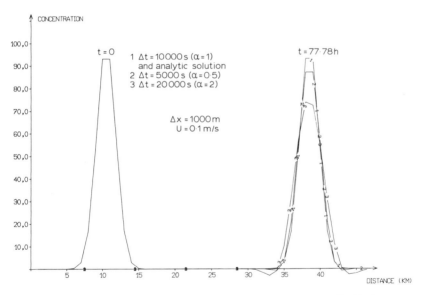

FIG. 6. Advection of a Gaussian in uniform flow using the Holly–Preissmann method.

To solve the complete equation of one-dimensional dispersion, eqn (3), the advection calculation stage will have to be followed at each time step by a stage of solution of the one-dimensional non-stationary diffusion eqn (7). Numerous finite difference schemes are applicable for this equation, solution of which is known to pose fewer problems than that of the advection equation. Since the scheme chosen for advection is stable regardless of the time step, preference will be given to an unconditionally stable scheme for diffusion. This could be a semi-implicit finite difference scheme such as that of Crank–Nicholson, which takes into account the concentration values at sets of three points, since the right side of eqn (7) is of 2nd order. An alternate implicit finite difference scheme is proposed herein, which considers only two adjacent points, introducing an additional variable. The equation of the 2nd order (7) is equivalent to the system of two equations of the 1st order:

$$A \frac{\partial \hat{C}}{\partial t} = \frac{\partial}{\partial x} (AF_x C\hat{X})$$

$$\frac{\partial \hat{C}}{\partial x} = \hat{C}X \tag{25}$$

$\hat{C}$ and $\hat{C}X$ being the dependent variables. Using the following notation $\theta =$ implication coefficient, $\Delta \hat{C}_i = \hat{C}_i^{n+1} - \hat{C}_i^n$, $\Delta \hat{C}X_i = \hat{C}X_i^{n+1} - \hat{C}X_i^n$, $\Delta x = x_i - x_{i+1}$ and a discretisation scheme devised by A. Preissmann adopting the approximations,

$$f(x, t) \approx \frac{\theta}{2} (f_i^{n+1} + f_{i-1}^{n+1}) + \frac{1-\theta}{2} (f_i^n + f_{i-1}^n)$$

$$\frac{\partial f}{\partial x} \approx \theta \frac{(f_i^{n+1} - f_{i-1}^{n+1})}{\Delta x} + (1-\theta) \frac{(f_i^n - f_{i-1}^n)}{\Delta x}$$

$$\frac{\partial f}{\partial t} \approx \frac{(f_i^{n+1} - f_i^n) + (f_{i-1}^{n+1} - f_{i-1}^n)}{2\Delta t}$$

the system (25) breaks down to the following discretised system:

$$a_1 \Delta \hat{C}_i + a_2 \Delta \hat{C}X_i = a_3 \Delta \hat{C}_{i-1} + a_4 \Delta \hat{C}X_{i-1} + a_5$$

$$b_1 \Delta \hat{C}_i + b_2 \Delta \hat{C}X_i = b_3 \Delta \hat{C}_{i-1} + b_4 \Delta \hat{C}X_{i-1} + b_5 \tag{26}$$

The coefficients a_i and b_i $(i=1,5)$ use the values of $\hat{C}$ and $\hat{C}X$ at different points at time t^n and the values of F_x and A at times t^n and t^{n+1}. These latter values depend only on the flow and are therefore known. The system (26) can thus be solved over the whole network by a classic double sweep algorithm. With this scheme it is possible to impose at each of the boundaries of the model any condition of the type

$$a\Delta \hat{C}_1 = b\Delta \hat{C}X_1 + d \tag{27}$$

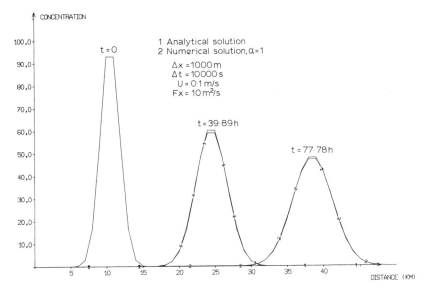

FIG. 7. Advection and diffusion of a Gaussian in uniform flow.

a, b and d being known coefficients. However, to avoid adversely affecting the preceding advection stage, it is generally considered that $\Delta\hat{C}_1 = 0$. Figure 7 shows the application of this numerical scheme to the transport by advection and diffusion of a pollutant distribution initially identical to that in Fig. 6. The diffusion coefficient is $F_x = 10\,\text{m}^2/\text{s}$.

3.2 Error Analysis

The linear analysis of stability developed by Von Neumann enables estimation of the error in phase and in amplitude of the scheme just described for solving the advection eqn (4). To this effect, it is assumed that any pollutant distribution can be written in the form of a Fourier series, of which only one component need be studied. Assuming the velocity $\hat{U}$ to be constant eqn (4) is linear, and the analytical solution for a given Fourier component is known. By comparison with this analytical solution it will be possible to determine the amplitude and phase coefficients for this component as advected by the numerical scheme. This analysis is described in detail by Holly and Preissmann[8] and Glass and Rodi;[6] here only the main results are presented.

Let $\hat{C}_i^n = \overline{C^n} \exp(j\sigma i)$ be the value of a Fourier component at point i, with $\sigma = (2\pi\Delta x/L)$, L being the wavelength of this component and

$j = \sqrt{-1}$. Calculation of the eigenvalues shows that there are two values λ such that

$$\begin{pmatrix} \bar{C}_i^{n+1} \\ \bar{C}X_i^{n+1} \end{pmatrix} = \lambda \begin{pmatrix} \bar{C}_i^n \\ \bar{C}X_i^n \end{pmatrix},$$

these two values are denoted λ_1 and λ_2. For the analytical solution only $\lambda_0 = \exp(-j\sigma\alpha)$ ensures pure advection (pure translation), with $\alpha = (\hat{U}\Delta t/\Delta x)$. The first eigenvalue λ_1 tends towards λ_0 when σ tends towards 0, i.e. for long wavelengths; this is called the primary mode. The second eigenvalue λ_2 deviates from λ_0 when σ tends towards 0; this is called the secondary or parasite mode. λ_0, λ_1 and λ_2 are complex values the moduli of which are such that $\bar{\lambda}_0 = 1 > \bar{\lambda}_1 \gg \bar{\lambda}_2 > 0$. The modulus $\bar{\lambda}_1$ represents the error in amplitude due to the primary mode of the numerical scheme, and the argument of the ratio λ_1/λ_0 represents the error in phase due to the same mode; the same applies to the secondary mode.

Figure 8 shows the variations of error in amplitude and in phase of the primary mode for different values of α, as a function of the ratio $L/\Delta x$, which is the number of calculation points per wavelength. These figures show that for $L/\Delta x$ greater than or equal to 7, the Fourier components

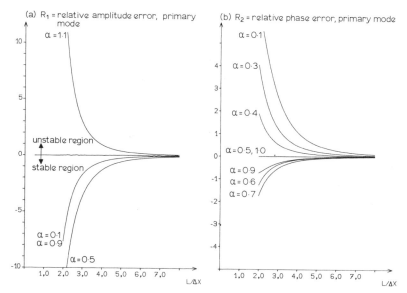

FIG. 8. Amplitude and phase portraits for one Fourier component advected by the Holly–Preissmann scheme.

are propagated by the numerical scheme practically without error for the primary mode. The error analysis also shows that any initial error in the derivative CX is soon damped in the course of the calculation. In practical cases it will nevertheless be advantageous to introduce initial values of CX that are consistent with the distribution of concentration. Otherwise the initial computation time steps could lead to erroneous values of concentration, which will then be transported correctly.

3.3 Application to Complex River Networks

As shown in the preceding sections, pollutant transport in rivers depends to a large extent on flow conditions, particularly as regards advection. This is why calculation of pollutant transport must be preceded by a calculation of the unsteady flow taking into account the complex topography of rivers and all types of hydraulic structures. In particular, the law of hydraulic continuity, eqn (2), must be respected at all points of flow, since validity of the dispersion eqn (3) depends on it. This calculation must solve the complete de Saint-Venant equations in one dimension, and must take into account the following particular features: transverse sections of any configuration; branched or looped river networks; hydraulic structures such as weirs, dams, gates, etc.; and alluvial plains in which flow is almost two-dimensional during floods. The first point mentioned above, associated with an unsteady regime, produces quite variable velocities and thus Courant-like numbers, which the dispersion calculation must accept.

As regards the second point, a hydrodynamic calculation scheme based on two points greatly simplifies the computation for branches. Such a scheme is described by Cunge et al.[5] For the diffusion eqn (7), for example, the use of a three-point scheme such as that of Crank–Nicholson would mean that conservation of diffusive flux in the branches can only be assured at the expense of simplifying assumptions. For processing of advection by the method described in Section 2.2, there must not be recirculation within a mesh over a given time step such that the Courant number exceeds 1 at every point of the mesh. For the iterative procedure to converge it is sufficient to reduce the time step or the length of a single section separating two calculation points in order to obtain a value of α less than 1 on the mesh.

It is known how to represent the hydraulic behaviour of a large number of structures. In order to model dispersion through these structures, a certain number of precautions must be taken. Taking for example the case of transport by diffusion over a weir, if there is no flow over the weir, then it acts as an impermeable barrier and it is legitimate

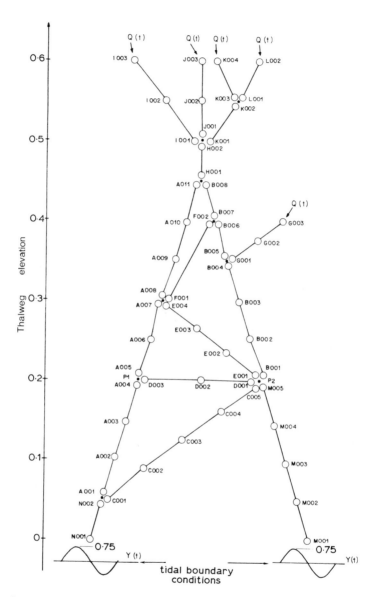

FIG. 9. Topological layout of a looped network of channels subject to tidal influence.

to impose $\hat{C}X = 0$ on either side. When there is free flow over the weir, the latter is permeable to diffusion from upstream (us) and impermeable from downstream (ds); it is possible to impose $\hat{C}_{us} = \hat{C}_{ds}$ and $C\hat{X}_{ds} = 0$. Finally, in a drowned flow regime, the weir is totally permeable to diffusion, and this is schematised by $C_{us} = C_{ds}$ and $CX_{us} = CX_{ds}$. However, such relationships will produce breaks of continuity on transition from sub-critical to super-critical flow or vice versa, which will no longer correspond to physical reality.

Cunge *et al.*[5] describe a method which enables the calculation of quasi two-dimensional flow in alluvial plains to be taken into account in a simplified manner. For pollutant transport by advection, an approximate calculation may be made, ensuring conservation of pollutant mass, supposing that the concentration is uniform in a flooded cell at each time step. However, in effect this means assuming diffusion in the cell to be instantaneous, whereas in real situations the pollutant arrives at one extremity and, on account of the slight currents in the cell, takes a long time to propagate. It is therefore illusory to try to simulate diffusion in a model comprising virtually two-dimensional zones, especially if these zones cover a large area and if the time step is short.

The CONDOR program, developed in 1982 by the French consulting engineering firm SOGREAH, enables the complete transport eqn (1) to be solved according to the principles set out in this chapter. It is part of the CARIMA programming system, which calculates unsteady flows in canal and river networks. An application of this program to a fictional case of a looped tidal river system is presented below.

The topological scheme of this river is that shown in Fig. 9. The distance separating adjacent calculation points is 1 km, and the bed slope is 0.05×10^{-3}. The upstream boundary condition is a constant fresh water discharge of $1 \, \text{m}^3/\text{s}$. The downstream boundary conditions are water levels varying in time according to a sinusoidal law with an amplitude of $0.75 \, \text{m}$.

The system is initially without pollutant. At the downstream boundary a constant concentration equal to 100 units is imposed, simulating salt intrusion. The model assumes concentration to be constant over a given cross-section; gravity effects are therefore ignored. Longitudinal advection and diffusion are considered, with a coefficient of diffusivity constant and equal to $10 \, \text{m}^2/\text{s}$. Figure 10 shows the time-dependent variations of concentration at several points of the model. Worth noting in particular is the variation of concentrations at point D3, where salt water is stored during the incoming tide and subsequently restituted to branch A1-A3 during the outgoing tide.

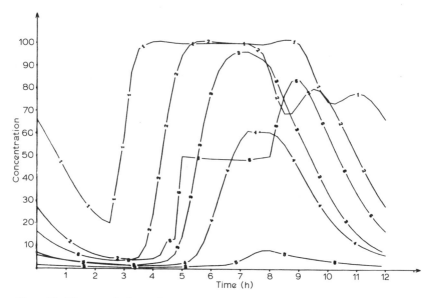

FIG. 10. Time variation of concentration at various points in the looped network. (1) Point A1, (2) point A3, (3) point A6, (4) point A8, (5) point A10, (6) point D3.

4   QUASI-TWO-DIMENSIONAL DISPERSION

4.1   General Principles

The one-dimensional dispersion eqn (1) is based on the assumption that any variable represents a mean value over each cross-section; this is a simplification, especially as regards the longitudinal velocity $\hat{U}(x, t)$ and pollutant concentration $\hat{C}(x, t)$. The assumption is acceptable for overall environmental studies, involving for example determination of the impact of a pollutant outfall in a river several tens or even several hundred kilometres from the outfall point. However, the distance between the outfall point and the point where the pollutant is distributed homogeneously may be several kilometres or even much more in the case of a river with very low flow. In river flow, the width is great by comparison with the depth, and homogeneous distribution is reached much more quickly vertically than horizontally over the river's cross-section. Consequently, it is often possible to assume that the contaminant is uniformly mixed over the depth.

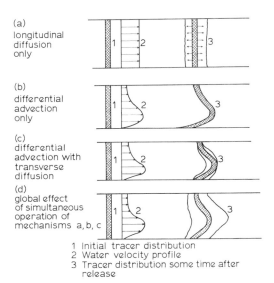

(a) longitudinal diffusion only

(b) differential advection only

(c) differential advection with transverse diffusion

(d) global effect of simultaneous operation of mechanisms a, b, c

1 Initial tracer distribution
2 Water velocity profile
3 Tracer distribution some time after release

FIG. 11. Conceptual view of dispersion as the combination of differential advection and transverse diffusion.

Figure 11 shows the various processes involved in depth-averaged dispersion of a pollutant in a river (d). It shows the deformation in plan of a pollutant band of initially homogeneous distribution over a transverse section. Diffusion is an equalising process which widens that band (b). Differential advection is due to transverse variation of longitudinal velocity (due for example to variable depths in a section), which causes deformation of the initial band (a). Transverse diffusion only takes place in the presence of transverse concentration gradients; this phenomenon therefore depends on differential advection, which creates transverse gradients (c). The quasi-two-dimensional cumulative discharge approach, described earlier in Section 4.3 of the previous chapter, allows these various phenomena to be taken into account. If transverse diffusion is ignored in eqn (76) of the previous chapter, the one-dimensional unsteady dispersion equation is valid for each stream tube, and may be solved by the fractional step method set out in Section 3. An additional computation step is then effected to process the transverse diffusion by an algorithm of implicit finite differences similar to that used for longitudinal diffusion. The algorithm enabling the two types of diffusion to be processed can also use a three-computation-points method, as in the

Crank–Nicholson scheme, since the problem of network branches does not arise.

For the computation of advection it becomes particularly important to use a calculation scheme with only slight numerical diffusion, regardless of the local Courant number. For the computation of transverse diffusion, zero diffusive flux is imposed on the right and left banks of the river, that is to say:

$$(E_z)_L = (E_z)_R = 0$$

L and R being indices of the left and right banks.

4.2 Example: Mixing of Contaminant from an Outfall Upstream of a Confluence

The stream tube algorithm has been incorporated in SOGREAH's POLDER program, which has been applied to a real case illustrated in Fig. (12).[12] There is a warm water outfall on the left bank of river A, at a point 1190 m upstream of the confluence with river B. The total discharge of these two rivers varies between 150 and 1000 m^3/s, river A transporting from 15 to 60% and B the rest. River B meanders between its containing embankments. At a point 370 m downstream of the outfall there is a bridge, the foundations of which generate to substantial turbulence in the flow, and 1280 m downstream of the confluence a small river discharges into river A on the right bank.

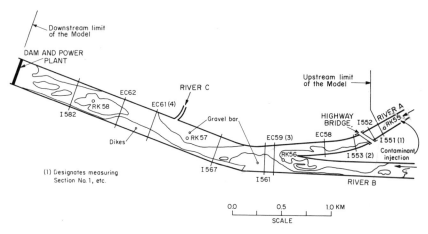

FIG. 12. Site plan for POLDER application.

Finally, construction of a dam is planned 4000 m downstream of the outfall, which will have the effect of reducing current velocities upstream. The mathematical model developed with the POLDER program was used to guide the field data collection program and enabled prediction of the consequences of construction of the dam on dilution of the outfall discharge. Figure 13 shows the velocity and concentration profiles, as

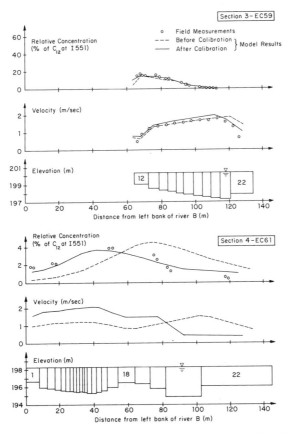

FIG. 13. Comparison of observations and computations using POLDER.

well as the depths per stream tube, at two cross-sections of flow before dam construction. The calculated values are compared with observations.

The parameters for calibration of the model are the bed roughness (Strickler coefficient), especially as it relates to the distribution of discharges in the stream tubes, and the coefficients of longitudinal and transverse diffusivity. These are generally written in the form of the following Elder formulae

$$K_x = \alpha_x u_* h \tag{28}$$

$$E_z = a_z u_* h \tag{29}$$

with $\alpha_x(x, y)$ and $a_z(x, y) =$ non-dimensional mixing coefficients. $h(x) =$ cross-sectional average depth, $u_*(x) =$ cross-sectional average shear stress, with $u_* = \sqrt{ghS}$, $S(x)$ being the slope of the energy line.

The coefficient a_z integrates the transverse mixing by secondary currents as discussed in Section 5.2 of the previous chapter. In the particular case of this river, these secondary currents proved to be particularly important in the natural state, leading to high values of the coefficient $a_z(x, y)$. The pebble banks existing in river A in the natural state will be submerged after commissioning of the proposed dam. This led the designers of the model to doubt its predictive capacity, since the coefficient a_z will probably have a much smaller value after attenuation of the secondary currents. The reader is referred to the article by Holly and Nerat[12] for more details on the study, and to Section 5.2 of the previous chapter for more discussion on the uncertainty about E_z.

5 CALCULATION OF FULLY TWO-DIMENSIONAL DISPERSION

5.1 Introduction

The one-dimensional solution (Section 3) or quasi-two-dimensional solution (Section 4) of the dispersion equation are useful tools for riverine dispersion problems. For coastal sites it is necessary to solve the fully two-dimensional, depth-averaged equation in two horizontal dimensions, eqn (66) of the previous chapter.

As in the case of one spatial dimension, this equation can be solved by a split-operator procedure which, in a given computation time step, considers two stages successively: (a) firstly the *advection*, solved by the characteristics method, associated with a Hermitian interpolation of the concentration at the foot of the characteristic and (b) then the *diffusion*, which is solved by an implicit scheme of finite differences, in order to ensure stability. The diffusion tensor (K) is constructed on the basis of the longitudinal and transverse diffusivities, which are related to the mean behaviour of the fluid by the Elder formulae.

This method, which was developed in 1981 by Holly and Preissmann[8] under support of SOGREAH, is outlined in the following paragraphs; a slightly different method has been developed by Glass and Rodi.[6] It is quite analogous to its one-dimensional counterpart described in Section 3. Details of the procedure can be found in ref. 10.

5.2 Advection Stage

The calculation network is that represented in Fig. 14. For any point B, the reverse characteristic calculation is performed from time $n+1$ to time n, even if the characteristic does not remain within a same mesh. The foot

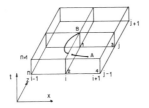

FIG. 14. Computational grid for numerical solution of the 2-dimensional dispersion equation.

A of the characteristic having been located, the concentration at A is calculated by bicubic interpolation using data at the four neighbouring nodes. Such interpolation requires 16 units of data, which are the values of $\tilde{C}$, $\partial\tilde{C}/\partial x$, $\partial\tilde{C}/\partial z$, $\partial^2\tilde{C}/\partial x\partial z$ at the four neighbouring nodes. Thus:

$$\tilde{C}_A = \sum_{k=1}^{4}\left[a_k\tilde{C}_k + b_k\frac{\partial\tilde{C}}{\partial x}\bigg|_k + d_k\frac{\mathrm{d}\tilde{C}}{\partial z}\bigg|_k + e_k\frac{\partial^2\tilde{C}}{\partial x\partial z}\bigg|_k \right] \tag{30}$$

Then, by integration along the characteristic, the value $\tilde{C}_A$ is assigned to point B.

For this procedure to be continued at the following time step, it is also necessary to transport $\tilde{C}X = \partial C/\partial x$, $\tilde{C}Z = \partial C/\partial z$ and $\tilde{C}XZ = \partial^2 C/\partial x\partial z$ along the characteristic. $\tilde{C}X$ and $\tilde{C}Z$ may be calculated at A by a polynomial of the same type as eqn (30). These values are then transported to B by integration along the characteristic of the differential equations equivalent to eqn (19) for one dimension:

$$\frac{d\tilde{C}X}{dt} = -u_x\tilde{C}X - v_x\tilde{C}Z$$

$$\frac{d\tilde{C}Z}{dt} = -u_z\tilde{C}X - v_z\tilde{C}Z \tag{31}$$

For $\partial^2\tilde{C}/\partial x\partial z$, a comparable operation would involve substantial computational effort with imprecise derivative estimates. It is preferable to calculate $\partial^2\tilde{C}/\partial x\partial z$ at point A on the basis of the values of $\tilde{C}X$ and $\tilde{C}Z$ obtained previously, through a finite difference approximation.

5.2.1 Boundary Conditions

For closed boundaries and for those through which the water leaves the field of integration, it is not necessary to provide a boundary condition, since the characteristics never cut through these boundaries. For those through which water enters the field, it is necessary to know $\hat{C}(t, T)$, T being the direction tangential to the boundary, and it must be possible to differentiate this boundary condition according to t and T. Thus it is possible to calculate $\partial\hat{C}/\partial t$ and $\partial\tilde{C}/\partial T$ then compute $\partial\tilde{C}/\partial N$, N being the direction perpendicular to the boundary, by the equation:

$$\frac{\partial\tilde{C}}{\partial t} + u_T\frac{\partial\tilde{C}}{\partial T} + u_N\frac{\partial\tilde{C}}{\partial N} = 0 \tag{32}$$

These values, obtained at the foot of the characteristic which intersects a boundary, are then transported by integration along the characteristic.

When this procedure is applied, it is obvious that the longer the time step (which means the longer the characteristic curve), the more difficult it is to accept that the diffusion and advection can be treated separately in a time step.

5.3 Diffusion Stage

This calculation stage must solve the pure diffusion equation in two spatial dimensions. It is written here in a general form for later use

$$h\frac{\partial\psi}{\partial t} = \frac{\partial}{\partial x}\left(h\varepsilon_{11}\frac{\partial\psi}{\partial x}\right) + \frac{\partial}{\partial x}\left(h\varepsilon_{12}\frac{\partial\psi}{\partial z}\right) + \frac{\partial}{\partial z}\left(h\varepsilon_{12}\frac{\partial\psi}{\partial x}\right) + \frac{\partial}{\partial z}\left(h\varepsilon_{22}\frac{\partial\psi}{\partial z}\right) + R_\psi$$

$$\tag{33}$$

when $\psi = \tilde{C}$ and $R_\psi = 0$, eqn (33) is merely the diffusion part of eqn (67) of the previous chapter. To be able to continue with the advection stage in the following time step, it is necessary to obtain $\tilde{C}X$ and $\tilde{C}Z$ at the end of the diffusion stage. To this effect the diffusion portion of eqn (67) of the previous chapter is differentiated with respect to X and with respect to Z. The equation obtained is then given by eqn (33) with $\psi = \tilde{C}X$ or $\psi = \tilde{C}Z$, respectively, and $R_\psi \neq 0$. To a first approximation, R_ψ can be ignored when $\psi = \tilde{C}X$ and $\psi = \tilde{C}Z$, which offers the advantage of using exactly the same procedure for the calculation of $\tilde{C}$, $\tilde{C}X$, and $\tilde{C}Z$. To avoid having to invert a large matrix, the following split-operator method is adopted

$$h\frac{\partial \psi}{\partial t} = \frac{\partial}{\partial x}\left(h\varepsilon_{11}\frac{\partial \psi}{\partial x}\right) + \frac{\partial}{\partial x}\left(h\varepsilon_{12}\frac{\partial \psi}{\partial z}\right)$$

$$h\frac{\partial \psi}{\partial t} = \frac{\partial}{\partial z}\left(h\varepsilon_{12}\frac{\partial \psi}{\partial x}\right) + \frac{\partial}{\partial z}\left(h\varepsilon_{22}\frac{\partial \psi}{\partial z}\right)$$

(34)

Each of these two equations may be solved on a line $x =$ constant or line $z =$ constant of the mesh using a classic Crank–Nicholson scheme, as described in ref. 4 for example, and an algorithm of elimination by a double sweep procedure on this line (see ref. 5).

5.3.1 Boundary Conditions
The parabolic nature of the diffusion eqn (33) implies that a condition must be provided for all boundaries of the integration domain. Moreover, the scheme adopted for the advection phase requires definition of the derivatives $\tilde{C}X$ and $\tilde{C}Z$ of concentration $\tilde{C}$ at the limits of the field, which may be considered as an overspecification of the boundary conditions. Generally, the variations of pollutant distribution due to diffusion are slight. Thus, to avoid adversely affecting the advection phase, the open boundary conditions of the field $\tilde{C}$, $\tilde{C}X$ and $\tilde{C}Z$ are taken as identical to the values obtained by the advection stage. On the closed boundaries the pure reflection of $\tilde{C}$, $\tilde{C}X$ and $\tilde{C}Z$ is imposed (null derivative on the perpendicular to the wall).

5.4 Treatment of Small Contaminant Clouds
In the case of effluent discharge through submerged outfalls, or of any other pollution source at a specific point, it is necessary to wait for a considerable time before the area of the pollutant cloud covers several

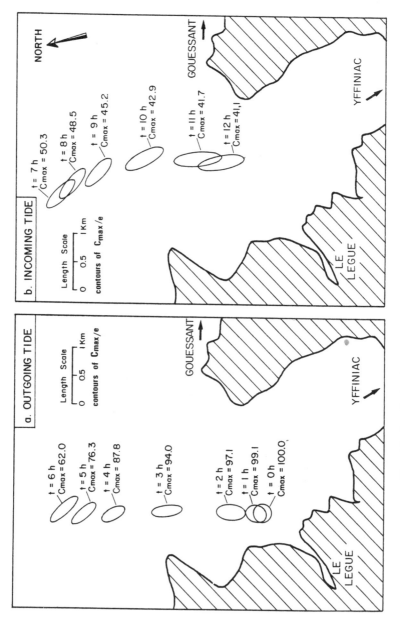

Fɪɢ. 15. Small cloud computations in the Bay of Saint-Brieuc.

cells of the computational grid (the grid cells cannot be too small for economic reasons). Moreover, the displacement of a small pollutant cloud may extend over as much as 20 km, which procludes the adoption of a finer grid locally. As in the one-dimensional case, the numerical precision of the algorithm provided above is only acceptable when the pollutant cloud covers several meshes of the model. Before this condition is fulfilled, a Lagrange-type solution of the dispersion equation may be performed, based on the following procedures.[10] (a) A cloud of small dimensions is assumed to be formed by ellipses of equal concentration, the values of concentration increasing from the edge to the centre; the distribution of concentration follows a Gaussian profile in any horizontal direction passing through the centre. (b) Displacement of the cloud is represented as the displacement of the point of peak concentration. (c) The cloud is then deformed by differential advection and by diffusion, both acting on the shape parameters of the jointly Gaussian distribution. The deformation operator is derived directly from the two-dimensional dispersion eqn (67) of the previous chapter.

When the cloud covers several meshes, according to a criterion defined by the user, it is allocated to the fixed computational grid, and application of the general procedure for 'large clouds', Sections 5.2 and 5.3, becomes possible. The small cloud procedure is fully described by Holly and Usseglio-Polatera.[10]

5.5 Application to Saint-Brieuc Bay

Saint-Brieuc Bay is situated in Northern Brittany (France), in an area where tidal currents are very strong. A mathematical model was developed for detailed calculation of the tidal currents in the bay, using the CYTHERE-ES1 programme.[3] The model was then used to study a series of test outfalls in the bay. Figure 15 shows the trajectory and deformation of a small pollutant cloud resulting from an outfall near Le Légué. Each ellipse corresponds to the contour of concentration C_0/e at the various simulated times (C_0 = concentration at the centre, $e = 2 \cdot 718$). Figure 16 clearly shows the variations of a large pollutant cloud in the course of a tidal cycle. These tests are also described in more detail in ref. 10.

6 DISPERSION OF NON-CONSERVATIVE POLLUTANTS

The term 'non-conservative' is applied to all pollutants which, contained

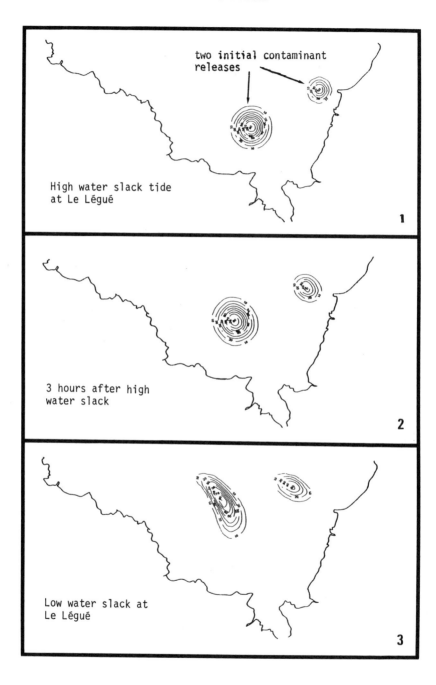

two initial contaminant releases

High water slack tide at Le Légué

1

3 hours after high water slack

2

Low water slack at Le Légué

3

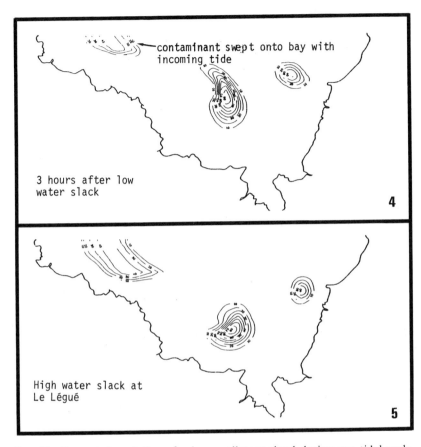

FIG. 16. Computed evolution of a large pollutant cloud during one tidal cycle (contours shown are lines of equal concentration in St Brieue Bay, France).

in an isolated volume of fluid, have a mean concentration which varies with time. This is the case with the great majority of pollutants. Temperature plays a special role; except in the proximity of industrial outfalls at specific locations, its variations are governed by thermal exchanges with the atmosphere. It has a significant effect on the laws of reaction of other pollutants. The reverse is not true, if phenomena of minor importance are neglected, as is shown in Fig. 17.

To construct a biochemical model of a river, the following stages must be followed. (1) Hydrodynamic model: calculation of flow velocities and

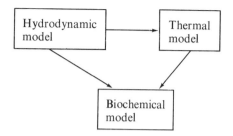

FIG. 17. Relationship between the different models representing operation of a water course (arrow indicates influence of one model on the other)

water depths. (2) Thermal model: heat is transported by advection and diffusion, and there are exchanges with the outside environment. (3) Biochemical model: pollutants are transported by advection and by diffusion, and they react among themselves according to local temperature conditions.

Certain pollutants, through chemical or physical reaction, form precipitate or colloidal solutions which are eliminated by deposition on the river bed. Others combine with animal or vegetable particles present in the river to form a complex ecosystem, in which oxygen plays a fundamental role.

There are thus a large number of substances in solution in a river. The model retains only the most important, since the reaction laws are often not well known and data necessary for the calibration of the model are scarce. Ecological models can attain a high degree of complexity (see e.g. ref. 18); the descriptions which follow are limited to only a few common processes.

6.1 A Few Decomposition Processes

6.1.1 Temperature: Natural Cooling at the Surface

The thermal behaviour of the river is a complex phenomenon,[20] involving a large number of meteorological parameters. This behaviour may be schematised by the following equation, if advection and diffusion are ignored:

$$\frac{dT}{dt} + \frac{\beta(T - T_e)}{\rho h C_n} = 0 \tag{35}$$

where T_e = equilibrium temperature of the water (K), obtained under constant weather conditions; ρ = density of the water (kg/m^3); h = mean depth (m); C_n = calorific capacity of the water (4180 J/kg/K) and β = coefficient taking into account the thermal exchanges between the water and atmosphere in the form of radiating energy, sensible heat and latent heat (in W/m^2/K).

Considering only mean daily exchanges, β may be expressed simply as a function of the water temperature and wind at the water surface:

$$\beta = 4{\cdot}48 + 0{\cdot}049\ T + f(u)(1{\cdot}12 + 0{\cdot}018\ T + 0{\cdot}0158\ T^2) \qquad (36)$$

with

$$f(u) = 4{\cdot}4 + 1{\cdot}82\ u_{10} \qquad (37)$$

u_{10} being the wind velocity (m/s) measured 10 m above the water surface.

6.1.2 Dissolved Oxygen (DO) and Biological Oxygen Demand (BOD)

The oxygen content of a water course is often selected as a criterion of water quality. Waste water discharged into a river contains a large quantity of organic substances (measured by the biological oxygen demand, or BOD), which oxidise in contact with the dissolved oxygen (DO) in the water. This oxygen comes mainly from exchanges through the air/water interface and from air entrainment in sections of supercritical flow or at weirs. As early as 1925, Phelps and Streeter[17] developed a model based on the following hypotheses: the decrease of BOD with time is exponential; the decrease of BOD and the decrease of DO proceed at the same rate and the rate of reoxygenation through the air/water interface is proportional to the oxygen deficit. This model leads to the following system of equations (advection and diffusion being neglected here)

$$\frac{dL}{dt} = -k_1 L$$

$$\qquad\qquad\qquad\qquad\qquad\qquad\qquad (38)$$

$$\frac{dC_d}{dt} = -k_1 L + k_2 (C_d - C_s)$$

where L = pollutant load = BOD concentration; C_d = dissolved oxygen concentration; k_1 = deoxygenation coefficient; k_2 = reaeration coefficient and C_s = dissolved oxygen concentration at saturation. The parameters k_1, k_2 and C_s are more or less complex functions of temperature depending on the author. The distributions of L and C_d as a function of

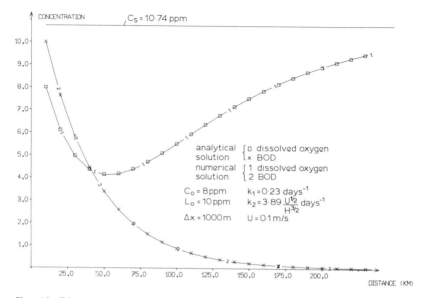

FIG. 18. Distributions of biological oxygen demand (×) and dissolved oxygen (□) as a function of distance in a steady flow.

distance obtained from a constant discharge of BOD into a steady flow take the form shown in Fig. 18 (obtained for initial values $L_0 = 10$ and $C_0 = 8$ by the CONDOR program developed by SOGREAH).

6.2 Computation of Non-conservative Processes

Thermal exchanges and the biochemical degradation process lead in most situations to systems of non-linear coupled equations involving the various pollutants. To solve the equations of transport by the three processes (advection, diffusion and non-conservative effects), it is therefore preferable to separate the processing of a computational time step into two stages. First, the equations of dispersion for each of the pollutants are solved separately, each of these equations taking the one-dimensional form of eqn (3) (see Chapter 3 for the numerical computation of this equation). Secondly, the system of non-linear coupled equations expressing the non-conservative processes is solved. This system can generally be written in the following form

$$\frac{\mathrm{d}\hat{C}_i}{\mathrm{d}t} + F_i(\hat{C}_1, \hat{C}_2, \ldots, \hat{C}_n) = 0 \qquad i = 1, n \qquad (39)$$

$\hat{C}_1, \hat{C}_2, \ldots, \hat{C}_n$ being the concentrations of the n pollutants involved, and F_i a non-linear function of these concentrations. F_i also takes into account the flow conditions (velocities, water surface area, etc.). In most non-conservative processes, the function F_i can be expressed in the following form:

$$F_i(\hat{C}_1, \hat{C}_2, \ldots, \hat{C}_n) = \sum_{j=1}^{n} a_{ij} \hat{C}_j + b_i \qquad (40)$$

The coefficients a_{ij} and b_i are linear functions of a third pollutant k, e.g.

$$a_{ij}(\hat{C}_k) = K_1 + K_2 \hat{C}_k \qquad (41)$$

K_1 and K_2 being constants.

Such a formulation enables representation of a large number of non-conservative processes of the 2nd order. It can be seen that in eqn (39) only time intervenes as an independent variable. This is a system of ordinary differential equations, which may be solved by a Runge–Kutta method or by the Newton–Raphson method[4] solving:

$$P(\mathbf{C}^{n+1}) = \mathbf{C}^{n+1} - \mathbf{C}^n + \Delta t \mathbf{F}(\mathbf{C}^{n+1}) \equiv 0 \qquad (42)$$

$\mathbf{C}$ being the vector of concentrations $(\hat{C}_1, \hat{C}_2, \ldots, \hat{C}_n)$ and $\mathbf{F}$ the vector of the functions $(F_1, F_2, \ldots, F_n)$.

7 PERSPECTIVES IN NUMERICAL MODELLING

Future progress in numerical modelling of contaminant dispersion will depend more on an improved understanding of the physical processes involved than on improved numerical methods. As has been mentioned in the previous chapter, the predictive capability of contaminant models is presently severely compromised by the inability of the commonly accepted functional form of the depth-averaged transverse mixing coefficient to incorporate the effects of transverse secondary flow, even in straight reaches. To be sure, accurate numerical methods such as those discussed herein must always be employed to minimise the purely numerical error. But there is a great need for fundamental research and analysis geared to development of complete description of depth-averaged transverse mixing.

The author's emphasis on finite-difference and characteristics method is not meant to suggest that finite-element methods are less attractive. For one-dimensional problems, however, simple finite-element methods are plagued by the same damping/phase error problems as finite-difference methods. Recent finite-element research devoted to the one-dimensional advection-diffusion problem has resulted in development of highly accurate schemes based on special test functions.[16] Since quite accurate characteristics schemes are available, and since finite elements appear to offer no other intrinsic advantages in one dimension, the author sees no strong reason for using one method over the other.

In two dimensions, by contrast, triangular finite elements offer a distinct potential advantage over characteristics and finite-difference methods: flexibility in fitting natural boundaries and extending a computational domain towards a distant boundary. The natural optimum behaviour of finite-element methods for the diffusion part of contaminant transport must be complemented by the use of highly specialised test functions to minimise advection error. Considerable research in finite-element methods is currently being devoted to this problem.

Although some effort is being devoted to the computation of three-dimensional dispersion using both finite-element and finite-difference techniques, it appears unlikely that three-dimensional modelling will receive a great deal of development in the foreseeable future. Of course three-dimensional computation places enormous demands on computer time and memory, but computing hardware is evolving so rapidly that time and memory constraints are fast disappearing. Of more fundamental significance is the fact that in the context of civil engineering applications one of two situations exists. Either (1) contaminant effects on ambient hydrodynamics are negligible, in which case vertical mixing occurs so rapidly that a two-dimensional approach is sufficient or (2) contaminant effects cannot be divorced from the ambient hydrodynamics, in which case a coupled contaminant dispersion/flow hydrodynamics model is required, such as in vertically stratified estuarine models. This latter area is an important area of research and will surely see further development in the years to come. But three-dimensional simulation of inert, neutrally-buoyant contaminant dispersion does not appear to merit a great deal of development at this juncture.

There are two areas of development which, although tangential to the inert contaminant dispersion problem discussed herein, are closely related to it. One is application of inert contaminant techniques to the computation of sediment transport in rivers. Most of the numerical techniques are directly transferable. But the significant new physical problem is that of predicting exchange of sediment between the water column and the bed. The second area concerns adaptation of numerical techniques for the accurate computation of linear contaminant advection to non-linear momentum advection. In particular, the Holly–Preissmann characteristics method may prove to be an attractive method for simulation of steep-front surges in power canals and river gorges following a dam break.

REFERENCES

1. ABBOTT, M. B. Computational hydraulics — a short pathology. *J. Hydraul. Res. IAHR*, **14** (4) (1976), 271.
2. BELLA, D. A. and DOBBINS, W. E. Difference modelling of stream pollution. *J. Sanitary Eng. Div. ASCE*, **94** (SA5) (1968), 995–1016.
3. BENQUE, J. P., CUNGE, J. A., HAUGUEL, A., FEUILLET, J. and HOLLY, F. M. JR. A new method for tidal current computation. *J. Waterways Harbors Div. ASCE*, **108** (WW3), Proceeding paper 17290, (1982), 396–417.
4. CARNAHAN, B., LUTHER, H. A. and WILKES, J. O. *Applied Numerical Methods*, John Wiley, New York, (1969).
5. CUNGE, J. A., HOLLY, F. M. JR and VERWEY, A. *Practical Aspects of Computational River Hydraulics*, Pitman, London, (1980).
6. GLASS, J. and RODI, W. A higher order numerical scheme for scalar transport. *Computer Methods in Applied Mechanics and Engineering*, **31** (1982), 337–358.
7. GRAY, W. G. and PINDER, G. F. An analysis of the numerical solution of the transport equation. *Water Resources Res.*, **12** (3) (1976).
8. HOLLY, F. M. JR and PREISMANN, A. Accurate calculation of transport in two dimensions. *J. Hydraul. Div. ASCE*, **103** (HY11) (1977), 1259–77.
9. HOLLY, F. M. JR and KOMATSU, T. Derivative approximations in the two-point fourth-order method for pollutant transport, *ASCE* 1983 Hydraulics Division Specialty Conference, Cambridge, Mass., 9–12 August.
10. HOLLY, F. M. JR and USSEGLIO-POLATERA, J. M. Dispersion simulation in two-dimensional tidal flow. *J. Hydraul. Eng. ASCE*, **110** (7) (1984), 905–926.
11. HOLLY, F. M. JR. Two dimensional mass dispersion in rivers. Hydrology Paper No. 78, Colorado State University, Fort Collins, (1975).
12. HOLLY, F. M. JR and NERAT, G. Field calibration of a stream tube dispersion model, *J. Hydraul. Eng. ASCE*, **109** (11) (1983), 1455–70.
13. IAEA Thermal Discharges at Nuclear Power Stations. Technical Report No. 155, Vienna, (1974).
14. LEENDERTSE, J. J. A water-quality simulation model for well-mixed estuaries and coastal seas. Vol. I. Principles of Calculation. Rand Corporation Memorandum, RM-6230-RC, February, (1970).
15. MARTIN, B. Numerical representations which model properties of the solution to the diffusion equation. *J. Comp. Phys.*, **17** (1975), 358–83.
16. MORTON, K. W. and PARROTT, A. K. Generalized Galerkin methods for first-order hyperbolic equations. *J. Comp. Phys*, **36** (2) (1980), 249–70.
17. PHELPS, E. B. and STREETER, H. W. A study of the Pollution and Natural

Purification of the Ohio River. *Bulletin 146*, US Public Health Service, Washington, D.C., 1925.
18. RINALDI, S., SONCINI-SESSA, R., STEHFEST, H. and TAMURA, H. *Modelling and Control of River Quality*, McGraw-Hill, New York, (1979).
19. SOGREAH/IIRCHA Etude de pollution de la Vienne — Etude Mathematique, Programme de Calcul. Annex 3, DGRST research contract, (1971).
20. SWEERS, H. E. A monogram to estimate the heat-exchange coefficient at the air–water interface as a function of wind speed and temperature—a critical review of some literature. *J. Hydrol.*, **30** (1976), 375–405.

Chapter 3

SEA OUTFALLS

John A. Charlton

*Department of Civil Engineering, University
of Dundee, UK*

1 COASTAL POLLUTION

Apart from marine accidents and disasters coastal pollution almost
always originates from land based sources. These pollutants reach the sea
via rivers and estuaries which carry waste from inland sources, and from
direct discharges into the sea from coastal sources. Man, being inherently
lazy, has used these routes to dispose of his liquid, and often solid,
rubbish from time immemorial. In moderation, and with a little luck,
water movement has conveniently moved and hidden this rubbish,
whether it be solid or liquid. The so-called industrialisation that accompanied the expansion of urban areas in the 18th and 19th centuries
continued to utilise waterways for dumping, in particular for the disposal
of raw sewage. In coastal areas, where it was inconvenient or difficult to
lay pipes across the tidal margin, discharges often occurred above the
low water mark with the unpleasant results that are familiar to most of
us.

Public conscience encouraged drainage authorities to lengthen many
of these outlets so that they discharged seaward of the low water mark.
These outfalls, made longer in hope rather than in design, took little
account of local water movement and did little to improve the coastal
and beach pollution situation. Increasing urbanisation, with its attendant
increase in wastewater discharges, then aggravated the problem.

The first half of the twentieth century had gone before a realisation by the public of the environmental deterioration of inland, estuarine and coastal waters prompted responsible authorities to increase expenditure on waste water treatment plants and on more effective methods of piping effluents away from our coasts.

The necessary new survey techniques and design methods required for the design of efficient long sea outfalls have also developed, but in the early stages were perhaps not entirely adequate for the purpose. Neither was there a full awareness of the necessity for a thorough understanding of the hydrodynamic characteristics of the coastal receiving water, if an outfall was to be designed for maximum efficiency. As a consequence some design surveys were inadequate, resulting in outfall designs which only worked either by luck, or gross overdesign. Indeed to the present day, conservative design is sometimes used to cover inadequacies in the design process.

However, it is now possible to design sea outfalls to work efficiently and assist in maintaining coastal water quality to the standard that is rightly expected.

The developments that have taken place over the last 10 years that make this statement possible range from a better appreciation of the marine environment and refinements in hydraulic design to an understanding of the complex interflow conditions that exist in two density systems. The design of outfalls encompasses these and many other factors.

2   THE MARINE TREATMENT OF BIODEGRADABLE EFFLUENTS

The discharge of any potential pollutant to the sea requires justification, particularly when the general public regards any such discharge as cumulative dumping. The coastal seas around us are often referred to as a 'resource' in terms of mineral recovery, or more particularly in terms of fisheries. A fishery may be regarded as being at the upper end of the food chain, which in turn is part of the greater natural process of life and decay, particularly in the marine environment. We are interested in the lower end of this cycle where biological processes return waste matter back into the food chain (Fig. 1). For this process to function the marine environment requires a good supply of oxygenated water, light, and a balanced bacterial and faunal population both in the water column and on the sea bed. Waste matter is transported in a suspended or dissolved state by water movement, which not only dilutes it but brings it into

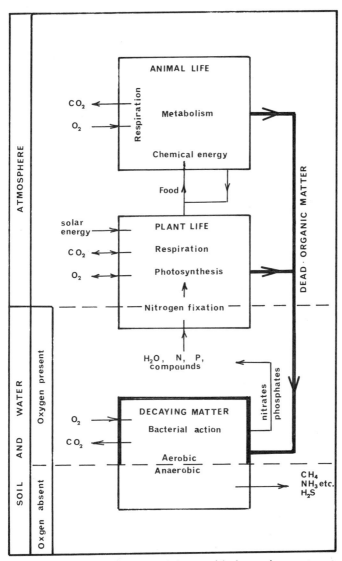

FIG. 1. The cycle of growth and decay, with the marine treatment section heavily lined.

contact with an abundant supply of oxygen to support the degradation process. Eventually sedimentation brings this new food supply to the benthic populations of the sea bed.

Far from being delicate, the marine living environment is highly adaptable to variations of waste input, whether it be from natural or man-made sources. However, there is an upper limit to the capacity of this environment to accept waste matter, and even its robust balance can be seriously upset by pollutants of a noxious or persistent character. Such pollutants may inhibit or modify the natural degradation process, accumulate in the food chain or physically blanket the sea bed. Some insecticides come into the first category, heavy metals into the second and mine process tailings into the third. This, unfortunately, is a gross over-simplification of a complex set of natural processes about which volumes[1] have been, and will continue to be, written.

Thus the discharge of domestic and other biodegradable effluents to the sea may be seen as part of the natural cycle of life and decay. It follows that the marine environment can legitimately be utilised, where appropriate, for the treatment of such sewage effluents. Indeed the once used term 'marine disposal' is now being replaced by the term 'marine treatment', in which an efficient discharge to the sea forms the first phase. Also, it is interesting to note that the Royal Commission on Environmental Pollution 10th report (1984)[2] recognises that current developments in sea outfall design and construction enable us to design efficient sea outfalls, which in many cases are environmentally preferable to the equivalent land based treatment.

The acceptance of the term 'marine treatment' imposes a responsibility on outfall designers and operating authorities. They need to understand and accept the conditions under which a coastal environment can accept a sewage discharge. At the risk of over-simplification, the necessary conditions are:

(a) That the receiving waters and sea bed are in a sufficiently 'healthy' condition to receive and 'treat' the effluent.
(b) That the effluent discharge is of such a quantity and character that the receiving water can accept and 'treat' the additional load.

The implications of these two statements are considerable.

Clearly the quantity of effluent from densely populated coastal or estuarial areas such as London or New York would overwhelm any coastal environment, and shore based treatment is essential in such situations. Similarly areas of low tidal energy such as the Baltic and

Mediterranean seas may need a rather different approach. However, provided the discharge criteria are suitably met, we may regard an area of coastal sea which is suitably used for the marine treatment of an effluent as a 'treatment area'. This area may be defined as the area surrounding an outfall discharge within which the effluent achieves a specified dilution, and within which the bulk of the treatment probably takes place. It follows that this area should not adversely impinge on parts of the sea or coast that are in any way sensitive, such as shell fishing areas, spawning grounds and recreation beaches. The sea outfall is a vital link in this process.

3 REGULATIONS FOR EFFLUENT DISCHARGE AND THE MAINTENANCE OF WATER QUALITY

In the late 60s and early 70s authorities in various parts of the world attempted to introduce quality standards for coastal waters, particularly where these were used for shell fishing or for recreation.

In the UK the Jeger report 'Taken for granted' was published in 1970.[3] In it the subject of 'sewage disposal to the sea' was given a balanced discussion. However, apart from recommending that all sea discharges should be controlled, its recommendations were presented in such general terms that the report was of little use as a design guide to drainage engineers and outfall designers.

One of the main problems in trying to establish standards for discharges into coastal waters is that although it can easily be shown that bacteria from sewage can accumulate in shell fish, there is very little epidemiological evidence available to show that humans are at risk from bathing in contaminated waters, unless the contamination is visibly severe.

In 1976, amidst a great deal of criticism the EEC published its Regulations for Bathing Waters[4] (Table 1) in which many of the contamination parameters were quantified under two grades, with exceedence limits. At about this time WHO[5] and several separate countries (e.g. Denmark and France) produced similar regulations which categorised recreational waters in terms of their pollution level. It is interesting to note that despite a continuing inability to specifically link disease with bathing water quality, all of these regulations use coliform bacteria as a primary quantified parameter.

By quantifying measurable levels of certain pollution parameters

TABLE 1
QUALITY REQUIREMENTS FOR BATHING WATER

Parameters		G (Guide)	I (Mandatory)	Minimum sampling frequency
Microbiological				
1 Total coliforms	(per 100 ml)	500 (80%)	10 000 (95%)	Fortnightly (1)
2 Faecal coliforms	(per 100 ml)	100 (80%)	2000 (95%)	Fortnightly (1)
3 Faecal streptococci	(per 100 ml)	100 (90%)	—	(2)
4 Salmonella	(per litre)	—	0 (95%)	(2)
5 Entero viruses	(PFU* per 10 litres)	—	0 (95%)	(2)
Physico-chemical				
6 pH		—	6 to 9 (0)	(2)
7 Colour		—	No abnormal change in colour (0)	(1)
		—	—	(2)
8 Mineral oils	(mg/litre)	—	No film visible on the surface of the water and no odour	Fortnightly (1)
		≤0·3	—	(2)
9 Surface-active substances reacting with methylene blue	(mg/litre) (lauryl-sulphate)	—	No lasting foam	Fortnightly (1)
		≤0·3	—	(2)
10 Phenols (phenol indices)	(mg/litre) C_5H_5OH	—	No specific odour	Fortnightly (1)
		≤0·005	≤0·05	(2)
11 Transparency	(m)	2	1(0)	Fortnightly (1)
12 Dissolved oxygen	(% satn)	80 to 120	—	(2)
13 Tarry residues and floating materials such as wood, plastic articles, bottles, containers of glass, plastic, rubber or any other substance. Waste or splinters.		Absence		Fortnightly (1)

(1) When a sampling taken in previous years produced results which are appreciably better than those in this Annex and when no new factor likely to lower the quality of the water has appeared, the competent authorities may reduce the sampling frequency by a factor of 2.

(2) Concentration to be checked by the competent authorities when an inspection in the bathing area shows that the substance may be present or that the quality of the water has deteriorated. Percentage values in ( )=proportion of samples in which the numerical values stated must not be exceeded.

*PFU =plaque forming unit — a method of counting viruses; one PFU may be regarded as one infective virus particle.

Extract from the EEC Directive on the Quality of Bathing Water (notably *E. coli*) these regulations have greatly assisted the outfall designer. At last he has 'numbers' as a design objective rather than vague words. Predicted effluent dilutions from an outfall can now be equated to bacterial counts and direct comparison made with regulation requirements.[6] Most of these regulations incorporate exceedence limits which give the designer an 'escape clause' to cater for adverse climatic conditions such as strong onshore winds. These allowances can also be adjusted to suit different sites where such an adjustment is applicable, and thus ensure that an outfall design is both economically and environmentally viable. It is also interesting to note that many of the criticisms levelled against such regulations are invalid when they are used in a design rather than a monitoring sense.

4 TREATMENT BEFORE DISCHARGE — HOW MUCH?

It is now accepted that the minimum amount of treatment required before an effluent is discharged to the sea should comprise grit removal and fine division of any other solid material.

The grit removal is to protect the outfall pipe and system from sedimentation, as it is unlikely that grit scouring velocities will be attained except during flood discharges. Any of the standard sewage treatment works preliminary processes are applicable. The fine division of suspended solid material reduces visible effects, but more important from the marine treatment angle is that a much greater surface area of the particulate material will be in contact with sea water after discharge.

The following are the main processes available.

Screening, which if used alone leaves a high volume residue which is both unpleasant and difficult to handle. Screening after maceration or comminution is to be preferred, with the removed screenings either being disposed of at this stage, or returned to the inflow and re-processed. However, multiple re-processing can result in non-decomposable floating matter being discharged through the outfall and creating a persistent visual effect that may not be a true indication of the outfall's real efficiency.

Screening should aim for a maximum particle size of 5–6 mm. The type of screens available to achieve this are either the 'Wedge Wire' screen with a bar spacing of 0·5–1·5 mm or the 'Rotating Drum Screen' with perforations down to 0·5 mm. Recent developments in the design of these drum screens using thick perforated plastic plates have virtually eliminated the problem of blockage through 'hair pinning' of fibrous material.[7]

As marine treatment via a sea outfall is being considered as an equivalent alternative to land treatment, it may equally be seen·as part treatment in conjunction with land treatment, with a consequent reduction in outfall costs. It may well be that the discharge of the full effluent load of suspended solids is environmentally unacceptable. In this case primary sedimentation may be incorporated into the pre-discharge processes. This may reduce the suspended solids load by up to 70% and the BOD by 30% but the coliform bacterial count by only 5% (Fig. 2). Clearly if the effectiveness of the outfall is to be measured in terms of bacterial counts the addition of primary treatment is not going to save very much on outfall length and therefore on construction costs.

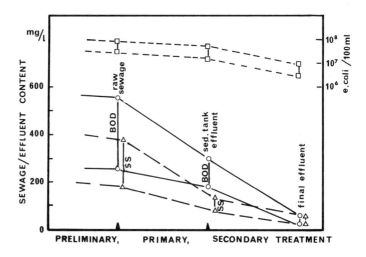

FIG. 2. Typical sewage parameter reductions achieved by land treatment.

Additionally, primary sedimentation produces sludge as an embarrassing by-product which is proving increasingly difficult and expensive to dispose of. Digestion may make it suitable for agricultural use but with industrial effluent components this may not be advisable, and in any case there is considerable resistance in the agricultural community to its use. Land disposal or incineration also presents many problems. Near to coasts sea disposal has its attractions and is frequently used; however, there appear to be influential agencies within such bodies as the EEC, promoting regulations which would severely restrict marine sludge dumping.

It would appear that when the solids component of a sewage effluent is discharged as part of the total effluent, the solids content (presumably finely divided) stands a far better chance of wide distribution than does the separated sludge when it is dumped 'en masse'. It is generally known that the continuous dumping of sludge in the New York Bight area has effectively blanketed the sea floor there. In contrast surveys have shown that similar (but rather smaller) discharges at a selected point in the Clyde Estuary have had little measurable environmental effect. It was a new departure when The Hague built its outfalls at Scheveningen comprising a long sea outfall for the main effluent, and an even longer outfall for discharging sludge from the primary treatment process. Unfortunately the latter outfall has proved unsatisfactory as undistributed sludge found its way shorewards again onto the beaches. It is interesting to speculate on the effectiveness of the system had this pre-discharge separation not taken place.

It would therefore seem prudent to consider very carefully the dubious merits of incorporating primary sedimentation in any treatment project involving a sea outfall, as the additional cost, land use, odour problems and other environmental problems may far outway any possible benefits. In many cases a slightly longer outfall, designed with the aid of thorough site surveys, may well be the preferred solution.

5   THE ROLE AND CHARACTERISTICS OF A SEA OUTFALL

An effective sea outfall may be defined as an engineering device designed to maximise the sea's 'marine treatment' capability, by discharging an effluent into areas which have the necessary water quality, good mixing and dispersion characteristics. Before finalising on the design of an outfall the following factors should be considered.

5.1   The Effluent Quantity and Variability of Discharge

Not only must the present discharge rate be assessed but forecast into the future life of the outfall (50 years?). The discharge may be fairly constant, or it may be highly variable if there is no separation of storm flows. It may also frequently have a seasonal variation at popular coastal resorts.

5.2 The Effluent Content

For a mainly biodegradable effluent from a primarily urban area we are looking towards a true marine treatment process from which we anticipate little permanent residue. However, if there is an element of nondegradable content (and as previously mentioned legislation is now able to limit this), we are looking for a receiving water with good long range dispersion characteristics to eliminate any possibility of undesirable sea bed blanketing or noxious substance build-up.

5.3 The Discharge Zone and Outfall Discharge Area

Man has virtually no control over the sea water characteristics of the discharge area. The designer must therefore use survey methods to look for areas of good turbulence, mixing characteristics and current systems that will disperse and dilute the effluent as rapidly as possible. Local eddy systems that may bring effluent shorewards, and bottom circulating currents that do the same quite obviously need to be avoided. Local current anomalies may equally be used to advantage. Currents generated by tides on a diurnal or semi-diurnal basis must be differentiated from occasional wind-induced or seasonal currents, and allowances made for them.

5.4 Initial or Rising Plume Dilution

Before the horizontal current mixing and dispersion phase, the buoyant effluent must rise towards the sea surface from its sea bed discharge point. The designer does have considerable control over this aspect of an outfall's performance. The dilution of a buoyant rising plume, or multiple plumes rising from a sea bed outfall to the sea surface is a function of discharge rate and efflux velocity, diameter of exit port, depth of water, fluid density difference and ambient current. The sea surface effluent dilution, for a given depth of water and current speed, may be varied by outlet port design and spacing, if multiple ports are to be used in a diffuser.

5.5 Receiving Water Density Stratification

Off many coasts which have the advantage of deep water, thermal variations, which may be seasonal, make it possible for a rising and diluting effluent plume to become entrapped below a certain density level or thermocline. Such entrapment may appear to have certain advantages. For instance the effluent is kept out of sight below the surface and may move with advantageous sub-surface currents. However, by being sub-merged the supply of oxygen is likely to be rapidly exhausted and the previously described form of aerobic marine treatment will be blocked. Anaerobic processes with their associated bacteria are then likely to take over in a rather different form of marine treatment, the by-products of which may not be quite so desirable. At the moment there appear to be two schools of thought on this aspect. One which says that surface aerobic marine treatment is essential and the other which says that either is valid. Unfortunately, thermoclines are not always stable, and an inversion of a stratified 'treatment zone' may bring to the sea surface a rather unpleasant and smelly by-product!

6   OUTFALL TYPES

Outfalls may be broadly classified under three main headings with tunnelled outfalls having important sub-classifications.

6.1   Piped Outfalls where the Pipe and Diffuser Section is Laid Entirely on or above the Sea Bed (Fig. 3(1))

Such an outfall may be constructed in a variety of materials and placed by the bottom tow, float and sink or *in situ* construction methods. The

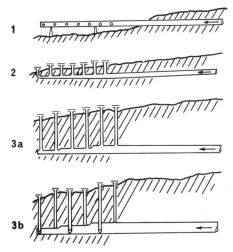

FIG. 3. The four main types of outfall and diffuser configuration.

diffuser section is generally a continuation of the outfall pipe, with a stepped area reduction, along which circular discharge points are cut into the pipe. In designing this type of outfall careful consideration must be given to its protection against ships anchors and trawled fishing gear. Otherwise this type of outfall is likely to be the simplest to maintain and the most reliable hydraulically.

6.2 Piped Outfalls where the Pipe is Shallowly Buried, and in which the Diffuser Section Consists of a Number of Short Riser Pipes Linked to Discharge Ports just above the Sea Bed (Fig. 3(2))

This is a very common type of outfall and is constructed very similarly to the previous sea bed type, except that the pipe is laid into a pre-dredged or excavated trench which is subsequently backfilled. Clearly these outfalls are well protected, but hydraulically may be considered similar to tunnelled outfalls with very short riser pipes.

6.3 Tunnelled Outfalls: (a) with the Diffuser Risers Connected to the Tunnel Soffit (Fig. 3(3a)); (b) with the Diffuser Risers Connected to the Tunnel Invert (Fig. 3(3b))

Under normal discharge conditions when the entire outfall system is full of fresh water the hydraulic behaviour of both sub-divisions is the same. However their behaviour under sea water intrusion conditions is significantly different and favours the (b) type (see Section 12).

There are a number of sub-classifications in which a tunnelled outfall may terminate in a sea bed pipe diffuser section, or the diffuser section of any type may take the form of two or more separate arms. The need for a multi-port diffuser should not be assumed, as there are certainly circumstances where its added design and operational complications are unnecessary.

7 SITE SURVEYS FOR OUTFALL DESIGN

The last decade has seen significant advances in the application of survey techniques which in many cases have been developed for research purposes. In addition, equipment commonly used in the offshore exploration industry has become available to the outfall designer.

Inevitably much of this equipment is expensive to use or hire and as the total site investigation cost has to be seen in relation to the overall project cost, the full panoply of this survey equipment may not in reality be available for the smallest project. Nevertheless, for effective design, a minimum of survey information is required. This minimum should include dye tracer tests (Section 7.4) as these tests give the most reliable prediction of an outfall's performance.

The siting of a projected outfall is often constrained by many factors, not least of which are the location of existing or projected sewer lines, construction access, etc. However, these constraints should not be allowed to unnecessarily dominate the outfall site, as a small shift of discharge area can, very often, improve an outfall's performance, or allow a shorter outfall to be used. In these cases an increase in known land construction costs may be preferable to a similar cost in less easily predicted offshore work.

A full site investigation now generally comprises the following.

7.1 Environmental Surveys

These surveys, generally covering the inter-tidal area, are required for control purposes, to assess the pre-construction state of the zone and then after construction to measure the changes in this zone. Clearly, if the new outfall is to replace a number of old short ones, as is frequently the case, a significant improvement will be expected (to better than EEC standards if the coastal zone is a recreational area). Alternatively, if a new outfall is to be constructed from an unpolluted coast it is important to record any additional impact on the coast.

The factors which may be recorded comprise:

(a) the type, distribution and cover density of seaweed and plant growth;

(b) a similar assessment of the animal life on rocks, and within the sands and muds;

(c) a tissue analysis of indicator species for heavy metals, pesticides and bacteria. This is important in areas where shell-fish may be harvested and

(d) bacteria sampling in the surf zone. This type of survey will be particularly important in assessing the effectiveness of an outfall on the recreational inshore zone. Any water sampling programme should take into account the seasonal weather and tidal state in the sampling area, to ensure that any results obtained may be truly comparable, as bacterial concentrations for the same sampling point have been known to regularly vary by a factor of over a 1000 during a 3 h period of flood or ebb flow.

7.2 Receiving Water Quality Assessment

Once again these measurements will be required for a pre- and post-construction comparison, but more importantly to assess the pre-discharge state of the receiving water. To accept the role of 'marine treatment' a receiving water clearly needs to be in a healthy state. We need to know what load the water is already carrying in the way of suspended solids, chemical and bacterial content, and the extent to which it may already be depleted of oxygen.[8]

7.3 Tide and Current Measurement

If we assume that the currents which are to disperse the discharged effluent are tidally generated (and this therefore excludes such areas as the Mediterranean and Baltic seas) the relationship between tides and currents will be regular and once measured predictable, with almost equally predictable variations for atmospheric variations, mainly in the form of superimposed wind driven currents.

At the outfall design stage it is necessary to have a clear idea of the regular tidal current patterns over the whole of the contemplated discharge and inshore area. Thus a synoptic view of these currents is required, preferably in the form of a tidal atlas in which the hour by hour current variation throughout the tidal cycle is shown.

The gathering of such site information from traditional current metering stations recording on an Eulerian basis is virtually impossible, as an impractical number of current meters would be required, and the resulting data handling would be particularly tiresome. A Lagrangian method of current measuring is therefore called for, the float–drogue method of current tracking being ideal for this purpose. Float–drogues have been used for a long time, but the traditional land theodolite tracking, or boat following methods of position fixing, limit the number of float–drogues that may usefully be deployed at any one time, thus reducing the synoptic value of the results. Radar tracking has enabled us to use up to 10 or 12 float–drogues at once, thus greatly increasing the value of the data.[9]

The system uses a land based radar (as its orientation and position must remain constant) to track the float–drogues over the survey area. A fast launch in touch with the radar operator by radio acts as a sheep dog would, collecting float–drogues as they leave the survey area and re-positioning them at the upstream boundary again, or alternatively deploying them to investigate any peculiarities or aberrations in the currents that the operator may have noticed. This latter point highlights a distinct advantage of the method. The radar operator has an immediate synoptic view of the currents developing in front of him and can react accordingly.

An effective form of float–drogue is shown in Fig. 4. The drogue may be suspended at almost any depth although 20 m would appear to be a practical limit. The cylindrical floatation collar is designed to minimise small wave action drift, while the minimum normal reflector size would appear to be about 300 mm.

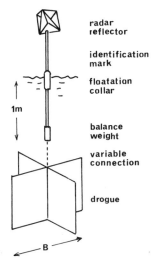

FIG. 4. Details of the TERC float–drogue.

It is possible to obtain radar equipment with the rotating aerial mounted independently and remotely from the viewing–control console with a cable connecting the two items. Thus the aerial may be mounted strategically on a wall or dune while the operator remains some distance away. It is also possible to offset the rotation centre within the circular viewing screen thus increasing the apparent survey area at any particular magnification. A parallax free plotting head enables direct plotting on transparent overlays to take place in real time. Position and timing of echoes on the screen will give path-lines and deduced current vectors (Fig. 5). The float–drogues, due to windage of the pole and reflector, will be subject to some wind drift. By calibrating the float–drogues for this drift in non-tidal waters any drift can be allowed for in the final current

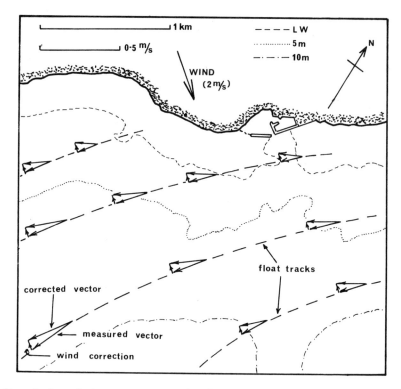

FIG. 5. A typical current survey showing the float–drogue tracks, deduced
velocity vectors, and normalised wind corrected vectors.

plot (Fig. 6). In practice we have found that there is a limiting wind speed
of about 4 m/s, above which wind drift becomes disproportionate. To
minimise this drift factor it is recommended that the drogue dimension B
in Fig. 4 should be not less than 0·5 m for currents between 0·2 and
0·5 m/s and 2 m for currents less than 0·2 m/s.

Eventually the data from a whole tidal cycle (spring, neap or intermediate) will be plotted progressively as the pages of a tidal atlas
(Fig. 6).

Funds permitting, a number of refinements to this system are possible.
Compact high gain, low windage radar reflectors are available built into
spheres or cylinders. Even more attractive is the powered radar re-
sponder which when triggered by a radar beam re-transmits a coded
signal which will identify the float on the radar screen. Sophisticated

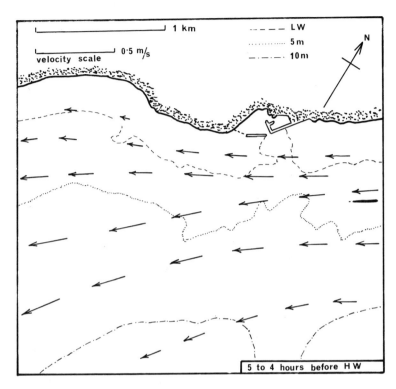

FIG. 6. Normalised and wind corrected currents plotted from Fig. 5. This would constitute one page of the site tidal atlas.

radar sets permit radar return signals to be identified and located electronically thus allowing data to be recorded for subsequent computer analysis.

However attractive many of these additional sophistications may be, they do tend to remove the operator one stage from the real action, raising the possibility of significant factors being missed.

Recent developments in other remote sensing techniques may be worth considering for future current surveys. Surface floats, which may be connected to drogues, can be fitted with small transmitters enabling their position to be reasonably accurately fixed by some of the orbiting navigation satellites. Although attractive, this technique is really more applicable to determining currents over a wider area than would normally be required in most outfall investigations. The observation of similar floats from aircraft or tethered balloons is also a possibility. A new radar technique is capable of measuring current velocities directly, but so far its spatial resolution is too coarse for practical outfall survey use. If this can be improved it promises to be a very powerful survey tool.

Other facets of water movement cannot be ignored in outfall surveys. Residual currents can play an important role in the ultimate dispersion of an effluent. Fixed recording current meters may be used for obtaining this information. However, once again the data, not being synoptic, are difficult to analyse. Perhaps the best compromise is to use a detailed analysis of the tidal atlas to obtain synoptic residuals, with confirmation from one or two fixed current meters.

Equally, bed drift by bringing light sediments shorewards, may affect an outfall's overall performance. The well tried Woodhead drifters are still the simplest method of determining bed drift although radioactive or fluorescent tracer particles have been used successfully. Many outfall sites will have a shoreward bed drift, but the relevance of this drift must be seen in terms of the drift time and the rate at which 'marine treatment' takes place.

7.4 Dispersion Assessment

A careful analysis of the current survey will enable the outfall designer to prepare a basic outfall design, position and termination. After the final stage of dilution in a buoyant rising plume, subsequent effluent dilution and dispersion is dependent entirely on the dispersion characteristics of the receiving water. Experience has shown this characteristic to be highly variable from site to site and indeed from one time to another at the same site, and more particularly between ebb and flood. Standard dilution equations are unlikely to cover all of these eventualities, and although useful in preliminary assessment, are no substitute for the *in situ* measurement of dispersion.

Effluent dispersion and dilution in a tidal stream is a function primarily of turbulent mixing. The degree of turbulence, and hence mixing, is a function of stream velocity and boundary conditions, but most importantly of the accelerating or decelerating conditions of the tidal stream. Accelerating tidal streams tend to be stable with low turbulence. Acceleration may be induced by a contracting channel or bed form, or by an increasing tidal stream at the beginning of a flood or ebb tide. Deceleration flows conversely occur in divergent channels, or over the second half of a flood or ebb period.

In practice the measurement of dispersion may be made in one of three ways: radioactive, fluorescent dye or bacteria tracers. The two former methods have comparable sensitivities, the dye tracer technique generally being favoured on account of its relative convenience and cost. Bacterial surveys in which a non-resident bacteria is introduced present considerable sampling and detection problems which generally limit their usefulness.

The dye technique usually uses the very powerful and concentrated rhodamine B dye for short term investigations, the more expensive WT variety often being preferred if multi-tidal observations are to be made, on account of its lower absorption and adsorption characteristics on organic matter.

Rhodamine dye being fluorescent is easily detected, down to concentrations as low as $1:10^{11}$, by standard fluorometry. Preferably the survey fluorometer should be the constant flow variety, self-balancing, and connected to an analogue recorder on board a survey launch. A sampling intake pipe and pump system is used to feed the fluorometer as the survey launch traverses the labelled survey area. These fluorometers tend to be very sensitive to air bubbles and therefore any pump in the system should be kept low down and feed the instrument under pressure to avoid inward air leaks, or gas coming out of solution in the sample flow.

The tracer dye is injected as a continuous surface stream at the proposed outfall point. It is metered and pre-diluted up to 1000 times by receiving water before discharge at 0·5–1 m depth below the surface. Surface discharge is adopted because it is the secondary surface spreading effluent plume that is being simulated by these tests.

The survey boat continuously monitors the spreading plume downstream of the injection point, mainly at 0·5–1 m depth, but with check traverses at lower depths to ascertain the three-dimensional spread of the plume.

Navigation of the survey boat has to be precise, necessitating the use of automatic electronic distance measuring or position fixing equipment.

A typical survey course is shown in Fig. 7 and selected transverse dye concentration profiles are shown in Fig. 8. The longitudinal section along the centre line of a dye plume shown in Fig. 9 illustrates the concentration variability due to turbulence and the exponential characteristic of dilution within the plume.

It is preferable that these dispersion surveys should be representative of fairly normal sea and wind conditions, and that they are not aberrated by excessive sea surface drift, although minor corrections are permissible.

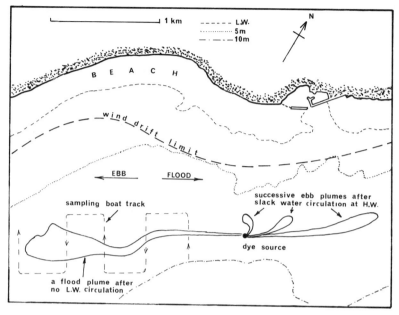

FIG. 7. Plotted dye plumes for the same site as shown in Figs 5 and 6.

(The converse of the process described in Section 7.5). Also, as these surveys are aimed at recording plume dilutions rather than long term spread, they are best conducted over half tidal cycles, usually about 7 h for a semi-diurnal tide. As the slack water period is the time when dilutions are at their lowest, the best period for a survey is generally from about 30 min before tide turn to the alternate tide turn. In this way the initial plume 'hammer head' shown in Fig. 7 (flood tide) may be effectively tracked, and tidal stream overlap is avoided. Local conditions may dictate different timings and where slack water circulations exist the hammer head situation may not exist (Fig. 7, ebb tide).

The organisation of this data requires painstaking desk and drawing office plotting, with care being taken to understand the sampling process used. For example, due to the turbulent mixing in the sampling pipe runs, the onboard fluorometer used in dye tests records a sharp and accurate start to a plume traverse, but a slower decay on exiting from this traverse (Fig. 10). This effect can be allowed for or eliminated by traversing the plume on the same line but in the reverse direction and superimposing the concentration plots. This particular sampling problem does not occur

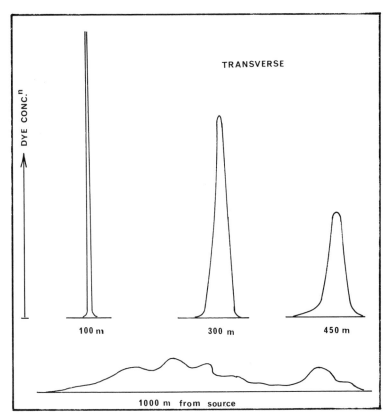

FIG. 8. Concentration profiles across a dispersing effluent plume.

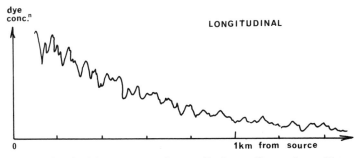

FIG. 9. A longitudinal dye concentration profile, in an effluent plume, illustrating turbulent mixing, and exponential concentration decay.

if towed *in situ* fluorometers are used, or if similar scintillation counters are used in radioactive tracer work.

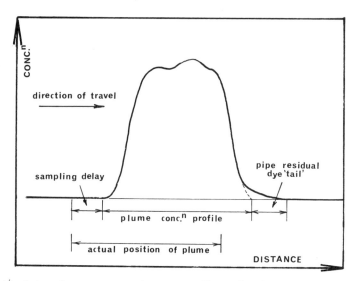

FIG. 10. A dye plume concentration traverse illustrating the sampling delay, and the 'false width' effect produced by residual dye.

7.5 Interpretation of Survey Data

The only survey data described in this section that require interpretation are the dispersion test data. *In situ* tracer testing is attempting to directly simulate an effluent discharge and thus bypasses any assessment of dispersion coefficients or calculations of that nature. This does not mean that the appropriate coefficients cannot be derived from the data if they are required.

Clearly the dye discharge, even initially diluted at 1:1000, does not reproduce the volume of effluent discharge that is contemplated. However, if the transverse cross-sectional area of the measured dye plume is plotted against distance from its source, it is possible to find a plume section which has a discharge flux equal to the predicted effluent flux at the surface boil point over the outfall. (In practice this has generally been found within 50 m of the dye injection point.) The plotted dye plume is then shifted upstream so that this apparent dye source coincides with the boil point. (Fig. 11). The dye plume now corresponds to, and predicts,

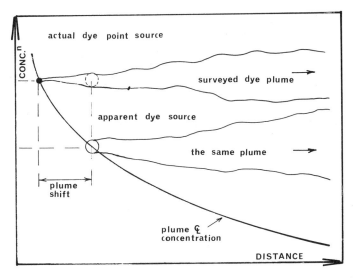

FIG. 11. The adjustment of a surveyed dye plume to match the source conditions of the real effluent plume.

the behaviour of the planned effluent plume, and dye concentrations can be equated to bacteria concentrations at the boil point. These surface boil point concentrations, which result from the rising buoyant plume dilutions, can be determined fairly accurately (Section 8). Subsequent dilutions and bacteria concentrations within the plume can now be estimated from the measured dye concentrations, and bacterial iso-concentration lines drawn. This analysis relates to the discharge from a single outfall port, its buoyant rising plume and current dispersion plume. By lineal multiplication the dispersion effect of a diffuser can be estimated.

In a field test conducted by the author from the Tay Estuary Research Centre, identical streams of dye were injected directly into an outfall flow before discharge, and from a standard dye dispensing unit anchored 50 m away from the single outfall port. The ensuing two parallel dye plumes were simultaneously surveyed for a distance of about 1·5 km downstream of the discharges. After applying the apparent dye source shift to the second plume, as described previously, the two plotted plumes were virtually identical in all respects.

So far effluent dispersion under normal conditions has been considered. The effects of onshore wind and its associated surface drift are

usually the limiting conditions for outfall design. In the open ocean
surface water drift speeds may be as high as 3–4% of the wind speed, but
in coastal waters an equivalent drift speed of 1·5–2·0% is now generally
accepted. Most water quality criteria (e.g. the EEC bathing water
regulations) have exceedence tolerances for sampling errors or excessive
onshore wind conditions. An analysis of local long term wind records
can establish the exceedence onshore wind limit, and hence the limiting
surface water drift speed. Figure 12 shows a coastal wind rose. The limit-

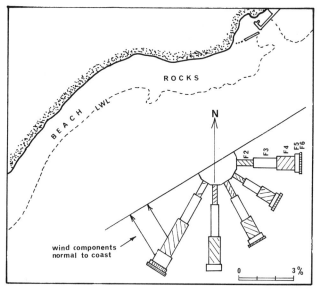

FIG. 12. A wind-rose for a survey area showing an example of the wind
components used in the exceedence curve.

ing wind speed is determined by obtaining the vector sum of all wind
components perpendicular to the shore line and plotting these against
their percentage occurrence values (Fig. 13). The limiting wind speeds
corresponding to the regulation limits are then read off from this graph.
The appropriate surface water wind drift can then be applied on the
drawing board to the plotted normal dye plumes and a new set of
bacterial iso-concentration lines drawn. These lines represent the limiting
performance condition for the projected outfall, the position of which
can now be optimised (Fig. 7).

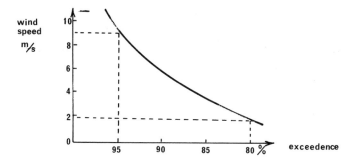

FIG. 13. An exceedence curve for the summed wind components normal to the shore.

This wholesale wind shifting of a plume does not take into account the transverse vertical shearing action that occurs in the wind drifted surface waters. The additional effluent dilution that this generates may be seen as a safety factor in the process as it is very difficult to quantify.

7.6 Bacterial Decay Rates

The mortality of bacteria originating from the effluent is measured by the usual T_{90} period and this decay may be incorporated into a combined dilution figure. However, caution should be exercised as the T_{90} period may vary between 0·5 h and 48 h depending mainly upon the intensity of sunlight (as it affects the u.v. levels) and the turbidity of the water (which filters out any sunlight)[8,10]

7.7 Standards for Tracer and Effluent Concentration Measurements

The concentration profiles across rising buoyant surface spreading plumes are ideally Gaussian, and certainly in the initial stages of dilution this has been found to be true. Unfortunately, quoted laboratory, and more particularly, field measurements, have frequently not been sufficiently clearly defined for sensible comparisons to be made. This is partly understandable from the practical difficulties of making these measurements. It is therefore recommended that quoted concentrations should refer to the Gaussian peak, or the concentration profile estimated peak.

7.8 Sites with Low Tidal Energies

The water currents in these areas tend to be seasonal where they form part of larger circulation patterns, and wind generated currents. Current and dispersion surveys in such areas are necessarily more protracted than previously described. They should aim to cover the less favourable conditions for outfall performance, and may need to carefully examine currents at all depths. As dispersion under these conditions tends to be more current orientated, rather than a direct function of turbulence, the use of mathematical models (Section 7.10) can be very helpful in examining the many possibilities of dispersion patterns. However, field work will be necessary to establish the primary parameters used in any model.

7.9 Physical Modelling

The use of physical hydraulic models for assessing secondary dispersion of effluents is not often attempted. To obtain any correlation of turbulent diffusion between model and prototype would generally require excessive model scales. The scale distortion of such a model also introduces unknown elements which must reduce their reliability. However, this does not rule out their use. It was discovered that the tidal model of the Tay Estuary (horizontal scale 1:1760, vertical scale 1:144) reproduced prototype dispersion plumes with surprising accuracy. It was successfully used to examine no less than 38 possible outfall sites within the estuary for sewage effluent discharge. Three of these were subsequently investigated *in situ* and confirmed the model's findings. Heat dispersion from projected power stations is successfully physically modelled and no doubt similar techniques could be used for other outfalls.

The initial dilution of a rising buoyant plume has frequently been modelled successfully on a straight Froudian relationship.[11-13] Similarly the modelling of sea water intrusion is basically a gravitational phenomena and is also amenable to Froudian modelling.[14]

7.10 Numerical Modelling

The use of numerical modelling in outfall siting studies is becoming an increasingly powerful tool. Nevertheless no model, however well it is constructed, is better than the control and boundary data that are fed into it. For a dispersion model this requires stream velocity data, i.e. a tidal atlas, and the appropriate dispersion coefficients which should be obtained from *in situ* testing, and as seen earlier these coefficients are liable to change both with time and location. In other words a full site survey, as previously described, is generally required to run a reliable numerical model. The correct choice and use of dispersion coefficients is vital in numerical modelling. They fall into three basic categories.

(1) Overall coefficients covering large areas used for multi-tide overall dilutions.

(2) Longitudinal coefficients representing the local dispersion along the axis of an effluent plume.

(3) Transverse coefficients which represent the dispersion transversely across the same plume, horizontally or vertically.

The longitudinal and transverse coefficients are used in local plume dispersion predictions parallel to the measurements described in Section 7.4.

Mathematical models may be usefully employed in a similar way to that described in Section 7.9 when their versatility may be utilised to explore a number of possibilities for outfall sites, a small selection of which would subsequently be tested *in situ* for confirmation and detail design purposes.[15,16]

8 OUTFALL DESIGN PROCEDURE

8.1 Port Sizing and Spacing

The processes for designing the actual outfall are now fairly well established. The initial design phase needs to start at the outfall discharge, as presumably the studies of the discharge area will have determined the initial surface dilution that is required. This initial surface dilution is generated by the turbulent mixing in the rising buoyant plume. That is the initial gravitational ascent of the fresh water effluent to the sea surface (or entrapment level). This process has been very fully studied both experimentally in the laboratory[11,12] and in the field,[17] as well as theoretically.[18]

The graphical representation of Abraham's work (Fig. 14) clearly illustrates the choices available to the designer at this stage. (Cederwall's equation[19] is an expression of the same data). Surface dilution is maximised, either at low or high discharge densimetric Froude numbers. The former implies low discharge velocities and consequent low driving heads, and the latter high velocities and large heads. As most outfalls are designed as gravitational systems, there are obvious advantages in designing for low densimetric Froude numbers, provided the lower critical limit of unity is not approached (see Section 8.3) and pipe scour velocities are maintained (Section 8.6). Over the last few years the discovery of various outfall malfunctions (Section 11) has highlighted the problems associated with low velocity design, and a few outfall designers and operators are now tending to think that the higher running costs (generally continuous pumping) of higher velocity discharging outfalls

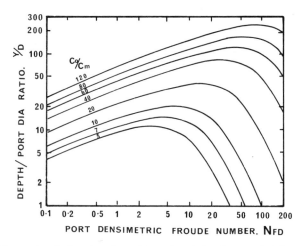

FIG. 14. General solution for three-dimensional jet (from ref. 11). N_{FD} = as in Section 8.3; Y = outfall port depth below surface; D = outfall port diameter and Co/Cm = port to surface dilution ratio (peak values).

may be worthwhile, if sedimentation and intrusion problems can be avoided.

Whichever basic philosophy is adopted, the use of the Abraham diagram (Fig. 14) or its equivalent will optimise the number of ports and their size. It is generally agreed that ports should not be less than 100 mm in diameter, and preferably not less than 150 mm.

Ports generally discharge horizontally for maximum dilution effect. Various discharge port modifications have been experimented with, such as swirl chambers and flow inducers,[20] but the small dilution improvements obtained have hardly justified the additional complexity. However, the simple orientation of ports may sometimes considerably improve initial dilution. It is possible to discharge at a slight downward angle close to and towards a smooth sea bed; jet attachment should then occur, when the inverted 'pointers tail' effect (Fig. 15) can increase the spread of the rising plume, and consequent dilution. The 'chimney stack' effect can also be utilised when a pipe port is discharging against the current. Effluent spreading round the pipe can be distributed along the back of the pipe in the low pressure wake (Fig. 16). Clearly tidally reversing currents may make these configurations only partly effective, but many outfalls need to have better dilution characteristics in one particular direction. The intrusion control diffuser outlet (Section 8.4) is also able to

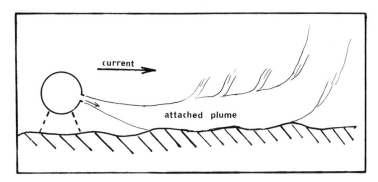

FIG. 15. The sea bed 'attached' effluent plume.

improve dilution by lowering the densimetric Froude number at higher discharges.

Port spacing is a function of rising plume geometry. Most outfall designers now opt for a spacing that keeps the buoyant rising plumes (based on still water analysis) separate until they reach the surface. Indeed a case can be made for increasing this separation to avoid interference of the spreading surface plumes for some distance downstream of the boil point. The geometry of the still water rising buoyant plume may be found from Fig. 17[21], a method which has adequately been confirmed by excellent Italian field work.[18]

Generally speaking piped outfalls have uniformly spaced ports along their diffuser length, whereas tunnelled outfalls, to minimise the number of riser pipes, tend to have clusters of ports at the head of each riser. Calculations and model tests have shown that multiple ports in such a riser head may be counter productive in maximising rising dilution due

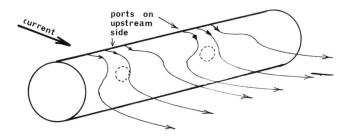

FIG. 16. 'Chimney stack' dilution enhancement from upcurrent facing ports.

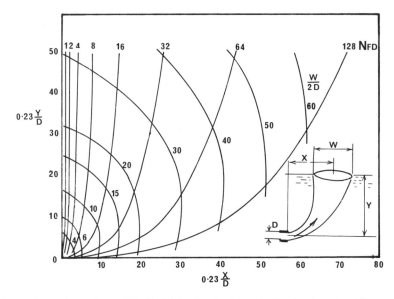

FIG. 17. Trajectories and half-widths for horizontal circular jets in still water (from ref. 21).

to rising plume interference. One such study showed that there was a strong case for a two port riser with the ports discharging at an angle to the current flow.

8.2 Diffuser Design

The problem of obtaining equal discharges from the multiple ports of a diffuser is a classic hydraulic design problem.[22,23] In an outfall, an additional problem is that the total discharge usually varies from DWF or less to flood flows, with a variation of anything up to 1:50. To maintain scouring flows within the diffuser section a tapered form, usually in steps, is now universally adopted. The many variables of geometry and flow within a diffuser system are an ideal subject for computer analysis. Any program developed for this should enable the pipe diameter, port diameters and spacing, as well as the overall discharge to be varied. For a constant port size and spacing, the variation of port discharge along the diffuser will vary in the way depicted in Fig. 18. Approximately uniform discharge along the diffuser may be obtained by varying the individual port sizes and/or their spacing. Practical considerations sometimes prevent this and the resulting variation of discharge is tolerated. However, it is important to ensure that at the lowest discharges the ports with least flow conform to the minimum densimetric Froude number criterion.

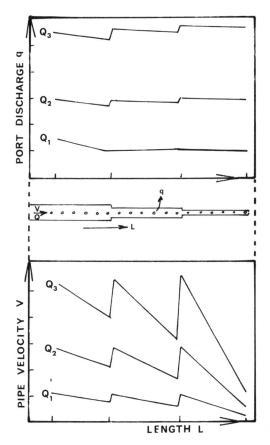

FIG. 18. Theoretical variation of port discharge and pipe velocities in a diffuser with two steps and equally spaced and sized ports.

8.3 Sea Water Intrusion

When an orifice discharges a lower density liquid, in this case usually fresh water effluent of relative density about 1·00, into a higher density liquid, i.e. sea water of relative density 1·024–1·030, there will be a low flow discharge at which the driving head across the orifice is less than the two liquid density difference on a vertical diameter of the orifice (Fig. 19).

Under the incipient conditions of this situation it can be shown that the orifice flow densimetric Froude number

$$N_{FD} = \frac{V_j}{\left(g\dfrac{(\rho_2 - \rho_1)}{\rho_1} D\right)^{1/2}} = 1$$

where V_j is the mean jet discharge velocity from the port; D is the port diameter and ρ_2 and ρ_1 are the two fluid densities.

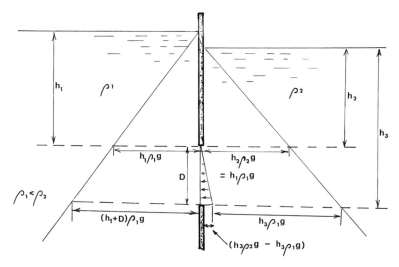

FIG. 19. Pressure distribution across an orifice for two liquids of different density, showing the limiting intrusive condition when the pressures on each side of the orifice upper surface are equal.

Once such a 'primary' intrusive situation has started a classical salt wedge situation develops (Fig. 20) and will continue to develop with decreasing effluent flow as long as there is horizontal space for it. However, if this salt wedge reaches a point where it can invade a vertical component of the system, usually a riser from a pipe or tunnel diffuser

(Fig. 20), a very different situation can arise in which one salt water intruded riser becomes out of hydraulic balance with its non-intruded neighbour and a circulating cell is formed in which the intruded riser goes into reverse flow. This may be termed 'secondary intrusion' (Fig. 21). The velocities which can be attained in this reverse flow are considerable. With this sort of salt water inflow it does not take long for other risers to entrain salt water, and in turn become out of balance and

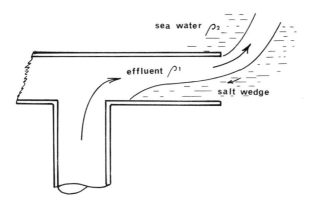

FIG. 20. Primary intrusion progressing along a horizontally discharging outlet.

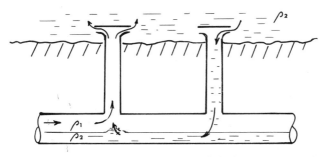

FIG. 21. Secondary intrusion occurring in a vertical 'riser' limb.

to go into reverse. Eventually an equilibrium situation will be reached in which a number of risers are flowing in reverse and the rest are flowing upward, some of which are discharging fresh water effluent mixed with entrained salt water. Continuity is thus maintained. In this condition the combined upward flow of mixed salt and fresh water requires a driving head equal to the differential head between the riser head colums of fresh and salt water ($z(\rho_2 - \rho_1)/\rho_1$ in Fig. 30).[24]

The discharge required to flush the system of secondary intruded salt water is consequently much greater than the discharge at which the intrusion process originally started. The head flow characteristic of the system takes a form similar to that shown in Fig. 30. (See also Section 12). Clearly it is important to avoid this situation occurring in the first place, as the requisite higher purging flows may not be available for sufficient time to clear all salt water from the system and reverse the situation to normal fresh water discharge.

The maintenance of an adequate discharge, such that all port discharges have densimetric Froude numbers reasonably in excess of unity, is an obvious way of avoiding this situation. However, this condition can fail under a number of circumstances.

(1) Poor diffuser design allowing big differences in port discharge.
(2) Port damage which adversely alters its discharge characteristics. Breakage or distortion can do this.
(3) Wave action in which sea bed oscillating hydrostatic pressures generate pulsating port discharge flows. Such wave-induced action can, if it happens to synchronise with a natural oscillating U tube frequency of a pair of risers, generate quite violent oscillating flow within the diffuser system. During the reverse flow phase, sufficient sea water may be drawn in to set up an intrusive condition.
(4) Tidal or other currents can also upset the balance of a two port riser in which one port faces upstream and the other downstream. The differential dynamic pressure between the two ports may induce all the effluent discharge to exit from the downstream port leaving the upstream port vulnerable to intrusion.

Most of these situations generate primary intrusion which, on its own, may not be too significant as it is completely reversible. The real trouble begins when secondary intrusion subsequently develops, as this is only reversible through a hysteresis loop and in some cases the necessary conditions to complete this loop may not be available. The hysteresis head differential is directly related to the vertical distance between the outfall pipe or tunnel and the sea bed discharge level (Fig. 30).

Secondary intrusion when it occurs can lead to a number of serious problems. Marine growth may be encouraged around the inside of ports, eventually causing physical blockage. Stagnant areas of a diffuser may also be created in which debris may settle out and lie undetected until total blockage occurs; such debris might even be carried into the outfall by intruding sea water.

A particular problem occurs with tunnelled outfalls when secondary intrusion feeds sea water into the tunnel, which for construction drainage purposes is often driven uphill from the shaft. This sea water is liable to accumulate in the tunnel as a dense layer or long wedge which is stable at appreciable flows. Unless high discharges can be maintained for long enough to either entrain this reservoir of sea water, and/or push the saline wedge to the diffuser section, the problem will return. Secondary intrusion will persist while any reservoir of sea water remains in the system.

A number of case histories of intrusion appear in Section 11.

8.4 The Prevention of Sea Water Intrusion

The maintenance of an adequate discharge under all circumstances has already been mentioned in Section 8.2. Unless high flushing flows are known to be available the shut down of outfall discharge may give rise to an irreversible intrusion condition. In fact the initial commissioning of an outfall may already contain this problem unless the whole system can be started up full of fresh water (a condition which is easier stated than managed).

However, before becoming too gloomy it must be stated that many outfalls function quite happily and can be designed to function thus, under intermittent intrusive conditions. Outfalls of type 1 (Section 6) are generally self-balancing with the salt water layer moving to accommodate the discharge (Fig. 22). There is very little hysteresis in the intrusion head characteristic of such an outfall but it is still necessary to ensure that full purging flows occur regularly. In an outfall of this type which is designed for long term population growth and discharge it is

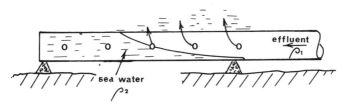

FIG. 22. Self-balancing intrusion in a type 1 outfall.

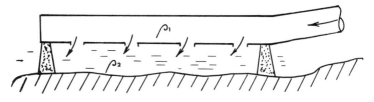

FIG. 23. An intrusion proof diffuser.

good practice to block off, until required, a proportion of the upstream ports.

The simplest form of intrusion prevention for type 1 outfalls is to have a horizontal diffuser section with downward facing ports (Fig. 23). This is a possible, although often less practical solution.

Alternatively, diffuser heads may have a separation weir in them (Fig. 24). The weir overlap (z) must be greater than any displacement likely through surge or wave action. Such a device is satisfactory for single riser systems. However in multiple riser systems the method may not be entirely satisfactory as the weirs must all be at exactly the same level, and even then differential gas accumulation is likely to upset the balance between different risers.

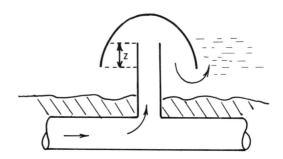

FIG. 24. An intrusion proof head.

A promising development in intrusion prevention has been the flexible duck-bill discharge valves developed by John Taylor & Sons (Fig. 25). These have been used successfully on a number of outfalls, notably the Weymouth tunnelled outfall. This is the nearest approach, outfall operators will accept,[25] to an underwater moving valve. Its long term use has yet to be proved, but it should be easy to replace if faulty or damaged.

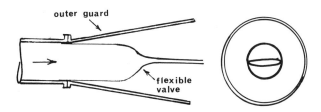

FIG. 25. Anti-intrusion flexible 'duck-bill' valve.

Separate from intrusion prevention is intrusion control, in which, under normal operating conditions, intrusion is blocked by hydraulic methods.

The SERC sponsored research programme at Dundee University has developed a number of methods of controlling sea water that is in a position to intrude into an outfall system. Once again these systems may be divided into primary and secondary control.

One primary control system involves discharging through a venturi shaped outlet port. This system combines the advantages of a large port having low efflux velocities, with a small diameter throat which restricts the intrusion of sea water. Figure 26a shows the device discharging at a flow which does not fill the outlet port and which would normally be intrusive and Fig. 26b shows it at full bore discharge. The limiting throat diameter will be about 100 mm and the whole outlet can be designed as a low loss venturi system.

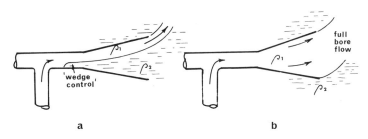

FIG. 26. A venturi discharge port acting as an intrusion control device.

The secondary control systems are designed to protect an outfall tunnel against the accumulation of sea water. Once again the venturi system has been used in a section just upstream of the diffuser section, and Fig. 27 shows a device limiting the advance of sea water into the

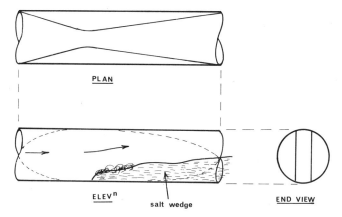

FIG. 27. The venturi intrusion control built into the Aberdeen sea outfall tunnel.

outfall tunnel. This device was developed for inclusion in the Aberdeen tunnelled outfall at a stage in its construction when it was too late to incorporate any other control method.

Neither venturi device will completely prevent the passage of sea water, but their threshold discharges will be considerably less than the full tunnel or port discharges. In addition, if due to abnormally very low flows or complete stoppage, sea water does pass through the tunnel venturi, successive flood flows of relatively short duration will be able to move the unwanted salt water through the venturi in such a way that return flow into the tunnel does not occur, and eventually complete purging becomes possible.

Another method limits intrusion to the diffuser section from which a single good flood flow should purge it. The tunnel section is joggled by one diameter (as a minimum) (Fig. 28). The no flow salt–fresh water interface is then as shown. To maintain this interface with no discharge in a rising tide situation either means the joggle offset must be the tunnel

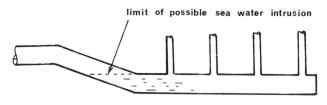

FIG. 28. A cranked tunnel-diffuser acting as an intrusion block.

diameter plus the tidal range, or a small fresh water flow must be maintained into the shaft sufficient to keep its water level above the tidal level.

8.5 Intermittent or Pumped Purging Flows

Although many outfall systems are gravity fed over large parts of the tidal cycle, flood flows or high water discharges may require pumped assistance. This leaves room for the storage of effluent and high rate intermittent discharge at velocities which will prevent sedimentation, and incidentally intrusion. Unfortunately for most outfall designs intrusion will occur during the intermediate no-flow phase. This may be acceptable if the volume of sea water entering the outfall can be purged on the next high flow, as in a simple type 1 piped outfall. However this condition may not occur in a type 2 outfall and is most unlikely in a normal tunnelled outfall.

In the Junk Bay outfall in Hong Kong which is a type 2 outfall fitted with the flexible duck-bill valves, initial very low discharges are augmented by weekly pumping phases at flows well above pipe scour velocities.

To avoid the transmittance of surge on starting or stopping it is good practice for pumped flows to discharge into an open head-pond or shaft in which the natural full discharge head can build up. Even under these conditions sudden changes in discharges may induce surge conditions due to the considerable fluid inertia of the outfall's discharge. Any non-return valves incorporated in the system would be liable to damage from such surges.

8.6 Pipe or Tunnel Hydraulic Design

Two main factors influence the design of the pipe or tunnel leading to the diffuser, head losses and scouring velocities. The determination of head losses is now a simple pipe flow problem using data from any of the more recent publications.[26] With the elimination of most of the grit at the headworks the main problem lies not with the organic material which is fairly easy to maintain in suspension, but with the finer mineral particles not removed in the grit removal process. These are likely to have an effective size of 0·1–0·2 mm with a density of about 2·65. A wall shear stress analysis suggests critical velocities of the order of 0·75 m/s. This is still higher than can be maintained in many systems at minimum discharge.[27,28] Under these circumstances, if diurnal variations do not achieve scouring velocities then augmented periodic discharge must be considered.

8.7 Headwork Design

The design of the headworks has largely been covered in Section 4. The headworks should incorporate a reliable method of flow measurement, which apart from the obvious records, is now seen as an essential element in outfall performance monitoring (Section 12). If primary treatment can be avoided the entire headworks may be enclosed[7] thus ensuring the environmental acceptability of the system.

9 OUTFALL MATERIALS

9.1 Steel

Steel is probably the most used material at the moment. It can be fabricated from sheet in a number of different ways to match a customer requirement for a specific size. Longitudinal welding has been used for a number of years but spiral welding is becoming increasingly popular, being a virtually continuous process. Steel outfall pipes have the advantage of great strength in tension, and as a consequence lend themselves to the popular 'bottom pull' laying method. Steel requires good corrosion protection. This is achieved on the exterior by paints and conventional wrappings of bitumen or resins. Internally paints, mortar linings and more recently resins have become popular. Most of these protection systems are applied at the factory during manufacture. With a 10 m pipe length transport restriction this necessitates a large number of *in situ* protection joints after welding has taken place. These joints are often the cause of lining failures. A recent innovation is to use the 'Permaline' sewer repair process on 200 m of pipe at a time at the launching site. In this process an un-set resin impregnated liner is literally unrolled into the pipe under water pressure and subsequently set and cured by heating the water. The reduction in internal joints is a major factor in the appeal of this process.

Steel pipelines are invariably concrete coated for additional protection and to give them weight stability during the laying process. This is an area where there has been considerable spin-off from the North Sea oil industry.

Additionally, cathodic corrosion protection is given either by sacrificial zinc anodes or by the impressed current method.

9.2 High Density Polyethylene (HDPE)

HDPE is occasionally being used in a similar way to steel, usually as a float and sink type where its flexibility is ideal for snake sinking into a trench. So far it has been available in diameters up to 1·2 m. The pipe may be butt welded using a heat process, and in diameters below 0·5 m can be laid in considerable lengths from a reel barge. Its tensile strength limitations do not make it suitable for a bottom tow method, and it must be anchored to the sea floor, usually with concrete anchor blocks. Within the UK HDPE outfalls have been laid at Milford Haven (diameter 595 mm), Hornsea (diameter 500 mm) and Guernsey (diameter 630 mm). Smaller diameters of HDPE pipe with wire wound reinforcement have been used for industrial effluents.

There may be a strong case for laying multiple lines of HDPE pipe, each section being progressively brought into use with increasing discharge. Such an approach would give some control over sea water intrusion.

Another attractive idea with HDPE pipe is that it could be refloated, by injecting air, for repair or maintenance purposes.

9.3 Reinforced Concrete

This material is not often used for piped sea outfalls, except as an outer cover for a steel tube and for the linings of outfall tunnels. However, the most recent outfall for San Francisco, which is 6700 m long and lies across the San Andreas fault is constructed of 7·3 m long, 3·65 m diameter pre-cast concrete segments. The segment joints are highly flexible and designed to accommodate sea bed movements of as much as 6 m (over a suitable length). The pipe sections are barge laid into a dredged trench, and then covered with stone.

Reinforced concrete has also been used for the new Portsmouth outfall. In this case a novel method has been used incorporating a rectangular section immersed tube construction technique. The 1200 m outfall uses 15 m long, 250 t units laid in a shallow trench from a purpose built catamaran barge.

10   CONSTRUCTION METHODS

10.1 Piped Outfalls

The 'bottom tow' is a well proven method and is now preferred where the site is suitable. In this method the transported pipes are welded together in parallel strings on a flat site in line with the eventual line of the outfall. A winch barge, anchored off-shore is then used to pull the first string into a pre-prepared trench. The second string is then rolled into line and welded to the first. The joints are made good, the second string pulled into the trench, and so on.

Sometimes the strings are launched through the surf zone on temporary tressles and subsequently lowered into a trench.

Winch barge pulling techniques now enable outfalls of several kilometres length to be pulled offshore in a pre-dredged trench. Over the last decade a number of outfalls of this type have been built — notably those at North Wirral, Whitstable, Littlehampton and more recently at Grimsby. This bottom tow method of keeping the pipe on the sea floor, or rather in a trench, during the pulling period of 1–2 weeks (while the various prefabricated lengths are joined) does keep most of the pipe out of any bad weather.

The float and sink technique used recently at Blackpool, where a 2·5 m diameter pipe, 920 m long was towed in a floating condition 36 km from its fabrication site and sunk in a pre-prepared trench within a 24 h period, appears to have advantages at sites where local land is not available for pipe string construction. The controlled sinking of such a pipe where flooding allows it to literally snake into the trench is a particularly elegant construction technique, provided the 'weather window' can be relied upon.

The relative flexibility of steel pipe is used in the reel–barge system used by the oil industry for quickly laying long lengths of pipe on the sea floor, and may be attractive for constructing outfalls. The biggest reel–barge to date operates out of Leith and is capable of laying 3·2 km of 0·4 m steel 1·9 mm wall pipe in a matter of hours. It is obviously capable of handling large quantities of plastic pipe.

The oil industry has its own method of bottom tow pipelaying in which a prefabricated length of pipe is towed to site along the sea floor. So far this method does not appear to have been used for outfalls, but looks promising.

10.2 Tunnelled Outfalls

Tunnels are generally used where surface access is poor, or rocky foreshores pose construction difficulties for piped outfalls. Notable cases in the UK are the Aberdeen outfall with a steep rocky landfall area, and the Weymouth outfall which had to cross the environmentally sensitive Chesil Beach. Hard and soft ground conventional tunnelling techniques are applicable, a practical minimum diameter of 2·5 m often being adopted with thick linings being used if an area reduction is necessary. Alternatively, interior pipes may be used as at Irvine where two outfall pipes are encased within the original tunnel. Tunnels are usually driven seawards with an upward gradient for construction drainage purposes. This is rather unfortunate from the point of view of sea water intrusion. Diffuser riser tubes may be driven downwards from a jack-up barge on the surface, or in some cases with soft ground, driven upwards from the tunnel. At Aberdeen the riser tubes were drilled astride the line of the outfall before the tunnel was driven, whereas at Weymouth they were driven after tunnel completion. This was fortunate as geological conditions necessitated a change of tunnel line. It is needless to say that there must be a generous allowance for geological surveys if tunnelling is used.

11 OUTFALL MALFUNCTIONS

Over the last few years the technical press has reported on a number of outfalls, which on close inspection have proved to have defects of one form or another. An examination of a few of these as case histories may illustrate some of the pitfalls that an outfall designer needs to avoid.

11.1 The Hastings Outfall (Constructed 1970)

This is a type 2 outfall 3 km long and 0·6 m diameter terminating in a non-tapered diffuser section 230 m long with 15 ports on short 1·3 m long risers. A larger end port was included to maintain scouring conditions (Fig. 29).

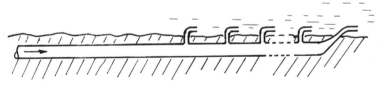

FIG. 29. Type diagram of the Hastings and North Wirral outfalls.

The outfall was designed to accommodate a considerable increase in population which did not materialise as rapidly as expected.

On inspection it was discovered that the end port and a number of the seaward ports were not functioning due to blockage of marine growth or sediment. Considerable accummulations of sediment were also found in the corresponding section of diffuser.[29]

An analysis of the outfall's flow characteristics revealed that, at the lowest flows, a number of ports had not been discharging at a high enough densimetric Froude number to prevent seawater intrusion which caused stagnation in the pipe and eventual blockage.

It is clear that if an outfall is overdesigned to cater for an increase in discharge over its planned life, then it should not be commissioned in its eventual form. In this case an appropriate number of landward ports could have been temporarily blanked off to await the forecast discharge increase.

It is also interesting to note that this outfall, even in its partially blocked state, was achieving its design standards.

11.2 The North Wirral Outfall (Constructed 1971)[30]

Once again this is a type 2 outfall 5 km long, 0·71 m in diameter with a non-tapered diffuser 61 m long and 10 ports similar in design to the Hastings outfall.

Inspection in 1983 revealed a similar state of affairs to that found at Hastings, with the addition of a broken diffuser head.

The causes in this case are probably two-fold. Firstly due to a lack of taper in the diffuser, scour velocities were not achieved at the seaward end, and secondly the broken diffuser head altered the hydraulic characteristics of the diffuser sufficiently to allow reverse flow into the diffuser from either the broken head, or by giving preferential discharge through the head, reverse flow occurred through the ports to seaward of it. The latter is the most likely explanation as the diffuser discharge appears to have stabilised with blockage and sedimentation occurring to seaward of the broken head.

While it is not always easy to prevent damage, more frequent inspections or continuous monitoring (Section 12) would have given a warning, and rapid remedial action would have saved the eventual expensive repairs. ·

This outfall was also performing satisfactorily in its damaged condition.

11.3 The Edinburgh Tunnelled Outfall (Constructed 1976)

This outfall discharges effluent which has had primary treatment. It is 2800 m long, 3·7 m diameter sloping downwards to the shaft. A 760 m long tapering diffuser discharges through 20 m long risers to sea bed diffuser heads which each have 4 ports. The author as part of his research programme has shown that this outfall is permanently operating in an intrusive condition with only 5 to 12 (depending on the discharge) of the 20 risers discharging upward at any time. It is probable, if blockage has not already occurred, that the outer risers are flowing in reverse, allowing sea water to enter the diffuser and tunnel at all times.

A fairly conclusive explanation of this outfall's behaviour has been made possible with the aid of hydraulic model tests carried out at the University of Dundee.[14]

This outfall was commissioned from a static salt water filled condition. It is now apparent that the duration of storm flows, even if they exceed the theoretical purging flow, do not last long enough either to entrain all the sea water contained in the tunnel, or to push the salt water wedge within the tunnel, as far as the diffuser, so that total sea water purging can occur. As soon as the flow reverts to a lower value the diffuser risers that are in reverse flow, re-charge the diffuser and tunnel and replace any sea water previously expelled during the high flow stage. This outfall operates in an equilibrium condition with enough risers operating to discharge the effluent such that the driving heads equal the out of balance intrusive flow heads.

Once again this outfall is operating to the required environmental standards, and dramatically improved local beach conditions when it was commissioned.

Each of these three cited outfalls apparently satisfies the environmental standards for which they were designed. That they are able to do this while operating in severely restricted circumstances indicates that the original designs were probably over conservative.

12. MONITORING AND MAINTAINING OF SEA OUTFALLS

Outfalls, being an engineering construction, should be monitored during their life for consistency of performance and efficiency. Pre- and post-construction environmental surveys will confirm the overall efficiency of an outfall and successive, if infrequent surveys, should be commissioned to check for the long term maintenance of water quality standards. However, as illustrated by the case histories in the previous section, a satisfactory environmental survey does not necessarily verify the hydraulic performance of an outfall. A study of possible monitoring systems

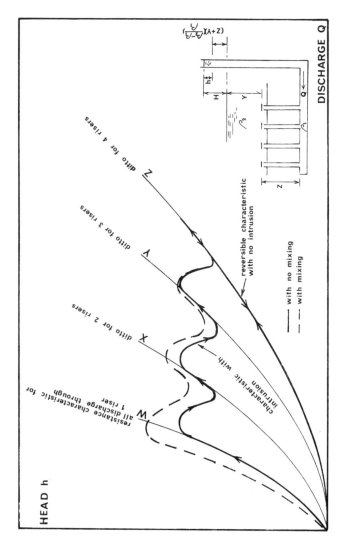

FIG. 30. The head/discharge characteristic for a four riser outfall with and without saline intrusion.

for the Weymouth outfall (1983) came to a very disappointing conclusion when it failed to recommend a potentially satisfactory system. It was apparent that there are virtually no detecting instruments that will work for any length of time within the flow conditions of an outfall. Fortunately the Dundee sea intrusion research programme has shown that a simple measurement of discharge flow and driving head measurement can be used diagnostically, and as a long term monitoring system.

An outfall will have the normal head loss discharge characteristics of a pipe–orifice system (Fig. 30). The particular characteristics will depend on how many discharge ports are being used. A new outfall discharging through all its ports having the reversible characteristic Z; or if this is its ultimate characteristic and a percentage of its ports are temporarily blanked off, it may have the reversible characteristic X. A deterioration of performance due to frictional increase (sedimentation or encrustation) will produce a permanent steepening of this reversible characteristic (e.g. Z would tend to Y).

If, however, a number of ports were subject to intrusion, the characteristic would move from Z to say W or X depending on the number of intruded ports.

Thus if the outfall's initial and possible characteristics are known or understood a simple recording of discharge and driving head could act as a sort of 'stethoscope' on the system.

Such a system would entail the fairly precise measurement, and recording, of flow and particularly head, to be successful. The head record requires the differential measurement between shaft, or equivalent level, and sea level. The ability to check datums at any time to ensure the long term compatability of measurements is vital to the success of this system. Interpretation of records which show irregularities or anomalies would require some experience or knowledge of the hydraulic characteristics but could indicate long term or sudden failures which require closer investigation, and thus avoid the damage that can easily occur between the normally infrequent diver inspections.

REFERENCES

1. JOHNSTON, R. (ed.) *Marine Pollution*. Academic Press, New York, 1976.
2. ROYAL COMMISSION ON ENVIRONMENTAL POLLUTION. Tenth Report. HMSO CMND 9149, London, Feb, 1984.

3. *Taken for Granted — Report of the working party on sewage disposal.* (Chairman: Lena Jeger). HMSO, 1970.
4. Official Journal of the European Communities Council Directive and Annex on the Quality of Bathing Water. OJ L31/1 (5.2.76).
5. WORLD HEALTH ORGANISATION, *Guides and criteria for recreational quality of beaches and coastal waters.* Bilthoven, Oct–Nov, EURO 3125(1). WHO Regional Office for Europe, Copenhagen. 1977.
   UNITED STATES ENVIRONMENTAL PROTECTION AGENCY. *Quality criteria for water.* July 1976. USEPA, Washington D.C.
6. CHARLTON, J. A. The design of sea outfalls with reference to E.E.C. amenity water pollution criteria. *J. IWES* **34** (1) (1980).
7. ROBERTS, D. G. M. and COOKMAN, I. J. R. *Pre-treatment Screenings and Detritus Removal. Coastal Discharges.* Thomas Telford, London, 1981.
8. JAMES, A. and EVISON, L. (eds). *Biological Indicators of Water Quality,* Chap. 11–15, Wiley, Chichester, 1979.
9. CHARLTON, J. A. The applications of E.E.C. bathing water standards to the design of sea outfalls. *Prog. Wat. Tech.* **12** (1) (1980).
10. GAMESON, A. L. H. (ed.) *Discharge of Sewage from Sea Outfalls.* Supplement to Progress in Water Technology, Pergamon Press, Oxford, 1975.
11. ABRAHAM, G. *Jet Diffusion in Stagnant Ambient Fluid.* Delft Hydraulics Laboratory, Publ. No. 29, 1963.
12. ANWAR, H. O. Behaviour of buoyant jet in calm fluid. *J. Hydraul. Div. ASCE,* **95** (HY4) (1969).
13. NOVAK, P. and ČÁBELKA, J. *Models in Hydraulic Engineering,* Pitman, London, 1981.
14. CHARLTON, J. A. Hydraulic modelling of saline intrusion into sea outfalls. *Proc. Int. Conf. on Hydraulic Modelling of Civil Engineering Structures.* B.H.R.A. Fluid Engineering, 1982.
15. KUO, E. Y. T. Analytical solution for 3-D diffusion model. *J. ASCE,* (EE4) (1976).
16. LEWIS, R. E. Modelling the dispersion of pollutants from marine outfalls. In *Mathematical Modelling of Turbulent Diffusion in the Environment.* (ed. on Harris). Academic Press. New York, 1979.
17. FAN, L. N. and BROOKS, N. H. *Numerical solutions of turbulent buoyant jet problems.* California Institute of Technology, Report No. KH-R-18, 1969.
18. VIGLIANI, P. G., SCLAVI, B., VISCONTI, A. and TARTOGLIA, G. F. An investigation of the initial dilution of sewage discharged through submarine diffusers. *Prog. Water Technol.* **12** (1) (1980), pp. 145–62.
19. CEDERWALL, K. *Hydraulics of Marine Waste Disposal.* Hydraulic Div., Chalmers Institute of Technology, Göteborg, Sweden. Report No. 42, 1968.
20. AGG, A. R. and WHITE, W. R. Devices for the pre-dilution of sewage at submerged outfalls. *Proc. ICE.* **57** (2) (1974), pp. 1–20, also Discussion **57** (2) (1974), pp. 747–64.
21. BROOKS, N. H. *Conceptual Design of Submarine Outfalls. I. Jet Diffusion.* Calif. Inst. Technol., W. M. Keck Lab. Tech. Memo. 70–1, 1970.
22. KOH, C. Y. and BROOKS, N. H. Fluid mechanics of waste-water disposal in the ocean. *Ann. Rev. Fluid Mech.* **7** (1975).
23. GRACE, R. A. *Marine Outfall Systems.* Prentice Hall, New Jersey, 1978.

24. CHARLTON, J. A. Salinity intrusion into multi-port sea outfalls. *Proc. 18th Int. conf. Coastal Engineering, ASCE*, 1982.
25. ROBERTS, D. G. M., FLINT, G. R. and MOORE, K. H. Weymouth and Portland marine treatment scheme: tunnel outfall and marine treatment works. *Proc. ICE.*, **76** (1984), pp. 117–44.
26. MILLER, D. S. *Internal flow systems.* BHRA, Cranfield, 1978.
27. ACKERS, P. Urban drainage, the effects of sediments on performance and design. *Proc. Int. Conf. on Urban Storm Drainage*, University of Southampton. 1978.
28. NOVAK, P. and NALLURI, C. Incipient motion of sediment particles over fixed beds. *IAHR J. Hydraul. Res.* **22** (3) (1984), pp. 181–97.
29. CRISP, E. W., STEWART, H. M. and FLETCHER, S. J. N. Design and construction of a submarine outfall at Hastings. *Proc. ICE*, **47** (1970), pp. 121–43.
30. ROBERTS, D. G. M. *et al.* North Wirral authorities and Hoylake U.D.C. long sea outfall. *Proc. ICE, Supplement (V) paper 7495S*, 1972.

TECHNICAL REPORTS: *TR 92 Application of coastal pollution research; TR 99 Investigations of sewage discharges to some British coastal waters.* Water Research Centre, Stevenage, 1978. *Waste discharge to the marine environment.* WHO–UNEP Pergamon, Oxford, 1982. *Rejets en mer par émissaire —* Guide pour l'étude du milieu marin. Sogreah, Grenoble, 1983.

Chapter 4

FLOOD ROUTING

ROLAND K. PRICE

Hydraulics Research Ltd, Wallingford, Oxon, UK

NOTATION

a_0	attenuation parameter
A	wetted cross-sectional area
B	surface width
B_c	channel half-width
c	wave speed
c_0	kinematic wave speed
C_0, C_1, C_2, C_3	finite difference coefficients
D_0, D_1, D_2, D_3	Muskingum–Cunge coefficients
f	variable
F	part of the section conveyance
F_r	Froude number
g	acceleration due to gravity
j	space counter
k	factor
K	storage or diffusion coefficient
L	length of reach
n	time counter
q	lateral inflow per unit length
Q	discharge
Q_0	kinematic wave solution
$\bar{Q}_0$	value of Q_0 for $\tau = 0$
Q_1	first-order solution
Q_1^*	attenuation of peak discharge

Q_a	average peak discharge or discharge amplitude
Q_b	base discharge
Q_{in}	inflow
Q_{out}	outflow
r	$\equiv \omega \Delta t / \Delta x$
s_0	bottom slope
s_f	friction slope
S	storage
t	time
T	time scale for synthetic hydrograph
T_p	time to peak
v	velocity
x	distance
y	depth
y_b	bankfull depth
y_c	channel depth
y_f	flood plain depth
z	horizontal distance across section
z_b	flood plain semi-reference width
β	curvature parameter
γ	Froude number squared
Δt	time increment
Δx	space increment
λ	constant
μ	constant attenuation parameter
ξ	distance
σ	wave number
σ^I	imaginary part of σ
σ^R	real part of σ
τ	characteristic time
χ	Muskingum proportionality parameter
ω	constant wave speed

A prime with a variable denotes the 0(1) part of that variable. Superposition of a bar over a variable denotes the scale of that variable.

1 INTRODUCTION

Our concern is with the movement of an abnormal amount of water along a river or channel. Such a situation may occur following excessive rainfall on the contributing catchments to a natural river or after the uncontrolled breaking of a dam. The possibly disastrous consequences accompanying these infrequent events lead to the need for the engineer to be able to trace the movement of the excess water and to predict the resulting peak water levels or discharges along the river. This need may arise in 'real-time' when the engineer has to forecast levels and flows in his river, or in design when he has to ascertain what effect civil engineering works for flood control have on events of prescribed frequency.

The advent of powerful computer hardware and corresponding software techniques have led to the solution of such problems using computational hydraulic models. The development and practical application of such models based on solutions of the full Saint-Venant equations for gradually varying flowing rivers is already well advanced.[1] However, the unthinking application of these sophisticated models can obscure the general behaviour of flood movement in rivers to the detriment of a better understanding of the phenomena involved. Additionally the models can be expensive to develop and apply, as well as being inaccurate or difficult to use, particularly for the unwary and inexperienced.[2,3] Simpler models of flood behaviour in rivers have been available for many years. Although less accurate than the more recent computational models and open to abuse by careless application, the simpler models continue to be a valuable tool for river engineers who want rapid access to a broad view of flood behaviour in their rivers.

The remainder of this chapter is dedicated to exploiting the potential of these simpler models to describe flood behaviour in natural rivers.

2 SIMPLE MODELS

The success of any model of a natural phenomenon is measured by how well it reproduces the more obvious and observable features of that phenomenon and the extent to which it enables the user to deduce other features which hitherto have been less obvious. In the case of flood movement in rivers the key features which any model has to reproduce are the translation of the flood peak downstream and the attenuation or 'subsidence' of the peak which is particularly apparent in the absence of any lateral inflow.

Attenuation of the flood peak can be conceived in terms of a reservoir where the control on the outfall and the storage available leads to a reduction of the peak inflow. The simplest model to describe this phenomenon is the linear reservoir in which the storage S is proportional to the outflow Q_{out}. Given the inflow Q_{in}:

$$\frac{dS}{dt} = Q_{in} - Q_{out} \qquad (1)$$

and

$$S = KQ_{out} \qquad (2)$$

where K is the storage constant.

These equations may be combined to give

$$K \frac{dQ_{out}}{dt} + Q_{out} = Q_{in} \qquad (3)$$

Simple inspection of this equation shows that the maximum peak outflow occurs when $Q_{out} = Q_{in}$ and is on the recession of the inflow hydrograph; see Fig. 1. This model therefore introduces the notions of

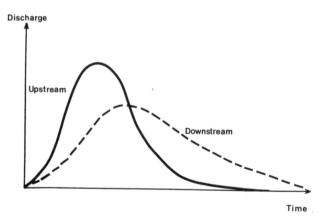

FIG. 1. Reservoir model.

both attenuation and translation. However, observations of flood hydrographs upstream and downstream of a river reach reveal that the flood peak downstream does not, in general, occur on the recession of the inflow hydrograph. The simple linear reservoir model therefore needs to be modified. The most straightforward and appropriate modification is to assume that S is a function not only of the outflow but also the inflow

$$S = K((1-\chi)Q_{in} + \chi Q_{out}) \qquad (4)$$

This form for S was originally proposed by McCarthy[4] in application of the resulting model to the Muskingum River. Subsequently the model has come to be regarded as the basis of the Muskingum method for flood routing.

If $\chi = 1$, eqn (4) reverts to eqn (3). Alternatively if $\chi = 0$ the combination of eqns (1) and (4) gives

$$Q_{in} - K \frac{dQ_{in}}{dt} = Q_{out} \qquad (5)$$

Simple inspection of this equation shows that the maximum of the peak inflow occurs when $Q_{in} = Q_{out}$, and is on the rise of the outflow hydrograph; that is, eqn (5) predicts a peak outflow which is greater than the peak inflow but which nevertheless occurs later (Fig. 2). So the

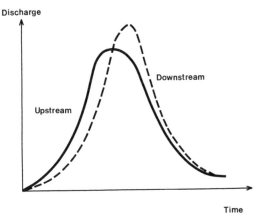

FIG. 2. Translation model.

Muskingum relationship predicts a translation of the flood peak, and, depending on the value of χ, the outflow peak can be greater than or less than the inflow peak. Because two parameters are available it is possible to fit the Muskingum model to an observed inflow and outflow such that the timing and magnitude of the outflow peak can be predicted accurately. This calibration is the traditional way in which the Muskingum method has been used.

The success of this and other simple models to describe the main features of flood behaviour has stimulated a large number of attempts to improve on these basic models. The search for improvements has concentrated on two areas; firstly, on ways of selecting appropriate values of the model parameters such as K and χ in terms of the physical characteristics of the river or channel and secondly, for alternative non-linear relationships between S, Q_{in} and Q_{out}.

The difficulty of relating the Muskingum parameters K and χ to the physical characteristics of the river or channel has stemmed from the conceptual nature of the basic model. This difficulty was made all the more disturbing by the successful early attempts to describe flood movement in terms of characteristic solutions of the hydraulically based Saint-Venant equations.[5] A synthesis between the two types of model was achieved by Cunge[6] in 1969 when he published an analysis of the Muskingum method in which he showed how the Muskingum equations are analogous to a simplified form of the Saint-Venant equations. This analysis leads to an identification of the Muskingum parameters in terms of the physical characteristics of a regular channel.

Cunge restricted his analysis to situations where K and χ do not vary significantly with the magnitude of the event. However, there are many cases, particularly in rivers with extensive flood plains, where an accurate simulation of an event using the Muskingum method with one set of parameter values is not repeated for another event of different magnitude unless the parameter values are changed significantly. The parameters may therefore be themselves functions of the inflow and outflow to the reach. This implies that the relationship between S, Q_{in} and Q_{out} is more appropriately a non-linear one rather than linear. One way of introducing the non-linearity is to define K and χ as functions of Q_{in} and Q_{out} though this approach has not generally been successful.[7] Some researchers have used other non-linear or three parametric functional forms for S in terms of Q_{in} and Q_{out} while retaining constant values of K and χ.[8,9] However, an alternative and more rigorous development of a non-linear Muskingum method is to take advantage of the analogy developed by Cunge and to begin with the Saint-Venant equations. The value of this approach is that the resulting non-linear method, although very similar to the traditional Muskingum method, is firmly based on identifiable physical characteristics of the river channel and the properties of the flood event. It is therefore possible to make reliable deductions of flood behaviour which have not previously been generally recognised.

3 THEORETICAL DEVELOPMENT

A hydraulic approach to flood routing includes not only a precise assessment of storage in the channel and its time rate of change but also an accurate account of the momentum of the water as it is affected by the channel geometry. A rigorous derivation of the continuity and momentum (or dynamic) equations for gradually varying flow in open channels can be found in any standard textbook; see for example, refs 1 and 10. The main assumptions are:

(i)   the flow is one-dimensional in the direction of the channel: that is, the velocity is uniform over a cross-section and the water level across a section is horizontal;
(ii) vertical accelerations are negligible;
(iii) steady state resistance laws may be used to model unsteady effects due to boundary friction and turbulence;
(iv) the average bed slope, s_0, of the channel is small such that the cosine of the angle made by the averaged bed profile with the horizontal can be regarded as unity.

With these assumptions and following Newton's second law we can derive the momentum equation in the form

$$\frac{\partial Q}{\partial t} + \frac{\partial}{\partial x}\left(\frac{Q^2}{A}\right) + gA\frac{\partial y}{\partial x} - gAs_0 + gAs_f = 0 \qquad (6)$$

where Q is the discharge; A is the cross-sectional area; y is the depth of flow; s_0 is the bed gradient; s_f is the friction slope; t is the time and x is the distance. The first two terms arise from the rate of change in momentum of the water, the third and fourth terms come from the change in the pressure forces and the fifth term describes the resistance effect. The storage or conservation of volume equation is

$$\frac{\partial A}{\partial t} + \frac{\partial Q}{\partial x} = q \qquad (7)$$

where q is the lateral inflow per unit length assumed to enter the channel normal to the general direction of flow.

Equation (6) is non-linear and cannot in general be solved without the aid of a computer. However the existence of several terms in the equation gives us the opportunity to see if some of the terms may be more important than others; if so we can simplify the equation and possibly find an analytical solution. We can resolve this by making a scale analysis of the equations using scales for the variables appropriate for a river in flood. We select scales typical of those in a UK river: $\bar{Q} \sim 500 \text{ m}^3/\text{s}$; $\bar{A} \sim 300 \text{ m}^2$; $\bar{y} \sim 5 \text{ m}$; $\bar{s}_0 \sim 10^{-3}$; $\bar{g} = 9\cdot81 \text{ m/s}^2$ and $\bar{t} \sim 10^5 \text{ s}$. Here the imposition of a 'bar' denotes the scale for the variable. $\bar{Q}$, $\bar{A}$ and $\bar{y}$ can be regarded as the bankfull discharge, cross-sectional area and depth, respectively, and $\bar{t}$ is the duration of the flood.

From eqn (7) the length scale $\bar{x}$ of the flood wave is

$$\bar{x} \sim \bar{Q}\,\bar{t}/\bar{A} \sim 1\cdot7 \times 10^{\,5}\text{m} = 170 \text{ km} \tag{8}$$

From the momentum equation

$$\left| g\,A\,\frac{\partial y}{\partial x} \right| \Big/ \left| g\,A s_0 \right| \sim \frac{\bar{y}}{\bar{x}} \Big/ \bar{s}_0 \sim 2\cdot0 \times 10^{-2} \tag{9}$$

$$\left| \frac{\partial Q}{\partial t} \right| \Big/ \left| \frac{\partial}{\partial x}\left(\frac{Q^2}{A} \right) \right| \sim 1 \tag{10}$$

$$\left| \frac{\partial Q}{\partial t} \right| \Big/ \left| g\,A s_0 \right| \sim \frac{\bar{Q}}{\bar{t}} \Big/ g\,\bar{A}\bar{s}_0 \sim 1\cdot7 \times 10^{-3} \tag{11}$$

It follows that we may write the conservation of momentum equation as

$$\frac{\varepsilon\gamma}{A'}\left[\frac{\partial Q'}{\partial t'} + \frac{\partial}{\partial x'}\left(\frac{Q'^2}{A'} \right) \right] + \varepsilon\,\frac{\partial y'}{\partial x'} - s_0' + s_f' = 0 \tag{12}$$

where

$$\varepsilon = \frac{\bar{y}}{\bar{x}} \Big/ \bar{s}_0 \tag{13}$$

$$\gamma = \frac{\bar{Q}^2}{g\,\bar{A}^2\,\bar{y}} \tag{14}$$

and a 'prime' denotes the 0(1) dimensionless part of the variable. ε is the ratio of the characteristic surface gradient (defined relative to the bed gradient) to the bed gradient, and γ is the square of the Froude number for the flow. ε is an event-based number in that it depends on the length scale for the event, whereas γ depends primarily on the nature of the channel. Generally for rivers $\gamma \leqslant \varepsilon \leqslant 1$, and therefore the first two terms in the momentum equation are significantly smaller than the third term which is significantly smaller than s_0 or s_f. We seek to exploit this feature by seeking an approximation to the basic equations of order ε; that is $0(\varepsilon)$. For ease of notation the original equations are used with the introduction of ε and γ to identify the terms of different order. Also to avoid unnecessary complications the channel is assumed to have a uniform cross-section and bed gradient. Note that no assumption is made about the shape of the cross-section or the bed roughness. An analysis including variations in cross-section and bed gradient along the reach would be similar to that proposed by the author in ref. 7.

If we assume $s_f = Q^2/(AF)^2$ then

$$Q = AFs_0^{1/2}\left\{1 - \frac{\varepsilon}{2s_0}\frac{\partial y}{\partial x} - \frac{\varepsilon\gamma}{2gAs_0}\left(\frac{\partial Q}{\partial t} + \frac{\partial}{\partial x}\frac{Q^2}{A}\right)\right\} + 0(\varepsilon^2) \tag{15}$$

This indicates that Q is a function of A, F and s_0 to zero order and of derivatives of y and Q to first order. We seek to remove the functional dependence of Q on y and its derivatives using eqn (7) so that we can derive an equation with Q alone as the dependent variable. To do this, we note first that by differentiating eqn (15) with respect to x then

$$\frac{\partial Q}{\partial x} = AFs_0^{1/2}\left(\frac{B}{A} + \frac{1}{F}\frac{dF}{dy}\right)\frac{\partial y}{\partial x} + 0(\varepsilon) = Bc\frac{\partial y}{\partial x} + 0(\varepsilon) \tag{16}$$

where

$$c = \frac{AFs_0^{1/2}}{B}\left(\frac{B}{A} + \frac{1}{F}\frac{dF}{dy}\right) \tag{17}$$

and B is the water surface width. Equation (11) now becomes

$$Q = AFs_0^{1/2}\left\{1 - \frac{\varepsilon}{2s_0 Bc}\frac{\partial Q}{\partial x} - \frac{\varepsilon\gamma}{2gAs_0}\left[\frac{\partial Q}{\partial t} + \left(\frac{2Q}{A} - \frac{Q^2}{A^2 c}\right)\frac{\partial Q}{\partial x}\right]\right\} + 0(\varepsilon^2) \tag{18}$$

Next we can differentiate eqn (18) with respect to t to give

$$\frac{\partial Q}{\partial t} = Bc\frac{\partial y}{\partial t} - \varepsilon\frac{\partial}{\partial t}\left\{\frac{Q}{2s_0 Bc}\frac{\partial Q}{\partial x} + \frac{\gamma Q}{2gAs_0}\left[\frac{\partial Q}{\partial t} + \left(\frac{2Q}{A} - \frac{Q^2}{A^2 c}\right)\frac{\partial Q}{\partial x}\right]\right\} + 0(\varepsilon^2) \tag{19}$$

From eqn (7)

$$B\frac{\partial y}{\partial t} + \frac{\partial Q}{\partial x} = q \tag{20}$$

So $B(\partial y/\partial t)$ in eqn (19) can be replaced by $(q-(\partial Q/\partial x))$. Unfortunately c in eqn (19) is a function of y. To remove this dependence on y we rearrange eqn (18) to give:

$$AFs_0^{1/2} = Q\left\{1 + \frac{\varepsilon}{2s_0 Bc}\frac{\partial Q}{\partial x} - \frac{\varepsilon\gamma}{2gAs_0}\left[\frac{\partial Q}{\partial t} + \left(\frac{2Q}{A} - \frac{Q^2}{A^2 c}\right)\frac{\partial Q}{\partial x}\right]\right\} + 0(\varepsilon^2) \quad (21)$$

Because A and F are functions of y alone, y is therefore a function of the expression on the right-hand side of eqn (21). Now, to order ε.

$$c(y) = c_0(Q) + \varepsilon\left\{\frac{Q}{2s_0 Bc_0}\frac{\partial Q}{\partial x} - \frac{\gamma Q}{2gAs_0}\left[\frac{\partial Q}{\partial t} + \left(\frac{2Q}{A} - \frac{Q^2}{A^2 c_0}\right)\frac{\partial Q}{\partial x}\right]\right\}\frac{\mathrm{d}c_0}{\mathrm{d}Q} \quad (22)$$

Replacing $B(\partial y/\partial t)$ and c in eqn (19) and simplifying the term of order ε we obtain

$$\frac{\partial Q}{\partial t} = c_0\left(q - \frac{\partial Q}{\partial x}\right) - \varepsilon c_0\frac{\partial}{\partial t}\left\{\frac{Q}{2s_0 Bc_0^2}\left[1 - \frac{\gamma B}{gA}\left(c_0 - \frac{Q}{A}\right)^2\right]\frac{\partial Q}{\partial x}\right\}$$

$$-\varepsilon\gamma\frac{\partial}{\partial t}\left(\frac{Q c_0 q}{2g As_0}\right) + 0(\varepsilon^2) \quad (23)$$

or

$$\frac{\partial Q}{\partial t} + c_0\frac{\partial Q}{\partial x} + \varepsilon c_0\frac{\partial}{\partial t}\left(\frac{a_0}{c_0^2}\frac{\partial Q}{\partial x}\right) = c_0 q - \varepsilon\gamma c_0\frac{\partial}{\partial t}\left(\frac{Qq}{2g As_0}\right) + 0(\varepsilon^2) \quad (24)$$

where

$$a_0 = \frac{Q}{2s_0 B}\left[1 - \frac{\gamma B}{gA}\left(c_0 - \frac{Q}{A}\right)^2\right] \quad (25)$$

Equation (24) is the basic flood routing equation and is valid for any typical Froude number. Before we look at a numerical method for flood routing based on eqn (24) we consider first some analytical consequences of the equation.

4 KINEMATIC WAVE

Equation (24) was derived under the assumption that the water surface slope defined relative to the bed gradient is small compared with the bed gradient. That is, terms identified by ε are small compared with the other terms. In the limiting case as $\varepsilon \to 0$ eqn (24) becomes

$$\frac{\partial Q}{\partial t} + c_0 \frac{\partial Q}{\partial x} = c_0 q \qquad (26)$$

If $q = 0$ this equation describes a kinematic wave,[11] that is, a wave which travels in the positive x direction with speed $c_0(Q)$ and without change in peak discharge. The fact that c_0 depends on Q means that the shape of the wave can vary. If the peak of the wave is travelling faster than the toe of the wave then eventually the wave will fold over on itself like a wave breaking on a beach (Fig. 3). Similarly if the peak of the wave is

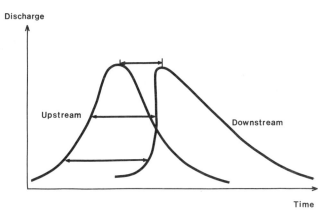

FIG. 3. Kinematic wave folding.

travelling slower than the toe of the wave the wave will fold back on itself. Both of these cases can tend to happen to a flood wave in a natural river. For example, the kinematic wave speed for the reach between Erwood and Belmont on the River Wye takes the form as shown in Fig. 4.[7] The shape of this curve is typical for all reaches of river with significant natural flood plains.[12] Generally the kinematic wave speed increases to some maximum value for a discharge less than the bankfull discharge. The curve can then drop steeply to a minimum value at approximately twice the bankfull discharge. Thereafter the wave speed increases with discharge as the flood plain width is taken up. For a small inbank flood in the Wye, the peak will travel faster than any other part of the wave profile. Similarly, the peak of an overbank flood which is less than twice bankfull will travel slower than other parts of the profile which are at or over-bank. However, in neither case will the flood wave

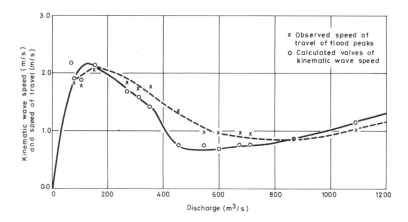

FIG. 4. Kinematic and observed wave speeds for River Wye.

actually fold over on itself, partly because the river reach is too short but more importantly because of the influence of factors neglected in the derivation of eqn (26), and particularly of those factors neglected with the terms of order ε. Lighthill and Whitham[11] indicated how in a long river the front of a flood wave in a river channel would approximate a monoclinal wave which is an exact solution of the full Saint-Venant equations.

5 MODIFICATIONS TO THE KINEMATIC WAVE

We now examine the way in which the terms of order ε in eqn (24) modify the kinematic wave. For simplicity we ignore lateral inflow, then eqn (24) becomes

$$\frac{\partial Q}{\partial t} + c_0 \frac{\partial Q}{\partial x} + \varepsilon c_0 \frac{\partial}{\partial t}\left(\frac{a_0}{c_0^2}\frac{\partial Q}{\partial x}\right) = 0 \qquad (27)$$

In its simplest form, with constant values for c_0 and a_0, eqn (27) becomes

$$\frac{\partial Q}{\partial t} + \omega \frac{\partial Q}{\partial x} + \frac{\mu}{\omega}\frac{\partial^2 Q}{\partial t\,\partial x} = 0 \qquad (28)$$

where ω replaces c_0 and μ replaces εa_0. This equation is very similar to the convection–diffusion equation originally proposed by Hayami[13] for flood routing, namely

$$\frac{\partial Q}{\partial t} + \omega \frac{\partial Q}{\partial x} - K \frac{\partial^2 Q}{\partial x^2} = 0 \tag{29}$$

where ω is the convection speed and K is an arbitrary diffusion coefficient. Hayami postulated this equation for flood routing (in depth rather than discharge) because it reproduces both the translation and attenuation of a disturbance and because it has a convenient analytical solution. The essential difference between eqns (28) and (29) is the form of the second derivative term. Equation (29) requires three boundary conditions, namely

$$\begin{array}{ll} \text{initial condition} & Q(x, 0) = Q_0(x) \\ \text{upstream condition} & Q(0, t) = Q_u(t) \\ \text{downstream condition} & Q(x, t) = Q_d \text{ as } x \to \infty \end{array}$$

However eqn (28), derived strictly from the Saint-Venant equations, requires only two boundary conditions, namely the initial and upstream conditions. The implication of this fact is that solutions of the basic hydraulic flood routing equation above are independent of any downstream effects. This conclusion is of crucial importance, not only because of its consequences for the development of a practical flood routing method but also because of the fact that any method based on eqn (27) (and therefore any similar method) ignores any backwater effect or downstream influence. Any attempt to use a convection–diffusion type model for flood routing and to regard that model as including backwater effects forces the model to be conceptual in nature and removes it from being based on strict hydraulic principles.[14]

To study eqn (27) further, we make the transformation

$$\tau = t - \frac{x}{c_0} \tag{30}$$

and

$$\xi = x \tag{31}$$

Then eqn (27) becomes

$$\frac{\partial Q}{\partial \xi} + \varepsilon \frac{\partial}{\partial \tau} \left[\frac{a_0}{c_0^2} \left(-\frac{1}{c_0} \frac{\partial Q}{\partial \tau} + \frac{\partial Q}{\partial \xi} \right) \left(1 - \frac{\xi}{c_0^2} \frac{dc_0}{dQ} \frac{\partial Q}{\partial \tau} \right)^{-1} \right] = 0 \tag{32}$$

Ignoring the term of order ε

$$\frac{\partial Q}{\partial \xi} = 0 \tag{33}$$

that is, Q is a function of τ only. If we now set

$$Q = Q_0(\tau) + \varepsilon Q_1(\xi, \tau) + 0(\varepsilon^2) \tag{34}$$

where Q_0 is the kinematic wave solution then the equation for Q_1 becomes

$$\frac{\partial Q_1}{\partial \xi} - \frac{\partial}{\partial \tau} \left[\frac{a_0}{c_0^3} \frac{dQ_0}{d\tau} \left(1 - \frac{\xi}{c_0^2} \frac{dc_0}{dQ_0} \frac{dQ_0}{d\tau} \right)^{-1} \right] = 0 \tag{35}$$

Integrating this equation, with $Q_1 = 0$ at $\xi = 0$,

$$Q_1 = -\frac{\partial}{\partial \tau} \left[\frac{a_0}{c_0} \left(\frac{dc_0}{dQ_0} \right)^{-1} \log \left(1 - \frac{\xi}{c_0^2} \frac{dc_0}{dQ_0} \frac{dQ_0}{d\tau} \right) \right] \tag{36}$$

An approximate value for the attenuation Q_1^* of the flood peak can be obtained by setting $(dQ_0/d\tau) = 0$ in eqn (36), hence

$$Q_1^* = \frac{a_0 \xi}{c_0^3} \frac{d^2 Q_0}{d\tau^2} \bigg|_{\text{peak}} \tag{37}$$

This expression for the attenuation was first derived by Forchheimer.[15] Because $(d^2 Q_0/d\tau^2)|_{\text{peak}}$ is negative and a_0 is positive for Froude numbers typical of most rivers Q_1^* is negative and denotes a decrease in peak discharge downstream. The attenuation is inversely proportional to the cube of the kinematic wave speed which highlights the sensitivity of the attenuation to variations in this parameter between different rivers. Typically c_0 is small for rivers with flat gradients and therefore the attenuation of flood peaks in such rivers is likely to be larger than in rivers with steep gradients.

If $a_0 \leqslant 0$, $Q_1^* \geqslant 0$ and the wave increases in amplitude. This is an unstable situation and the limiting case is when $a_0 = 0$, that is

$$\frac{B}{gA} \left(c_0 - \frac{Q}{A} \right)^2 = 1 \tag{38}$$

(γ has been removed here as we have been using it to indicate the order of the term only.) This equation can be rewritten as

$$c_0 = v + \sqrt{\frac{gA}{B}} \tag{39}$$

where $v = Q/A$. In other words the kinematic wave speed is equal to the dynamic wave speed downstream. For a wide rectangular channel with the Chezy friction law $c_0 = 3v/2$ and the limiting condition is $v\sqrt{(B/gA)} = F_r = 2$. Similarly for the Manning friction law, $F_r = 3/2$.

The peak does not travel with precisely the speed $c_0(Q_0)$.[16] The peak at $x = \xi$ actually occurs when $(\partial Q/\partial t) = 0$, or, to first order ε, when

$$\frac{dQ_0}{d\tau} + \frac{\varepsilon \partial Q_1}{\partial \tau} = 0 \tag{40}$$

To investigate this further, consider a Taylor expansion of Q_0 about the peak

$$Q_0 = \bar{Q}_0(0) + \frac{1}{2!}\frac{d^2 Q_0}{d\tau^2}\bigg|_{\tau=0} \tau^2 + \frac{1}{3!}\frac{d^3 Q_0}{d\tau^3}\bigg|_{\tau=0} \tau^3 + 0(\tau^4) \tag{41}$$

Substitution from eqns (36) and (41) in eqn (40) gives

$$\frac{c_0 \tau}{\xi} = -\varepsilon \frac{Q_1^*}{c_0}\frac{dc_0}{dQ_0}\bigg|_{Q_0 = \bar{Q}_0} - \varepsilon \frac{\xi a_0^2}{c_0^4 Q_1^*}\frac{d^3 Q_0}{d\tau^3}\bigg|_{\tau=0} + 0(\tau^2, \varepsilon\tau) \tag{42}$$

Consequently the propagation speed of the flood peak becomes

$$c_0\left(1 + \frac{c_0 \tau}{\xi}\right)^{-1} = c_0 + \varepsilon Q_1^* \frac{dc_0}{dQ_0}\bigg|_{Q_0 = \bar{Q}_0} + \varepsilon \frac{\xi a_0^2}{c_0^3 Q_1^*}\frac{d^3 Q_0}{d\tau^3}\bigg|_{\tau=0} + 0(\tau^2, \varepsilon\tau) \tag{43}$$

There are two terms in this equation modifying the kinematic wave speed c_0. The first is proportional to the attenuation Q_1^* and the gradient of the wave speed with discharge. A linear flood routing model would obviously not be able to include this effect. The second term is proportional to the third derivative with respect to τ, thereby introducing an effect due to the skewness of the hydrograph about the peak. Because the sign of $d^3 Q_0/d\tau^3$ at the peak will normally be positive for small inbank and large overbank discharges where dc_0/dQ is also positive, and negative for intermediate discharges, then the observed wave speed will tend to be less than the kinematic wave speed for the small inbank and large overbank discharges and greater than the kinematic wave speed for intermediate discharges. This interpretation accords with studies of the Erwood to Belmont reach of the River Wye[7] (Fig. 4).

In modelling this reach of river the travel times T_p of flood peaks were extracted from records at the two gauging stations. Values of L/T_p were then plotted against the average discharge along the reach and the curve for L/T_p as a function of discharge was defined through the plotted points. Some scatter of the plotted points about the averaged curve had to be accepted because for a given average discharge L/T_p depends on the shape of the hydrograph. Having defined the averaged curve for L/T_p the kinematic wave speed was deduced from the equation:

$$c_0(Q_a) = \frac{L}{T_p}\bigg|_{Q=Q_a} + Q_1^* \frac{d}{dQ}\left(\frac{L}{T_p}\bigg|_{Q=Q_a}\right) \tag{44}$$

where $(L/T_p)|_{Q=Q_a}$ is the observed propagation speed for the flood peak with average discharge Q_a. This expression for c_0 in terms of observed propagation speeds was first proposed by the author in 1973[17] but was not based on any rigorous proof. Although not in the same form as eqn (43) the expression for c_0 in eqn (44) reveals the same dependence on the gradient of the curve. Additionally eqn (44) is derived for long reaches of river and is not restricted to a theoretically short length of reach as in eqn (43).

An effective numerical demonstration of the validity of eqn (44) was devised by the author[18] using a synthetic river model having a rectangular channel

$$0 \leqslant z \leqslant B_c, \ 0 \leqslant y_c \tag{45}$$

with the domain

$$B_c \leqslant z, y_b + y_f \tan\left[\left(\frac{z-B_c}{z_b-B_c}\right)\tan^{-1}\frac{y_b}{y_f}\right] \leqslant y_c \tag{46}$$

used for storage only (Fig. 5).

It was assumed for simplicity that the level of water in the channel is the same as the level over the flood plain at the cross-section. The curve for the kinematic wave speed was defined by

$$c_0 = \frac{Q}{\lambda B_c y_c}\left[1 + \frac{2}{3}\left(1 + \frac{2y_c}{B_c}\right)^{-1}\right] \tag{47}$$

$$Q = \frac{B_c y_c s_0^{1/2}}{n_c}\left[y_c\left(1 + \frac{2y_c}{B_c}\right)^{-1}\right]^{2/3} \tag{48}$$

and

$$\lambda = \frac{z_b}{B_c}\left[\tan^{-1}\left(\frac{y_c-y_b}{y_f}\right)\bigg/\tan^{-1}\frac{y_b}{y_f} + 1\right] \tag{49}$$

Figure 6 shows c_0 for $B_c = 50$ m, $s_0 = 0.001$, $n_c = 0.035$, $z_b = 150$ m, $y_b = 4$ m and $y_f = 0.5$ m.

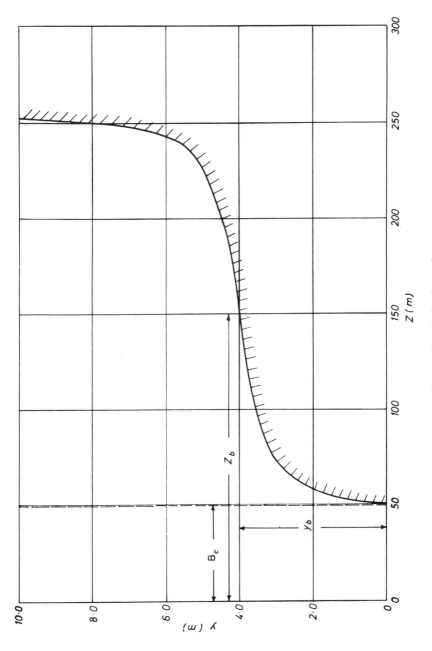

FIG. 5. Synthetic channel.

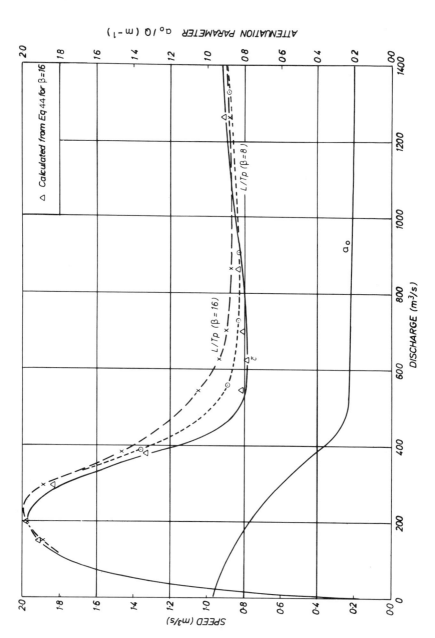

FIG. 6. Kinematic wave speed and attenuation parameter curves for synthetic channel.

Flood hydrographs of the form

$$Q(0,t) = Q_b + Q_a \left[\frac{t}{T} \exp\left(1 - \frac{t}{T}\right) \right]^\beta \tag{50}$$

were routed along the synthetic river using the iterative four point implicit method of Amein[19] for the full Saint-Venant equations, and values of L/T_p were determined for each flood. These values were correlated with the average peak discharge along the reach. Figure 6 also shows the curves for L/T_p as a function of Q for the case $Q_b = 100 \, \text{m}^3/\text{s}$, $T = 24 \, \text{h}$ and $\beta = 16$ and 8.

The results confirm some important features given by eqn (44). For example, $d(L/T_p)/dQ$ is approximately zero where the curve for c_0 intersects the curves for L/T_p. Also, for smaller value of β and so for smaller values of the curvature at the peak of the upstream hydrograph, the curve for L/T_p is closer to the curve for c_0. Finally, values of c_0 calculated from eqn (44) and using the 'observed' peak propagation speeds agree well with the known kinematic wave speed for the channel.

6   EQUIVALENT RIVER MODEL CONCEPT

The flood routing model above is based on the two parameters c_0 and a_0, which are non-linear functions of the discharge and are peculiar to each river reach. Both of these parameters, and in particular the kinematic wave speed c_0, are functions of the river geometry alone and are independent of any flood hydrograph shape, that is, the flood event. In this sense $c_0(Q)$ and $a_0(Q)$ are parameters which describe the river geometry and roughness.

The above derivation of the basic routing equation assumed that the channel has a uniform cross-section, gradient and roughness. This, however, is rarely the case. For practical application the routing reach could be divided into a number of sub-reaches, each of which have approximately uniform cross-sections, and the routing model could be applied to each sub-reach in succession. It would be preferable, however, to apply the model to the whole reach if possible, using some form of averaging process. The possibility of this approach has been demonstrated by the author in ref. 7 where it is shown that a similar, if simpler, routing equation can be applied to a long reach of river with c_0 interpreted as the kinematic wave speed for the reach and a_0 calculated in terms of integral along the reach. In particular for small Froude numbers a_0 takes the approximate form

$$a_0 = \frac{Q}{2} \left\{ \frac{1}{L} \int_0^L \frac{B}{s_0^{1/3}} \, dx \right\}^{-3} \frac{1}{L} \int_0^L \left(\frac{B}{s_0} \right)^2 \, dx \tag{51}$$

where L is the length of the reach. The significance of the second integral is that the integrand is the square of B/s_0. This implies that large scale irregularities in channel width and bottom slope can make a significant contribution to a_0 over and above the value generated for a uniform channel with the same average width.

Given a uniform channel with constant slope it is a simple matter to calculate the functional forms of c_0 and a_0 as in the previous section. In other words, c_0 and a_0 can be regarded as an alternative way of defining a channel rather than in terms of its cross-section, roughness and gradient. It is therefore pertinent to ask whether we can deduce the average cross-section and roughness of a given river c_0, a_0 and the gradient. This possibility has been explored by Price and Kawecki[20] who, beginning with curves for the River Wye as shown in Fig. 7,

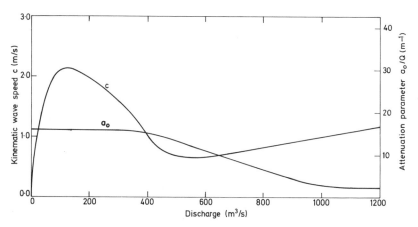

FIG. 7. Kinematic wave speed and attenuation parameter curves for River Wye.

deduced an averaged cross-section and associated Manning roughness for the channel and flood plain (Figs 8 and 9). The cross-section shape is distorted primarily because of the irregular nature of the river channel and flood plain. Having deduced an averaged form for the cross-section

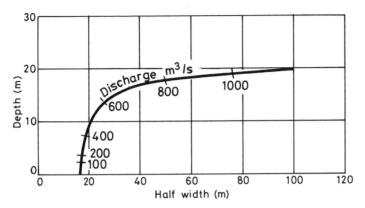

FIG. 8. Equivalent river model channel for River Wye.

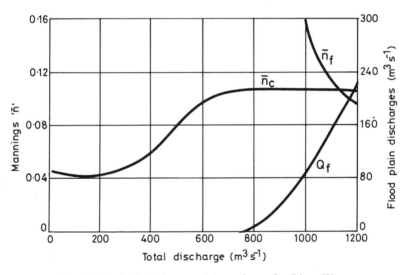

FIG. 9. Equivalent river model roughness for River Wye.

the authors proceeded to deduce modified cross-sections for certain design improvements to the river. Then by routing observed flood hydrographs through the existing and modified reaches they could assess the performance of the design improvements. This approach offers excellent possibilities for assessing the effect of design improvements to a river reach on floods.

Because c_0 and a_0 can be deduced in terms of an averaged cross-section for a river reach the parameters can be interpreted generally as defining an equivalent river model.

7 NUMERICAL FLOOD ROUTING MODEL

The analytical solutions described above are not in a convenient form for general application. Instead it is preferable to return to eqn (24) and solve it numerically using finite differences. Equation (24) can be rewritten in the conservative form

$$\frac{\partial}{\partial t}\int \frac{dQ}{c_0} + \frac{\partial Q}{\partial x} + \frac{\partial}{\partial t}\left(\frac{a_0}{c_0^2}\frac{\partial Q}{\partial x}\right) = q - \frac{\partial}{\partial t}\left(\frac{Qq}{2g\,As_0}\right) \tag{52}$$

where we neglect all terms of order ε^2 and remove the labels ε and γ. For optimum accuracy we adopt a centralised four point finite difference scheme where

$$\frac{\partial f}{\partial t} \sim \frac{1}{2\Delta t}(f_j^{n+1} + f_{j+1}^{n+1} - f_j^n - f_{j+1}^n) \tag{53}$$

$$\frac{\partial f}{\partial x} \sim \frac{1}{2\Delta x}(f_{j+1}^{n+1} + f_{j+1}^n - f_j^{n+1} - f_j^n) \tag{54}$$

in which

$$f_j^n \equiv f(j\Delta x, n\Delta t) \tag{55}$$

Equation (52) becomes

$$C_0\,Q_{j+1}^{n+1} + C_1\,Q_{j+1}^n + C_2\,Q_j^{n+1} + C_3\,Q_j^n + C_4 = 0 \tag{56}$$

where

$$C_0 = \frac{1}{c_{0j+1}^{n+(1/2)}} + r + \frac{2}{\Delta x}\left(\frac{a_0}{c_0^2}\right)_{j+(1/2)}^{n+1} + \left(\frac{q}{2g\,As_0}\right)_{j+(1/2)}^{n+1} \tag{57}$$

$$C_1 = \frac{-1}{c_{0j+1}^{n+(1/2)}} + r - \frac{2}{\Delta x}\left(\frac{a_0}{c_0^2}\right)_{j+(1/2)}^{n} - \left(\frac{q}{2g\,As_0}\right)_{j+(1/2)}^{n} \tag{58}$$

$$C_2 = \frac{1}{c_{0j}^{n+(1/2)}} - r - \frac{2}{\Delta x}\left(\frac{a_0}{c_0^2}\right)_{j+(1/2)}^{n+1} + \left(\frac{q}{2g\,As_0}\right)_{j+(1/2)}^{n+1} \tag{59}$$

$$C_3 = \frac{-1}{c_{oj}^{n+(1/2)}} - r + \frac{2}{\Delta x}\left(\frac{a_0}{c_0^2}\right)^n_{j+(1/2)} - \left(\frac{q}{2g\,As_0}\right)^n_{j+(1/2)} \qquad (60)$$

$$C_4 = -2\Delta t q_{j+(1/2)}^{n+(1/2)} \qquad (61)$$

and $r = \Delta t/\Delta x$

Note that $C_0 + C_1 + C_2 + C_3 = 0$.

Given Q_j^n for all j and Q_0^{n+1} eqn (56) can be used to deduce Q_1^{n+1}, $Q_2^{n+1}, \ldots$, in order. However, $c_{0j+1}^{n+(1/2)}$ and $(a_0/c_0^2)_{j+(1/2)}^{n+1}$ are functions of Q_{j+1}^{n+1} and therefore require an estimate of Q_{j+1}^{n+1}. Such an estimate may be obtained as $Q_j^{n+1} + Q_{j+1}^n - Q_j^n$, with subsequent iteration if the estimated and predicted values for Q_{j+1}^{n+1} differ by an unacceptable amount. Because c_0 and a_0 are generally slowly varying functions of Q the first estimate is usually sufficient.

The above approach to solving the finite difference equations may be termed the forecasting algorithm where Q is calculated for all spatial points at a given time (Fig. 10). Correspondingly Q may be calculated at all relevant times for a given spatial point. This could be termed the design algorithm (Fig. 11).

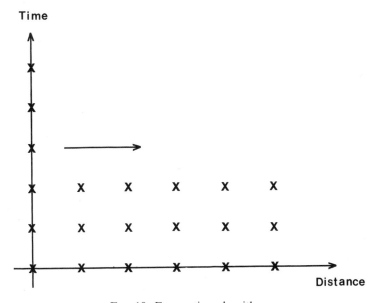

FIG. 10. Forecasting algorithm.

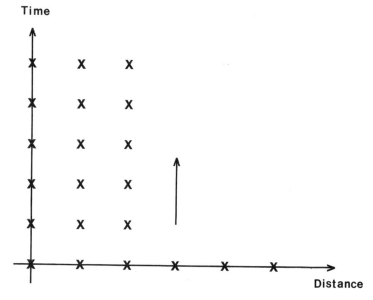

FIG. 11. Design algorithm.

Equation (56) has the same form as the finite difference equation for the Muskingum method,[4] except that C_0, C_1, C_2 and C_3 are not constants. Consequently, eqn (56) can be regarded as a true non-linear form of the Muskingum method.

8 ACCURACY OF THE ROUTING MODEL

Any finite difference approximation of an analytical equation introduces a numerical error which is a function of the space and time increments. A proper choice of these increments must be made if the accuracy of the scheme in reproducing solutions of eqn (52) is to be maintained. A basis for the choice of the space and time increments is a comparison between the analytical solutions to the linearised form of eqn (52) and the corresponding form of the finite difference eqn (42).

Returning to the linearised analytical equation

$$\frac{\partial Q}{\partial t} + \omega \frac{\partial Q}{\partial x} + \frac{\mu}{\omega} \frac{\partial^2 Q}{\partial t\, \partial x} = 0 \qquad (62)$$

the corresponding finite difference equation is

$$D_0 Q_{j+1}^{n+1} + D_1 Q_{j+1}^n + D_2 Q_j^{n+1} + D_3 Q_j^n = 0 \tag{63}$$

in which

$$D_0 = 1 + \frac{\omega \Delta t}{\Delta x} + \frac{2\mu}{\omega \Delta x} \tag{64}$$

$$D_1 = -1 + \frac{\omega \Delta t}{\Delta x} - \frac{2\mu}{\omega \Delta x} \tag{65}$$

$$D_2 = 1 - \frac{\omega \Delta t}{\Delta x} - \frac{2\mu}{\omega \Delta x} \tag{66}$$

$$D_3 = -1 - \frac{\omega \Delta t}{\Delta x} + \frac{2\mu}{\omega \Delta x} \tag{67}$$

These in fact are the equations for the Muskingum–Cunge method.[6] Unlike the original Muskingum–Cunge method developed by Cunge, there is no upper limit on μ other than to preserve the accuracy of the original equation with respect to the Saint-Venant equations. We now seek solutions of eqns (62) and (63) in the form $Q \equiv \bar{Q} \exp\{i(\sigma x + \beta t)\}$. We then compare solutions using the measures of the percentage phase speed and attenuation errors defined by:

$$\text{percentage phase speed error} = 100\,(1 - \sigma'^R/\sigma^R)$$

$$\text{percentage attenuation error} = 100\,[\exp\{(\sigma'^I - \sigma^I)\Delta x\} - 1]$$

where $\sigma \equiv \sigma^R + i\sigma^I$ and $\sigma' \equiv \sigma'^R + i\sigma'^I$ are solutions of eqns (62) and (63), respectively. This analysis is similar to that developed by Jones[21] for the convection–diffusion equation.

It can be shown that

$$\sigma^R \Delta x = -\frac{\beta \Delta t \cdot \dfrac{\Delta x}{\omega \Delta t}}{1 + \left(\dfrac{\mu}{\omega \Delta x} \cdot \dfrac{\Delta x}{\omega \Delta t} \cdot \beta\right)^2} \tag{68}$$

$$\sigma^I \Delta x = \frac{\dfrac{\mu}{\omega \Delta x} \left(\dfrac{\Delta x}{\omega \Delta t}\right)^2 (\beta \Delta t)^2}{1 + \left(\dfrac{\mu}{\omega \Delta x} \cdot \dfrac{\Delta x}{\omega \Delta t} \cdot \beta\right)^2} \tag{69}$$

and

$$\tan \sigma'^R \Delta x = \frac{2 \cdot \dfrac{\omega \Delta t}{\Delta x} \tan \dfrac{1}{2} \beta \Delta t}{\tan^2 \dfrac{1}{2} \beta \Delta t - \left(\dfrac{\omega \Delta t}{\Delta x}\right)^2 - \left(\dfrac{2\mu}{\omega \Delta x}\right)^2} \tag{70}$$

$$e^{-2\sigma'^I \Delta x} = \frac{\left[\tan^2 \dfrac{1}{2} \beta \Delta t - \left(\dfrac{\omega \Delta t}{\Delta x}\right)^2 - \left(\dfrac{2\mu}{\omega \Delta x}\right)^2\right]^2 + 4\left(\dfrac{\omega \Delta t}{\Delta x}\right)^2 \tan^2 \dfrac{1}{2} \beta \Delta t}{\left[\left(\dfrac{\omega \Delta t}{\Delta x}\right)^2 \tan^2 \dfrac{1}{2} \beta \Delta t + \left(1 + \dfrac{2\mu}{\omega \Delta x}\right)^2\right]^2} \tag{71}$$

These expressions may then be used to define the percentage errors for the phase speed and attenuation. Figure 12 shows a plot of the errors with $\beta = 2\pi/10\Delta t$ and for $\mu/\omega \Delta x \leqslant 1$. To achieve accuracy of within 5% for both phase speed and attenutation it is adequate to take

$$\frac{1}{\omega r} \leqslant 1 \cdot 6 \tag{72}$$

giving $\Delta x \leqslant 1 \cdot 6 \, \omega \Delta t$.

So provided the time increment Δt is selected to be less than 1/10th of the duration of the flood then Δx can be defined as being the order of $1 \cdot 6$ $c_{0\min} \Delta t$ where $c_{0\min}$ is the minimum value of c_0 for discharges greater than bankfull. Usually Δt will be defined such that $\Delta x \geqslant \mu/\omega$, for rivers. However, the choice of Δt for flood waves in artificial channels and particularly storm sewers may force Δx to be considerably less than μ/ω, and some care may be needed to avoid inappropriate values for both Δt and Δx.

The accuracy of the finite difference scheme with respect to the full Saint-Venant equations is a separate issue. Returning to the scale analysis of Section 3 we can require

$$\left| \frac{1}{s_0} \frac{\partial y}{\partial x} \right| \leqslant \frac{5}{100} \tag{73}$$

From eqn (16)

$$\left| \frac{1}{s_0 B c_0} \frac{\partial Q}{\partial x} \right| \leqslant \frac{5}{100} \tag{74}$$

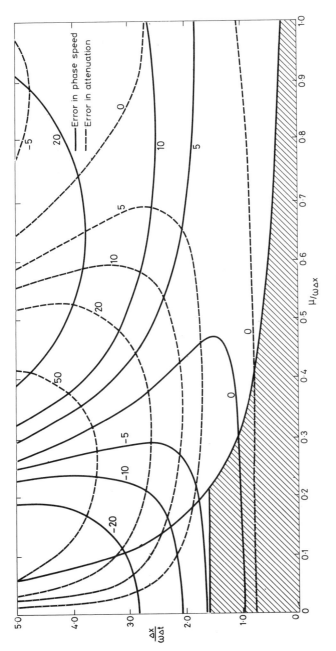

FIG. 12. Percentage phase speed and attenuation errors for $\beta = 2\pi/10\Delta t$.

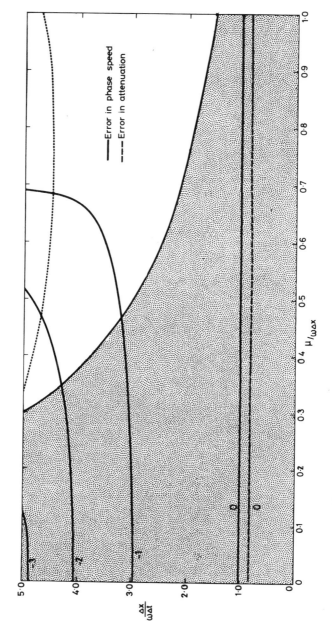

FIG. 13. Percentage phase speed and attenuation errors for $\beta = 2\pi/50\Delta t$.

or

$$\frac{2\mu}{\omega\bar{x}} \leqslant \frac{5}{100} \qquad (75)$$

The length scale $\bar{x} \sim \bar{Q}\bar{t}/A = \bar{u}\bar{t}$, and we can take $\bar{t} = 2\pi\beta$ and $\bar{u} = k\omega$ where $k = 3/5$ for a friction slope based on Manning's equation with a wide rectangular channel. Equation (75) then becomes

$$\frac{\mu}{\omega\Delta x} \cdot \frac{\Delta x}{\omega\Delta t} \leqslant \frac{2\pi k}{20\beta\Delta t} \qquad (76)$$

If $\beta\Delta t = 2\pi/10$

$$\frac{\mu}{\omega\Delta x} \cdot \frac{\Delta x}{\omega\Delta t} \leqslant \frac{k}{2} \sim 0.3 \qquad (77)$$

The shaded region in Fig. 12 shows the region in which $\Delta x/\omega\Delta t$ and $\mu/\omega\Delta x$ may lie. This region is restricted, however the choice of a smaller time increment improves the situation; see Fig. 13 which shows the corresponding case of $\beta = 2\pi/50\Delta t$. For a more detailed investigation of accuracy for the finite difference scheme see de Souza and Price.[22]

9   APPLICATIONS

River Wye

The reach of the River Wye between gauging stations at Erwood and Belmont is a valuable reach on which to test flood routing methods, not only because the two gauging stations have reliable records and ratings but also because the intervening reach usually has negligible lateral inflow, the reach is reasonably long (70 km), and it has extensive flood plains which considerably attenuate the larger floods. This reach was the subject of an original study by the author in 1973.[17] The routing of two particular floods highlights some important features of flood wave propagation and of the benefits and deficiencies of the flood routing model.

The two flood events of interest occurred in December 1960 and January 1965; see Figs 14 & 15. Both floods had approximately similar peak discharges at Erwood (1080 m³/s, and 1210 m³/s, respectively), yet the peak discharges at Belmont downstream were 980 m³/s and 620 m³/s, respectively. This large difference in the peak discharges downstream is

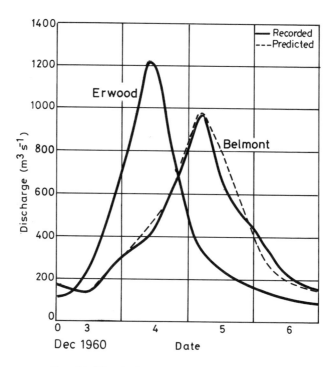

FIG. 14. Flood of December 1960, River Wye.

attributable primarily to the shape of the discharge hydrographs. The 1965 event was considerably more peaked than the 1960 event, and hence, following Forchheimer's formula in eqn (37), the peak would attenuate more rapidly downstream.

Closer examination of the 1960 event shows how significant is the time of travel of different parts of the wave profile. Although the attenuation of the peak does lead to a (symmetrical) distortion of the hydrograph about the peak there is a pronounced increase in time of travel of the hydrograph profile between inbank and overbank discharges. This is particularly pronounced in the region of $400 \, \text{m}^3/\text{s}$ which is approximately the bankfull discharge for the whole reach. The differential in travel time and therefore the shape of the hydrograph can only be properly simulated using the flood routing method above; attempts to use the Muskingum–Cunge method with fixed parameters may lead to accurate values of the peak discharge downstream, provided

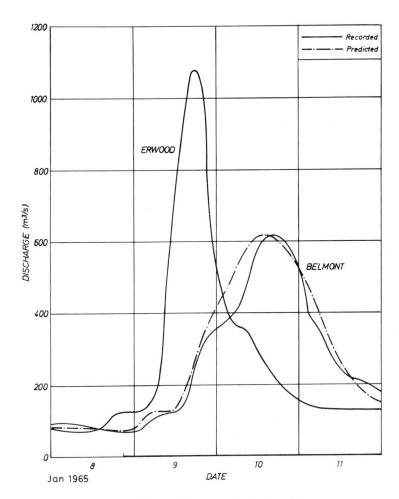

FIG. 15. Flood of January 1965, River Wye.

the parameters are correctly chosen for each separate event, but the shape of the hydrograph is difficult to reproduce.

A deficiency with the routing model is exposed in the simulation of the recession of the large flood events. For example in the 1960 event the simulated discharge is generally too large on the recession of the hydrograph for discharges greater than the bankfull discharge and too small for lesser discharges. This feature is primarily a consequence of the

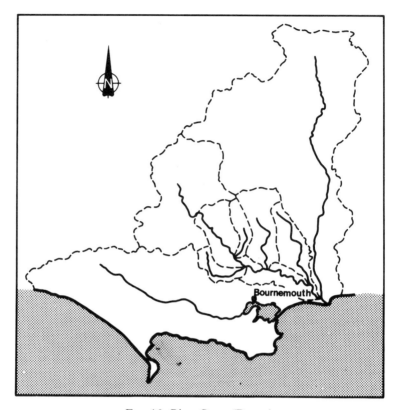

FIG. 16. River Stour (Dorset).

assumption that the lateral drainage of water off the flood plain is instantaneous, that is, the water surface across the river channel and adjacent flood plains is uniform and horizontal. This is not generally the case where extensive flood plains are involved. It follows that the routing model would need to be refined further if it were to reproduce this phenomenon on the recession of the hydrograph for large flood events. However, the primary need of flood routing methods is to accurately reproduce the rise and peak of the hydrograph, and it is questionable whether the additional refinement would be worthwhile.

River Stour

Two severe flood events occurred in the River Stour during 1979. A simulation of these floods was done using the river flood catchment model FLOUT.[23] This model simulates flood hydrographs in a river channel network and either generates input flows from rainfall using the Flood Studies unit hydrograph model[24] or can accept observed flows.

The model of the Stour covered the reach from the gauging station at Hammoon Weir down to the confluence with the Moors River and included six distinct routing reaches, each with their own prediction of lateral run-off generated from the observed rainfalls which caused the flood event; see Fig. 16. Because of the significant lateral inflows, such as for the event in May 1979, there are some problems in calibrating the model for the lateral inflows, particularly in reproducing the peak downstream. Indeed the calibration of a model for ungauged lateral inflow is probably now the most difficult part of a flood routing exercise: whereas the hydraulics of the flow can be modelled deterministically the accuracy of the routing model is generally limited by the stochastic modelling of run-off. The results of the model in application to the River Stour confirm, however, that with care, reasonable agreement can be obtained between predicted and observed flows, and the model may then be used with confidence in design; see Figs 17 & 18.

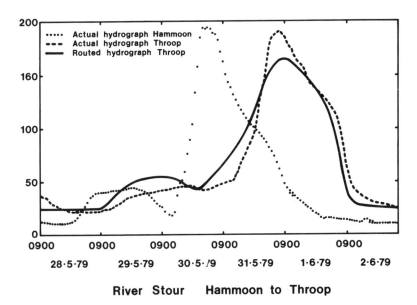

River Stour   Hammoon to Throop

FIG. 17. Flood of May 1979, River Stour.

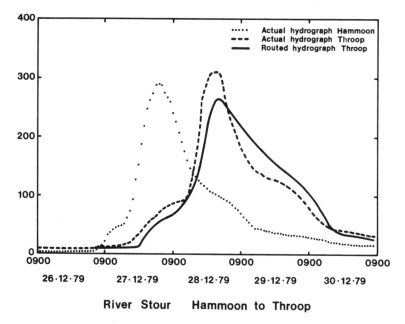

FIG. 18. Flood of December 1979, River Stour.

River Soar

Another valuable aspect of the simple routing model which has been the subject of this chapter is its use in assessing a river prior to the development of a more sophisticated model based on the full Saint-Venant equations. Such an assessment can identify the degree of attenuation along the river and the location of reaches where particular attention needs to be given to data collection. The first of these two points was the subject of a study of the River Soar.

This river, between Leicester and its confluence with the River Trent (Fig. 19), is prone to flooding due to a number of structures on the river controlling flow for navigation in connection with the Grand Union Canal. Additionally the river is comparatively flat with extensive flood plains. Intuitively, one could anticipate that the attenuation of major floods along the river would be significant and therefore any model set up to reproduce water levels as well as discharge should simulate unsteady rather than steady flow if accurate results are to be obtained. Unfortunately, the complexity of the river geometry and the need for fine

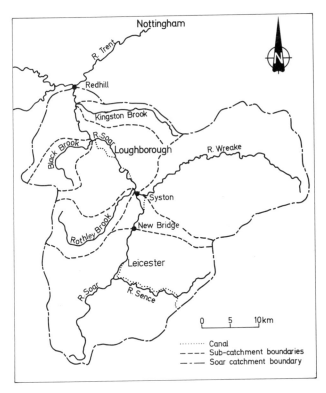

Fig. 19. River Soar.

resolution of water level variation over the flood plains would make a
steady flow model easier to develop and apply than an unsteady model.
To resolve the question of whether the attenuation was significant or not
and thus whether an unsteady rather than a steady flow model would be
required, a FLOUT model of the river was developed. This model is
described in more detail elsewhere;[23,25] it is sufficient to recall the results
for a 50 year design event in the existing river as shown in Figs 20 and 21.

To demonstrate the magnitude of the attenuation at the downstream
end of the reach, that is at Redhill, the model was re-run for the same
event but with a negligible attenuation parameter. The difference in peak
discharge at Redhill is about 5% of the existing peak flow showing that a
steady flow model for overbank events would give an adequate
simulation for design. Closer examination of the results also reveals that

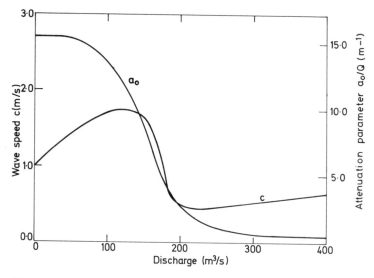

FIG. 20. Kinematic wave speed and attenuation parameter curves for River Soar.

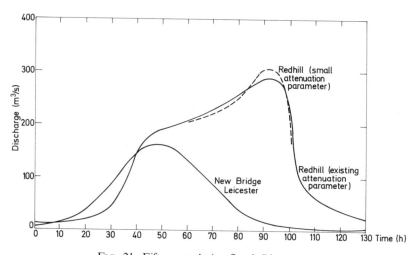

FIG. 21. Fifty year design flood, River Soar.

the key reason why the attenuation is so small is the flatness of the discharge hydrograph. This flatness is induced primarily by the lag between the peaks from the main river and from the River Wreake. In turn this phenomenon highlights the importance of the interaction of

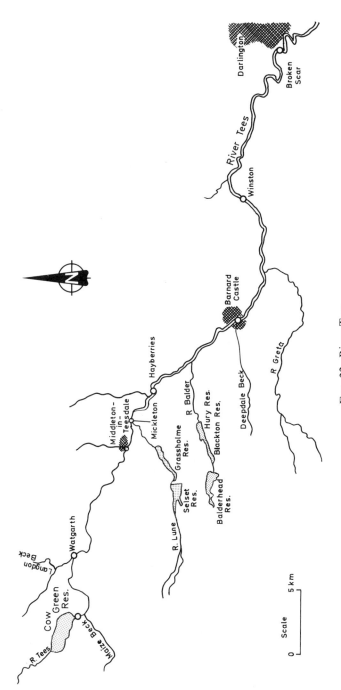

FIG. 22. River Tees.

flows from tributaries with that in the main river. In many rivers the timing of the interaction of flows is more important in affecting peak flows downstream than the 'natural' attenuation of the hydrograph.

River Tees

A further illustration of the versatility of the non-linear routing model is in its application to superimposed step releases from Cow Green Reservoir on the River Tees (Fig. 22). The releases were made under drought conditions when the flow depth in the river was the order of the roughness height. Observations were made at a number of sites downstream of the reservoir.[26] A particular feature of the experiment

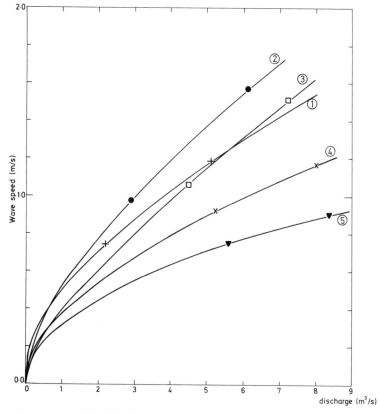

FIG. 23. Wave speed curves for River Tees.

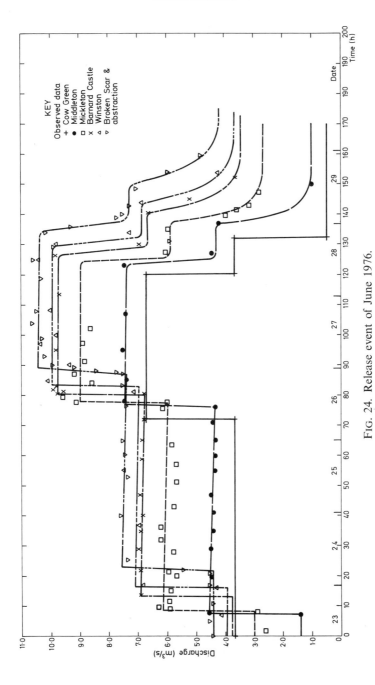

FIG. 24. Release event of June 1976.

was that after the first step release the flow was kept constant for 72 h and then a second release was made. The second release was observed to travel significantly faster than the first release, so confirming the non-linear behaviour of the flow under these conditions.

The kinematic wave speed curves for each model reach were derived from observed data, plotting the speed against discharge corresponding to half the step in each case;[27] see Fig. 23. The attenuation parameters a_0 for each reach were calculated assuming fixed values of channel width and slope.

The recorded discharge hydrograph at Cow Green was used as input and lateral inflows were determined from the observed recession curves at each gauging station. A time increment of 5 min was necessary to retain adequate definition of the stepped releases. Good agreement between observed and predicted hydrographs was obtained with only minor adjustments to the speed–discharge curves (Fig. 24).

10   CLASSIFICATION OF ROUTING MODELS

The flood routing model developed above is based on strict hydraulic principles and is therefore deterministic provided it is operated within the constraints imposed by the assumptions made in its development. Beginning with the Saint-Venant equations for open channel flow the key assumption for the method is that the characteristic surface slope defined relative to the bed slope, ε, is small compared with the bed slope: no assumption is made about the Froude number (or rather about the square, γ, of the Froude number). A classification of *hydraulic* routing models then follows in terms of the pair of parameters ε and γ (Table 1).

TABLE 1

$\gamma \backslash \varepsilon$	$O(1)$	$\ll 1$	~ 0
$O(1)$	Complete dynamic wave	Complete diffusion wave	Kinematic wave
$\ll 1$	Non-inertial dynamic wave	Non-inertial diffusion wave	Kinematic wave

The complete dynamic wave model can be regarded as the standard flood routing model in that, based on the complete Saint-Venant equations for open channel flow, it is theoretically the most accurate and versatile. See Cunge *et al.*[1] for an extensive survey of the various models developed for studying flows in natural rivers.

The non-inertial dynamic model should properly be restricted in its use to rivers with small gradients. As an example of this type of model, see Akan and Yen.[28]

The term 'complete diffusion wave' model is used to identify the model developed and described in this chapter. The 'non-inertial diffusion wave' model is the parallel of the diffusion analogy model identified in various reviews such as those of Weinmann and Laurenson[29] and Miller and Cunge.[30] Strictly, the diffusion analogy model is derived from arguments other than those based upon the Saint-Venant equations, and is commonly based on a convection–diffusion equation (cf. eqn (29)). The original version of this model is that developed by Hayami,[13] though a number of other researchers have studied similar linear and non-linear versions of the model; for example see Henderson,[31] Thomas and Wormleaton,[32] Price[17] and Keefer and McQuivey.[33]

Models based on the diffusion analogy may be regarded as one of several classes of models which are in essence conceptual in nature and are not therefore included in the classification of the hydraulic based models above. These classes include kinematic wave, storage, diffusion (as above) analogy and empirical methods.

Miller and Cunge[30] observe that the theory of kinematic waves in flood movement was given by Boussinesq[34] who in turn referred to previous authors. The classic paper is however that by Lighthill and Whitham.[11] Various models based on linear and non-linear forms of the kinematic wave equation have been used extensively for flood routing; see for example Wooding,[35] Kellerhals,[36] Koussis,[37] Smith[38] and Wiltshire and Novak.[39]

Storage methods are based on the continuity equation, as described in Section 2 of this chapter. The most notable methods of this class are Muskingum (McCarthy[4]), Kalinin–Miljukov (Kalinin and Miljukov[40]) and SSARR (Brooks, Davis and Kuehl[41]). These methods all have a common basis and are carefully analysed by Miller and Cunge.[30] Cunge's[6] own analysis of the Muskingum method in relation to the kinematic wave and diffusion methods has been referred to above, as have several of the variants of the Muskingum method. Other analyses of the Muskingum method and the vexed problem of the choice of parameters for the method are given by Koussis,[42,43] Nash,[44] Laurenson[45] and Ponce and Theurer[46] among others.

Finally, some methods have been based on an empirical analysis of data for particular rivers. Most of these methods rely on a logging of the inflow with rules relating the discharge to the rate of change of stage.

11 CONCLUDING REMARKS

All routing models require some degree of calibration when used in practical application. The hydraulically-based models, provided they are operated within the constraints imposed by their assumptions, can be calibrated using observed physical parameters and should be more reliable than the conceptual models when applied to events outside the range of calibration. Any operation of the hydraulically-based models outside these constraints will invalidate the deterministic basis of the model and results may therefore be inaccurate. The form of the results will, however, in general appear reasonable because of the capacity of the models to reproduce translation, attenuation and the deformation of a flood hydrograph. Care must therefore be exercised to ensure that an apparently sensible end result of applying the model is achieved within appropriate constraints on the parameters, and in particular on the space and time increments. Where the model is applied outside the constraints, reasonable results may still be obtained, but in this case extrapolation to other events in the range for which the models are not calibrated should be made with caution.

The development of the simpler routing models (as opposed to the sophisticated numerical models based on the full Saint-Venant equations) has reached a stage where the main problems are not ones of theory but rather of practice and, in particular, of application to flooding problems in rivers with inadequate data. The uncertainty in the estimation of rainfall–run-off, particularly along a routing reach, can often force an engineer seeking reliable routing models to adopt the simplest model commensurate with the quality of his data. Sufficient information on the various models is now available for a responsible choice of the model best suited to a particular set of circumstances.

ACKNOWLEDGEMENTS

This chapter is published with the permission of the Managing Director of Hydraulics Research. The author is grateful for the considerable assistance given by many colleagues in developing and applying the model described above.

REFERENCES

1. CUNGE, J. A., HOLLY, J. F. M. and VERWEY, A. *Practical Aspects of Computational Hydraulics*, Pitman, London, 1980.
2. EVANS, E. P. Behaviour of a mathematical model of open channel flow. *Proc. 17th Congress of IAHR*, Baden-Baden, 1977.
3. SAMUELS, P. G. Computational modelling of open channel flow. An analysis of some practical difficulties. *Report IT 273*, Hydraulics Research, Wallingford, UK, June, 1984.
4. MCCARTHY, G. T. The unit hydrograph and flood routing. *Proc. Conf. of the North Atlantic Division of the US Corps of Engineers*, June, 1938.
5. THOMAS, H. A. The hydraulics of flood movements in rivers. *Carnegie Inst. Tech. Eng. Bull.*, 11–70, 1937.
6. CUNGE, J. A. On the subject of a flood propagation method (Muskingum method). *J. Hydraul. Res. IAHR*, **7** (1969), 205–30.
7. NATURAL ENVIRONMENT RESEARCH COUNCIL. *Flood Studies Report — Volume III — Flood Routing Methods*. NERC, London, 1975.
8. STRUPCZEWSKI, W. G. and KUNDZEWICZ, Z. Choice of a linear, three-parametric conceptual flood routing model and evaluation of its parameters, *Acta Geophys Polon.* **28** (2) (1980), 129–41.
9. STRUPCZEWSKI, W. and KUNDZEWICZ, Z. Muskingum method revisited. *J. Hydraul*, **48**, (1980), 327–42.
10. HENDERSON, F. M. *Open Channel Flow*. MacMillan, New York, 1976.
11. LIGHTHILL, M. J. and WHITHAM, G. B. On kinematic waves, I. *Proc. R. Soc. London, Series A*, **229**, (1955), 281–316.
12. WONG, T. H. F. and LAURENSON, E. M. Wave speed — discharge relations in natural channels. *Water Res. Res.* **19** (3) (1983), 701–6.
13. HAYAMI, S. On the propagation of flood waves. *Bulletin No. 1. Disaster Prevention Research Institute*, Kyoto University, Japan, December, 1951.
14. GOOGE, J. I., KUNDZEWICZ, Z. W. and NAPIORKOWSKI, J. J. On backwater effects in linear diffusion flood routing. *Hydrol. Sci. J.* **28** (3) (1983), 391–402.
15. FORCHHEIMER, P. *Hydraulik*, 3rd Edn, Tuebner, Leipzig and Berlin, 1930.
16. PRICE, R. K. A non-linear theory of flood wave propagation. *Appl. Math. Modelling*, **6**, (1982), 338–42.
17. PRICE, R. K. Flood routing methods for British rivers. *Report IT 111*, Hydraulics Research, Wallingford, UK, March, 1973.
18. PRICE, R. K. Variable parameter diffusion method for flood routing. *Report IT 115*, Hydraulics Research, Wallingford, UK, July, 1973.
19. AMEIN, M. An implicit method for numerical flood routing. *Water Res. Res.* **4**, (4) (1968), 719–26.
20. PRICE, R. K. and KAWECKI, M. W. Equivalent river models. *Proc. Int. Symp on Unsteady Flow in Open Channels*, BHRA, Paper K4, Newcastle, 1976.
21. JONES, S. B. Choice of space and time steps in the Muskingum–Cunge flood routing method. *Proc. Inst. Civ. Eng.* **71**, (2) (1981), 759–72.

22. DE SOUZA, P. A. and PRICE, R. K. The Saint-Venant equations: a linearised analysis. *Report IT 203*, Hydraulics Research, Wallingford, UK, September, 1980.

23. PRICE, R. K., FLOUT, A river catchment flood model. *Report IT 168*, Hydraulics Research, Wallingford, UK, January, 1980.

24. NATURAL ENVIRONMENT RESEARCH COUNCIL. *Flood Studies Report. Vol. 1. Hydrological Studies*, NERC, London, 1975.

25. PRICE, R. K. Flood routing methods for British rivers. *Proc. Inst. Civ. Eng.* **55** (12), (1973), 913–30.

26. NORTHUMBRIAN WATER AUTHORITY. Cow Green Reservoir releases experiment. 23–28 June, 1976, NWA, 1977.

27. PRICE, R. K. Hydraulics of low flows in shallow rivers. *Report IT 117*, Hydraulics Research, Wallingford, UK. May, 1978.

28. AKAN, A. O. and YEN, B. C. A non-linear diffusion wave model for unsteady open channel flow. *Proc. 17th Congress of IAHR*, Baden-Baden, Vol. 2, 1977, 181–90.

29. WEINMANN, P. E. and LAURENSON, E. M. Approximate flood routing methods: A review. *J. Hydraul. Div. ASCE*, **105** (HY12) (1979), 1521–36.

30. MILLER, W. A. and CUNGE, J. A. Simplified equations of unsteady flow. In: *Unsteady Flow in Open Channels*, ed. M. Mahwood and V. Yevjevich, Vol. 1 Chap 5, 1975, 183–257.

31. HENDERSON, F. M. *Open Channel Flow*, New York, MacMillan, 1966.

32. THOMAS, I. E. and WORMLEATON, P. R. Finite difference solution of the flood diffusion equation. *J. Hydraul.*, **12**, (1971), 211–21.

33. KEEFER, T. N. and McQUIVEY, R. S. Multiple linearization flow routing model. *J. Hydraul. Res. ASCE*, **100** (HY7), (1974), 1031–46.

34. BOUSSINESQ, J. Essai sur la théorie des caux courantes (Treatise on the theory of flowing water). *Academic Science (Paris) Memoirs*, **V. 23**, (1977), 261–529, (in French).

35. WOODING, R. A. A hydraulic model for the catchment stream problem — kinematic wave theory. *J. Hydraul.* **V3** (1965), 254–67.

36. KELLERHALS, R. Runoff routing through steep natural channels. *J. Hydraul. Div. ASCE*, **96** (HY11), (1970), 2201–17.

37. KOUSSIS, A. D. An approximative dynamic flood routing method. *Proc. Int. Sym. on Unsteady Flow in Open Channels*, Paper L1, Newcastle-upon-Tyne, 1976.

38. SMITH, A. A. A generalised approach to kinematic flood routing. *J. Hydraul.* **45** (1980), 71–89.

39. WILTSHIRE, S. E. and NOVAK, P. An evaluation of the performance of a finite difference approximation of the kinematic wave speed equation. *J.IWES*, **38** (1) (1984), 61–9.

40. KALININ, G. P. and MILJUKOV, P. I. Approximate computation of unsteady flow, Trudy CIP, V66, Leningrad, 1958 (in Russian).

41. BROOKS, K. N., DAVIS, E. M. and KUEHL, D. W. Program description and user manual for SSARR — streamflow synthesis and reservoir regulation. *North Pacific Division Corps of Engineers*, Portland, Oregon, December, 1972.

42. KOUSSIS, A. D. Theoretical estimations of flood routing parameters. *J.*

Hydraul. Div. ASCE, **104** (HY1), (1978), 109–15.
43. KOUSSIS, A. D. Comparison of Muskingum method difference schemes. *J. Hydraul. Div. ASCE*, **106** (HY5), (1980), 925–29.
44. NASH, J. E. A note on the Muskingum flood routing method. *J. Geophys. Res.* **64** (1959), 1053–56.
45. LAURENSON, E. M. A catchment storage model for runoff routing, *J. Hydraul.* **2** (1964), 141–63.
46. PONCE, V. M. and THEURER, F. D. Accuracy criteria in diffusion routing. *J. Hydraul. Div. ASCE*, **108** (HY6) (1982), 747–57.

Chapter 5

ICE AND RIVER ENGINEERING

Ö. Starosolszky

Institute of Hydraulic Engineering, Research Centre for Water Resources Development, Budapest, Hungary

NOTATION

a	constant of Shulyakovskiĭ's method
A	surface area of the ice floe
b	width of the structure
B	width of a river cross-section
c	specific heat
Cv	Chézy's velocity coefficient
Ca	Cauchy number
C	drag coefficient
d	diameter
D	dispersion coefficient
D_t	thermal diffusivity
E	Young's modulus of elasticity
f	friction factor
F	force
Fr	Froude number
G	shear modulus
g	acceleration due to gravity
h	ice thickness
h_0	heat transfer coefficient
h_f	flying height
H	water depth, mean depth of flow
H_i	head loss

I inertia momentum
k Strickler's roughness coefficient $(k = 1/n)$
k_s absolute roughness
k_p pile form parameter
k_t thermal conductivity
K constant
l length, characteristic length on elastic foundation
L length of the ice floe
M momentum
n Manning's roughness coefficient
N power (output)
N   Nusselt number
P wetted perimeter, loading force
P   Prandtl number
q specific discharge per unit width, specific heat flux
Q flow discharge (Q_i ice discharge)
Q_h heat flux
Q_h^* heat loss, change in heat storage
R hydraulic radius
Re   Reynolds number
s strip width
S slope (water surface)
t time
T temperature
u average flow velocity: velocity component perpendicular to cross-section
u_* shear velocity
v velocity component
V velocity vector ($V(u, v, w)$)
w width of frozen ice floe; velocity component
W wind velocity; W_1 work
x longitudinal coordinate, distance
X non-dimensional distance (e.g. $X = x/H$)
y vertical coordinate; boundary layer thickness
Y parameter of ice stability on wide rivers
z transverse coordinate

α wedge angle, α_1 parameter
β slope angle
γ constant (ice cover stability)

δ   constant (ice cover stability)

ε   strain

ζ   coefficient (reduction of discharge)

η, ξ   Beltaos' parameters

λ   scale factor of physical models

μ   friction factor, dimensionless coefficient that depends on the internal friction of the ice jam

ν   Poisson ratio

ρ   density

σ   strength, stress

τ   shear stress

φ   surface heat flux

Subscripts

a   air

b   bottom

i   ice

h   heat

o   initial

w   water

1 INTRODUCTION

River engineers in several countries, mainly in the Northern Hemisphere, are confronted during the winter period with problems due to the solid form of water, i.e. the natural freshwater ice. The occurrence of ice on rivers depends on the climatic and hydraulic conditions at a particular site.

The principal problem in river engineering is the prediction of the time and location of ice formation and of the thickness of the ice cover. As far as ice movement is concerned, distinction must be made between frazil ice moving in the entire cross-section and ice floes moving at the surface. Under certain conditions the development of solid ice packing will influence the discharge capacity of the river; flow is retarded compared with ice free conditions, which — in extreme cases — may lead to ice jamming and to devastating floods. Depending on its mechanical properties, the impact of ice transmits forces to the banks and hydraulic structures, which must be protected against this force, or else special control measures must be adapted to prevent the development of such forces. In some instances it may become necessary to exploit the load bearing capacity of the ice cover.

The above phenomena and related problems will be dealt with in this chapter with emphasis on their relation to river engineering. International understanding of ice problems was promoted by the IAHR Multilingual Ice Terminology,[55] which contains the basic terms in 21 languages.

2 PROPERTIES OF RIVER ICE

There are several properties of ice interesting from the point of view of river engineering. The formation and classification of freshwater ice can be seen in Fig. 1.[35] An ice cover may be a continuous sheet or an unconsolidated ice accumulation. In rivers with turbulent flow above a certain velocity the dynamic formation is dominant and frazil slush, pancake ice and ice floes can be found. Ice jam is a major accumulation, it can be refrozen as hummocked ice cover. If slush accumulates under the ice cover, it forms an underhanging dam.

The solid ice cover can be divided into three layers: primary, secondary and superimposed ice. Primary ice has a uniform structure and texture, in turbulent water it may consist of frozen frazil slush. Congealed snow slush can also be its part. Secondary ice forms parallel to the heat flow direction. Its structure may be columnar, frazil or snow slush, deposited under primary ice. Superimposed ice forms on top of primary ice due to flooding, sometimes as snow ice.

The crystal orientation is determined by preparing a thin section and observing it between crossed polaroid sheets. There are three basic types of primary, four of secondary and three of superimposed ice. Natural river ice is mostly an agglomeration of various ice types and forms. The grain size and the orientation of the crystal axis can vary between wide limits. Mechanisms of frazil ice formation were discussed by Osterkamp,[41] Ashton[3] and Müller.[37] Although the variation of the structure of river ice can be considerable and ice properties[14] involved in fluvial processes are thus variable, they are usually assumed as constants for design computations.

The basic properties of river ice can be summarised as follows. Density of ice (ρ_i) shows a linear increase with decreasing temperature T_i

$$\rho_i = 916 \cdot 55 - 0 \cdot 14 . T_i \, [\text{kg/m}^3] \tag{1}$$

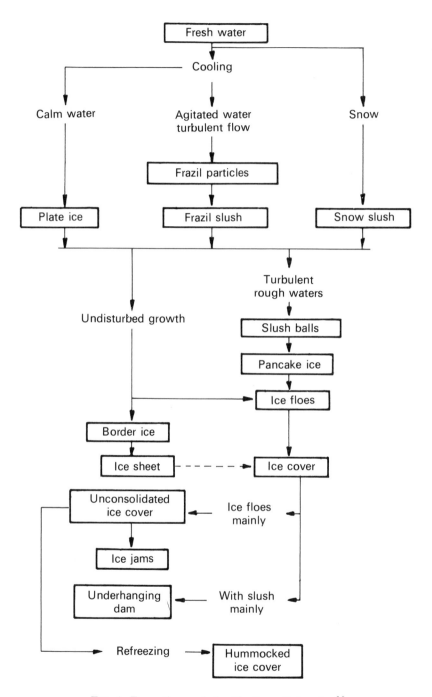

FIG. 1. Formation and classification of river ice.[35]

For approximative calculations the density of ice can be considered as $920 \, kg/m^3$.

Creep of ice takes a predominant role in comparison with its elastic response to loading and unloading. In engineering problems loading is usually at a constant high rate and the creep curve is steep at the origin with primary creep not significant. The behaviour of ice can, thus, be simplified for both tension and compression (Fig. 2).

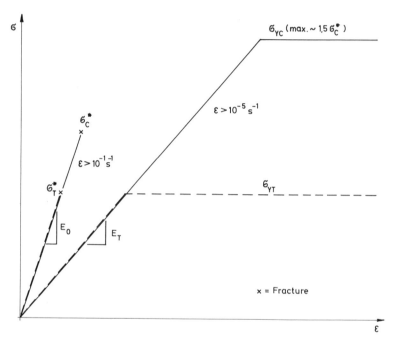

FIG. 2. The simplified behaviour of ice at tension and compression.

For very high loading rates (where the rate of change of strain is higher than $10^{-1} \, s^{-1}$) the ice behaves as a perfectly elastic material and fails by cracks.

The specific heat (c_i) is given by

$$c_i = 2 \cdot 45 - 1 \cdot 97 \, Jg^{-1} \, {}^\circ C^{-1} \tag{2}$$

The mean value of heat required to melt 1 g of ice is

$$c_i = 2 \cdot 12 \, Jg^{-1} \, {}^\circ C^{-1}$$

The thermal conductivity of pure ice can be calculated by

$$k_t = 2\cdot21 - 0\cdot011\, T\,(\text{Wm}^{-1}\,{}^{\circ}\text{C}^{-1}) \tag{3}$$

The thermal diffusivity

$$D_t = 2\cdot3 \times 10^{-7} - 12\cdot8 \times 10^{-7}\,\text{cm}^2\,\text{s}^{-1} \tag{4}$$

Strength is the property of ice of immediate engineering interest, specifying the ice forces. Strength is a function of test conditions (loading rate, test system, specimen size), basic material properties (temperature, ice type, grain size, air content) and failure mode (ductile or brittle). Testing standards have been established by IAHR[46] and uniform loading conditions have been specified for uniaxial compression or tension for shear stress or flexural strength determination, etc. The strength values suggested for usage in river engineering are given in Table 1.

Ice responds elastically if the loading time is less than 100 s for stresses σ, less than 1 MNm^{-2}, or if loaded to failure within 2 s and follows Hooke's Law $\sigma = E\varepsilon$. Young's modulus (E) depends on several factors (temperature, density, grain size, direction of loading, etc.).

TABLE 1
AVERAGE STRENGTH PARAMETERS OF FRESH WATER ICE AT $T_i = -5{}^{\circ}\text{C}$

Name of parameter	Unit	Symbol	Parameter value
Density	kg/m^3	ρ_i	918–875
Modulus of elasticity			
dynamic	MN/m^2	E_d	8 300–10 300
static	MN/m^2	E_{st}	7 300–8 800
Shear modulus			
dynamic	MN/m^2	G_d	2 100–3 600
static	MN/m^2	G_{st}	250–2 300
Poisson ratio			
dynamic		v_d	0·34–0·4
static		v_{st}	0·28–0·37
Compression strength			
dynamic	MN/m^2	$\sigma_{c,d}$	2·0–2·9
static	MN/m^2	$\sigma_{c,st}$	2·2–3·4
Tensile strength			
dynamic	MN/m^2	$\sigma_{t,d}$	8·0–12·0
static	MN/m^2	$\sigma_{t,st}$	1·2–1·5
Shear strength			
dynamic	MN/m^2	τ_d	0·9–2·0
static	MN/m^2	τ_{st}	1·0–1·8
Flexural strength	MN/m^2	σ_f	1·4–2·0

Variation of tensile strength σ_t with grain size d (m) was investigated by Michel[36] with the following result

$$\sigma_t = \frac{K_i \sqrt{\pi}}{2} \cdot \frac{1}{\sqrt{d}} \tag{5}$$

The mean value for K_i is $88 \cdot 3 \pm 14 \cdot 2 \, \text{kN m}^{-3/2}$.

3 THERMAL REGIME AND ICE FORMATION

The ice regime of rivers depends on the thermal regime which is the temperature distribution in the river and its variation in time and space. This temperature variation is caused primarily by heat exchange through the water surface and the ice cover.

Heating and cooling of water masses follows an annual cycle and ice is affected by the winter thermal regime. Particularly ice production and development of ice cover are affected by the preceeding cooling period with thermal effects due to human activities (e.g. release of cooling water, selective withdrawal from storage reservoirs). The knowledge of the thermal regime is, therefore, a prerequisite to the prediction of ice phenomena. Water in a stream receives heat from shortwave radiation (Q_R), from the geothermic heat supply of the earth (Q_G), by advection from inflowing groundwater (Q_{GW}) and the heat generated by friction along the bottom (Q_F). Heat losses are due to longwave radiation (Q_B), evaporation (Q_E), conduction and convection (Q_H) and occasionally snowfall (Q_S).

The above terms can be combined into the heat budget equation with Q^* denoting the change in heat storage of water

$$Q^* = Q_R - Q_B - Q_E - Q_H - Q_S + Q_G + Q_{GW} + Q_F \tag{6}$$

Thermal conditions for significant ice formation are found north of the 40th northern latitude and south of the 40th southern latitude.

In stream waters turbulent mixing generally prevents thermal stratification. The temperature is characteristic for the whole cross-section unless artificial effects are involved (e.g. thermal plumes). A typical temperature development for a river is shown on Fig. 3. During the winter the water temperature is theoretically 0°C, at least within the ordinary accuracy of 0·1°C. In typical rivers, in particular before a

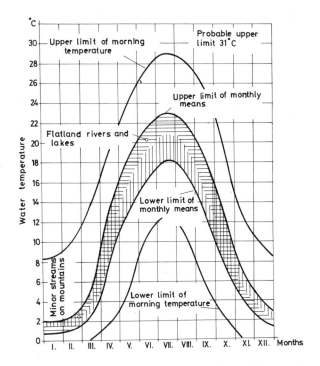

FIG. 3. Temperature development for rivers (Hungary).

constant ice cover develops, the actual temperature can be somewhat less than 0°C due to supercooling which is the reason for frazil ice formation. Usually no temperature distribution along the verticals can be observed, only slight deviations in lateral directions. Temperatures below 0°C can be attributed to freezing point depression due to dissolved substances.

When a stream becomes ice covered the heat loss from the water to the air is reduced by insulation effects of the ice cover which may be substantially increased by snow cover.[47]

The temperature field in the turbulent heat transfer is governed by the equation

$$\frac{\partial T}{\partial t} + u \frac{\partial T}{\partial x} + v \frac{\partial T}{\partial y} + w \frac{\partial T}{\partial z} = D \nabla^2 T \tag{7}$$

where $V(u, v, w)$ is the velocity vector of the flow, $T(x, t)$ is the space and time variant temperature and D is the thermal diffusivity.

The heat balance is controlled in a decisive manner by heat exchange occurring across the surface. Empirical formulae for estimating the gain or loss in heat have been employed for a long time and they are still used in practice. The basic equations used for estimating specific heat loss from the surface (q^*) can all be reduced to the form

$$q^* = h_0 (T_w - T_a) \qquad (8)$$

where h_0 is the heat transfer coefficient and T_w and T_a are the water and air temperatures, respectively. The value of h_0 is generally higher if the shortwave radiation is lower than the heat loss by evaporation and lower if the heat loss by evaporation is smaller than shortwave radiation. The fundamental deficiency of empirical formulae is that they apply to lakes only and disregard the particular properties of turbulent mixing.

Starosolszky[52] applied the relationships of thermodynamics to turbulent flow between parallel plates with only one side exposed to heat influence (heat transfer occurs across the ice only); in the range of ice formation, i.e. at the Prandtl number $P \sim 14$ the relationship

$$N = 0.058 \, \mathrm{Re}^{0.83} \qquad (9)$$

has been established, where N is the Nusselt number of heat flow and Re the Reynolds number of water flow. The change in the water temperature near to $T_w = 0$ is

$$\frac{T_w - T}{T_w - T_o} \sim \frac{T}{T_o} = e^{-E\mathrm{Re}^{-0.2} X} \qquad (10)$$

where E is an experimental constant (in this case $E \sim 0.0126$) and $X = x/H$, the relative distance, with H denoting the water depth and x the distance. Using this formula the drop of the water temperature along the river, or the effect of heating — e.g. against frazil ice formation — can be calculated.

Warm water (e.g. cooling water outfalls) released into rivers with ice covers causes suppression of the ice cover by melting or by preventing its initial formation. The vertical, horizontal and longitudinal mixing processes of the river influence the geometry of the ice free (open) water and reduce ice cover thickness. Effects of warm water release can be calculated on the basis of the energy budget equation

$$\frac{\partial(\rho c \, T_w)}{\partial t} + U \frac{\partial(\rho c \, T_w)}{\partial x} = \frac{\partial}{\partial z} \left[D_z \frac{\partial(\rho c \, T_w)}{\partial z} \right] - \frac{\phi}{H} \qquad (11)$$

where ρ is the density of the water, c is the specific heat, t is the time, x is the longitudinal coordinate, z is the transverse coordinate, D_z is the transverse (lateral) dispersion coefficient, H is the depth and ϕ is the heat flux at the surface. It is assumed that mixing is complete over the depth and lateral mixing due to secondary currents and longitudinal mixing can be neglected.

The heat flux can be calculated by the heat transfer coefficient. The non-dimensional dispersion coefficient for ice covered rivers was found by Beltaos:[10] $D_z/Ru_* = 0.35 - 2.50$ where R is the hydraulic radius and u_* is shear velocity.

Ashton[4,5] developed a numerical method including lateral dispersion, ice growth and melting, and the unsteady effects of air temperature.

His equation can be simplified when complete mixing at the inflow may be assumed; introducing the transformation $udt = dx$ results in:

for open water conditions

$$\frac{T_w - T_a}{T_{w,o} - T_a} = \exp\left[\frac{-h_{owa}(x - x_0)}{\rho c U H}\right] \qquad (12)$$

and for ice conditions

$$\frac{T_w - T_a}{T_{w,o} - T_a} = \exp\left[\frac{-h_{owi}(x - x_0)}{\rho c U H}\right] \qquad (13)$$

where T_w is the water and T_a is the air temperature, $T_{w,0}$ is the water temperature at distance x_0, c is the specific heat of water, and h_{owa} is the heat transfer coefficient for water–air interface and h_{owi} for water–ice interface.

For steady state conditions, such as constant air temperature, the approximate location of the ice edge by assuming that this corresponds to $0°C$ isotherm is given by

$$x - x_{0_{T_w = 0°C}} = \frac{-\rho c U H}{h_{owa}}\left[\log_e\left(\frac{-T_o}{T_{w,o} - T_a}\right)\right] \qquad (14)$$

Ashton[4] discusses also cases when the steady state and $0°C$ isotherm assumptions are not valid.

Unsteady flow water temperatures have been modelled by Chaudry et al.[18] by integrating the one-dimensional Saint-Venant equations using an implicit finite difference method. Time varying lateral inflows and cross-section variations can be included in the model. Dispersion coefficients under ice cover are given by Beltaos.[11]

4   OBSERVATION OF ICE PHENOMENA

In order to ensure safe navigation, river regulation, safe operation of hydraulic structures and protection against ice flooding, prompt and reliable reports are necessary on ice conditions in rivers.

Usually the following observations are required:[59] date of ice appearance, shore ice, ice drifting and its intensity, onset of ice break-up, formation of ice jams. The following parameters can be measured directly: ratio of drifting ice surface to open water surface (ice cover ratio), ratio of drifting ice surface to stationary ice surface, velocity of drifting ice floes and usually ice thickness. When stationary ice is present, ice thickness can be measured regularly. Dimensions of ice jams (the ice mass in the jam) can be calculated on the basis of several ice thickness measurements. From time to time, photogrammetric measurements can be taken of ice conditions on larger rivers.

Observations of ice phenomena cannot be separated from water stage and temperature readings, in many cases regular ice observations are therefore made by the water gauge observers. Ice thickness measurements by impact gauges should be carried out in the vicinity of the water gauge at ice holes. On lakes and reservoirs ice holes should be placed in five locations in a line of approximately 200 m perpendicular to the shore. An ice pick or drill is usually used for holing the ice sheet. Under certain conditions, ice thickness measurements are carried out by the ice breaking service from the ice breakers. An up-to-date technique is the measurement of the ice thickness by a subsurface radar which senses non-destructively the bottom of ice cover.

Ice thickness and ice cover ratio are usually recorded in the hydrological observation log. Ice phenomena are designated in code established by the World Meteorological Organization. The use of the code ensures uniform processing and evaluation of ice data.

When organising ice observations accident prevention instructions should be given to the personnel involved. Special patrols can also be deployed once or twice a day to observe ice phenomena along rivers, in particular during intensified ice drifting and jamming. Once defensive measures (e.g. breaking or blasting) are undertaken, ice observation should be made by the defence service also. For fixing the observed locations the kilometre signs of navigable rivers or dykes may be used, particularly dangerous conditions (ice jams) must be pin-pointed in relation to other landmarks (bridges, river regulation structures, harbours). The date of patrol observations should also be recorded and transmitted to the appropriate authorities.

Determination of exact quantitative characteristics of ice phenomena can be collected by regular photogrammetric survey from a location on the shore or by occasional aerial photography. For surveying the ice conditions over a reach a strip width(s) and a flying height (h_f) can be determined as a function of focal length (L_f) of the camera used and the effective width (l) of the film frame: $h_f = s(L_f/l)$. Since the L_f is a camera constant which is near to 1·0 the flying height could be approximately equal to the strip width. By repeating aerial photography every few minutes the velocity of the ice drift can also be determined as well as the

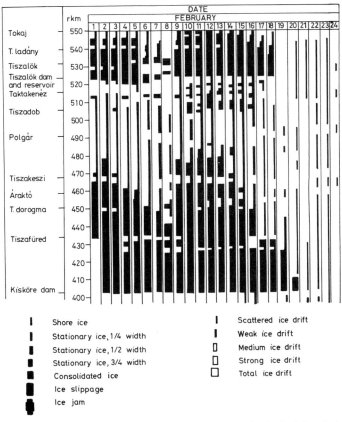

FIG. 4. Recording observed data (Hungarian Hydrological Service).

density of cover and the ice discharge (throughput). Knowing the ice thickness value, the quantity of ice can also be calculated.

The regular primary processing of the data collected in this way comprises decoding of information, checking of decoded data, correction of faulty data, graphical representation of ice phenomena and determination of characteristic dates and duration of ice phenomena.

Figure 4 provides a simplified method for checking and recording observed data.[58] The figure can also be prepared in colour.

5 ICE FORECAST

Exact relationships for calculating thermal and ice regime are available, but their application to ice forecasting is severely limited by the stochastic nature of parameters governing the equations which vary over the time span between the forecast and the event predicted. Ice regime forecasts may be classified as follows.[61,62]

Short term forecasts: date of appearance of ice on rivers; commencement of freeze-up; build-up of the ice cover; ice thickness; break-up of the ice cover; ice jams and date of disappearance of ice.

Long term forecasts: date of ice appearance and date of break-up.

The most important forecast, the date of appearance of ice on the water surface, can be made by the method proposed by Shulyakovski[47] which is based on the inequality between the two heat fluxes:

$$\alpha_n T_{wn} \leqslant -Q_m^* \quad \text{or} \quad T_{wn} \leqslant -\frac{Q_m^*}{\alpha_n} \tag{15}$$

where T_w is the mean temperature of water flow, α is the heat yield coefficient of the water body, Q^* is the heat loss through the air–water interface, and n refers to the time when this inequality appears. The calculation of α, T_w and Q^* needs several meteorological and hydrological parameters. The method can be used if forecasts are available on air temperature several days ahead, and its accuracy is affected mostly by errors in the air temperatures anticipated. The original method could be improved especially in two aspects: the time increment can be increased according to the actual observation period (e.g. for 12 h) and the variation of the time of travel and the average depth over the reach can also be taken into account.

Important results were achieved at the USSR Hydrometeorological

Centre,[21] where a method has been developed for long term forecasts on freezing-up and breaking-up of the ice on the rivers in Siberia, the Soviet Far East and the North-European territory. The basis of this method is:

— Synoptic analysis of the processes giving rise to the freezing-up of rivers, dividing the Northern Hemisphere into typical regions.
— Obtaining quantitative parameters for atmospheric processes, expanding meteorological fields by orthogonal functions.
— Use of multiple correlations to determine relationships between the time of ice occurrence and the coefficients of the expressions for the appropriate meteorological fields.

Ginsburg[21] applied a long term forecasting method based on Shulya-kovskii's results for the reservoirs on the Volga River. It was possible to forecast the dates of increase of the ice cover to thicknesses of 10, 15 and 20 cm. The accessibility to ships during the thawing period depends not only on the thickness, but also on the strength of the ice cover. Consequently long term forecasts on the rate of ice strength loss are also issued on the basis of regression equations calculated from long time series.

Empirical formulae have been derived to predict frazil ice formation for hydropower stations using available forecasts on air temperature and winds. An example of a similar relationship is shown in Fig. 5.[21]

The operation of water management schemes under winter conditions should be founded on appropriate reports and forecasts. An ice oriented hydrological network should be organised,[53] which can be operated

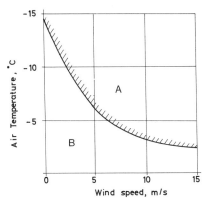

FIG. 5. Prediction of frazil ice formation. (A) Slush possible, and (B) no slush.

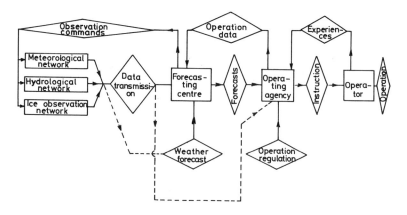

FIG. 6. Ice forecasting system.

according to the requirements of the scheme and the forecasting centre (Fig. 6). Regular feedback from the operator to the forecasting centre is also necessary.

Efforts are being made to apply the World Weather Watch (WWW) of WMO for hydrological data collection and a successful pilot exercise on the Saint John River[62] may be mentioned as a good example of international cooperation in the field of ice observations and forecasts.

A simplified form of the Shulyakovskiĭ[47] equation is successfully used for the Danube:[24]

$$(T_w)_n = (T_w)_o e^{-na_0} + \left[\bar{T}_a + \frac{d}{k} + \frac{(\alpha + h_0)q_b}{\alpha h_0} \right](1 - e^{-na_0}) \qquad (16)$$

where

$$a_0 = \frac{\alpha h_0 t}{(\alpha + h_0)Hc\rho}$$

$(T_w)_o$ initial water temperature selected within the interval corresponding to the flow time of travel through the upper portion of the reach

e   base of natural logarithm

α heat transfer coefficient between water mass and water surface approximating by $\alpha_n = (1745\bar{u}_n + 106\bar{W}_n)\,4 \cdot 1868$

$\bar{u}$ mean flow velocity in the reach during period n

$\bar{W}$ mean wind velocity during n

h_0 heat exchange coefficient between the water surface and the air $(J/cm^2\,Cd)$

H average water depth of the reach (m)

d specific heat exchange coefficient at a temperature equal to that of the water surface $(J/cm^2 d)$

$\bar{T}_a$ daily mean air temperature values during the period (°C)

q_b specific heat flux from the river bed to the water $(J/cm^2 d)$

c specific heat of water $(kJ/kg\,°C)$

t time unit used in the calculations (1 day)

The resultant of the heat exchange process between the water and the atmosphere Q_m^* can be expressed by the following empirical formula

$$Q_m^* = h_0\,\bar{T}_a + d \qquad (17)$$

For the determination of the critical temperature (T_{cr}) required for freeze-up the following functional relation is recommended

$$\frac{T_{cr}\dfrac{\partial \rho_w}{\partial T}}{B\rho_w} = f\left(\frac{u^2}{gB}\right) \qquad (18)$$

where $\partial \rho_w/\partial T = 1\cdot000\,kg/m^2\,°C$; $\rho_w = 1\cdot000\,kg/m^3$; $g = 9\cdot81\,m/s^2$; $u = $ average velocity (m/s) and $B = $ width of the river section (m). The average error on the Danube was about 3 days and the standard deviation ± 5 days.

Ice thickness can be predicted by

$$\Delta h_i = 6\cdot2\frac{\Sigma D_{surf}}{h_i} \text{ (cm)} \qquad (19)$$

where $\Delta h_i = $ growth in ice thickness,

$$h_i = h_{ii} + \frac{k_{ti}}{k_{ts}}\,h\text{(cm)}$$

where h_{ii} is the initial thickness, k_{ti} the heat conduction quotient of ice, k_{ts} the heat conduction quotient of snow, h_s the thickness of snow cover on ice and $D_{surf} = $ expected total negative temperature at the ice surface (degree-days) calculated from the day when ice thickness was first measured to the day when ice thickness is to be predicted.

6 EFFECT OF ICE ON DISCHARGE CAPACITY.
BACKWATER DUE TO ICE

For estimating the reduction in conveyance discharge capacity, and the increase in energy loss due to ice cover, methods developed by Lászlóffy[30] and Devik[20] can still be applied. The discharge at uniform steady flow for wide channels $(R \cong H)$ without ice cover is:

$$Q = kH^{2/3} S^{1/2} \cdot HB = kH^{5/3} S^{1/2} B \tag{20a}$$

and with an ice cover

$$Q' = \bar{k} R'^{2/3} S^{1/2} (H-h)B = \bar{k} \left(\frac{H-h}{2} \right)^{2/3} S^{1/2} (H-h)B \tag{20b}$$

Introducing βH for $(H-h)$ the ratio of conveyances, Q'/Q becomes.

$$\frac{Q'}{Q} = \frac{\bar{k}}{k} \frac{\left(\dfrac{\beta H}{2} \right)^{2/3} S^{1/2} B \cdot \beta H}{H^{5/3} S^{1/2} B} = \frac{\bar{k}}{k} \frac{\beta^{5/3}}{2^{2/3}} \tag{21}$$

thus

$$Q' = \zeta Q$$

where R is the hydraulic radius, H is the mean water depth, h is the ice thickness, B is the width of water surface, k is Strickler's roughness coefficient, β is the ratio $(H-h)/H$, S is the slope of energy gradient, $\bar{k}$ is the coefficient for the cross-section under ice cover.

The discharge under an ice cover is considerably reduced mainly due to the change of velocity distribution (Fig. 7), which is the consequence of the flow under pressure. The water surface in front of the ice cover is thus raised, i.e. the river is backed up. From eqn (21) the ratio of head losses becomes

$$\frac{H'_l}{H_l} \sim \left(\frac{Q'}{Q} \right)^2 = \left(\frac{\bar{k}^{5/3}}{k 2^{2/3}} \right)^2 = \left(\frac{\bar{k}}{k} \right)^2 \frac{\beta^{10/3}}{2^{4/3}} \tag{22}$$

Beltaos[9,10] supposing a wide channel with uniform ice thickness (h) under free flotation and uniform flow conditions calculates the approximate ratio of water depths as follows

$$\frac{H_{\text{cov}}}{H_{\text{open}}} = \left(2^{2/3} \frac{n_0}{n_{\text{b,open}}} \right)^{3/5} \tag{23}$$

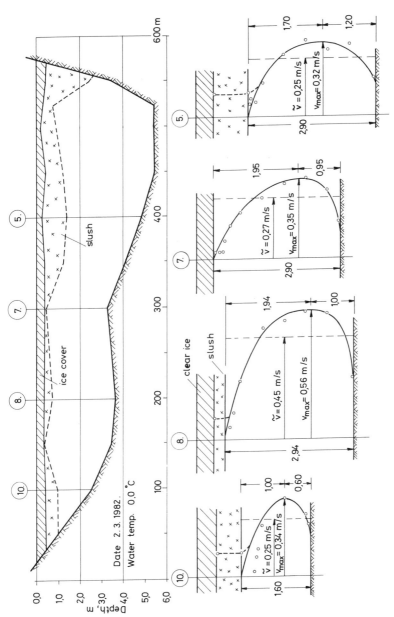

FIG. 7. Velocity distributions under ice cover.

where n_0 is the composite roughness coefficient.

Assuming for simplicity that $n_{b,open} \sim n_{b,cov} \sim n_b$

$$\frac{H_{cov}}{H_{open}} = \left[1 + \left(\frac{n_i}{n_b} \right)^{3/2} \right]^{2/5} \tag{24}$$

Figure 8 shows the effect of an ice cover on flow depth, assuming uniform steady flow and $n_{b,open} = n_{b,cov} = n_b$.

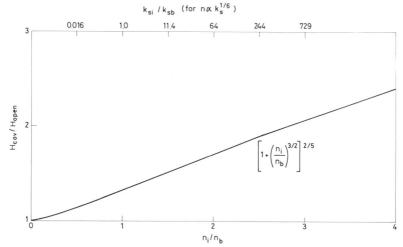

FIG. 8. Effect of ice cover on flow depth at uniform steady flow.

When $n_i = n_b$, $H_{cov} = 1 \cdot 3\, H_{open}$. The total depth under ice H'_{cov} can be calculated by adding $0 \cdot 92\, h$ to H_{cov}:

$$\frac{H'_{cov}}{H_{open}} = \frac{H_{cov}}{H_{open}} + 0 \cdot 92 \frac{h}{H_{open}} \tag{25}$$

The ice jam may have a large effect on water stage, particularly because the ice jam is very rough ($n_i > n_b$), and usually its thickness is several times the thickness of the individual floes.

It should be noted that when the ice cover is moving, its effect on stage and discharge is smaller than with a stationary cover.

The hydraulic resistance of the ice cover depends on the configuration of the underside of the ice and varies during the year. The resistance reaches high values at the beginning of freeze-up, because the ice is unconsolidated. Nezhikhovskii[39] estimated the n_i roughness coefficients for slush ice as: loose slush, frazil, $0 \cdot 01$–$0 \cdot 06$; dense slush, ice flocks, $0 \cdot 02$–$0 \cdot 09$ and ice floes $0 \cdot 02$–$0 \cdot 10$.

At mid-winter the resistance drops because bottom irregularities are smoothed out and n_i may fall to 0·008–0·015. Hanging dams cause roughness coefficients up to 0·06.

In late winter the hydraulic resistance may increase due to ripple like features (up to 300 mm); the roughness depends on the height of these ripples (n_i up to 0·03). When ice jams have formed, it is difficult to measure flow parameters and n_i can be between 0·04 and 0·10.

Velocity distribution under ice cover can be calculated on the basis of the turbulent boundary layer. The shear stress and the shear velocity along the ice surface can be calculated, as follows

$$\tau_i = \rho g H_i S_f, \quad u_{*i} = \sqrt{g H_i S_f} \tag{26a}$$

and along the bottom

$$\tau_b = \rho g H_b S_f, \quad u_{*b} = \sqrt{g H_b S_f} \tag{26b}$$

where S_f is the slope of the energy gradient.

The velocity in the two layers can be calculated by introducing the equivalent sand roughness height, the measure of average surface roughness, and applying the universal velocity distribution law

$$v_i = 2 \cdot 5 \, u_{*i} \ln\left(30 \frac{y_i}{k_{si}} \right) \tag{27a}$$

$$v_b = 2 \cdot 5 \, u_{*b} \ln\left(30 \frac{y_b}{k_{sb}} \right) \tag{27b}$$

where y_i and y_b are the boundary layer thickness corresponding to the ice cover and to the bottom, respectively, and k_s is the absolute roughness of the ice and the bottom.

The friction factor is

$$f = \left[2 \cdot 12 + 2 \cdot 04 \log_{10}\left(\frac{H}{k_s} \right) \right]^2 \tag{28}$$

the Chézy coefficient

$$C = \sqrt{\frac{8g}{f}} \tag{29}$$

the Manning roughness coefficient

$$n = \sqrt{\frac{f}{8g}} H^{1/6} \tag{30}$$

and

$$f = [\text{const}] \cdot k_s^{1/6} \left[5 \left(\frac{H}{k_s} \right) 700 \right] \tag{31}$$

From eqn (27) it can be concluded that over the normal ranges of k_{si}/k_{sb} ($0 \cdot 01 < k_{si}/k_{sb} < 10 \cdot 00$) the average velocities v_i and v_b are not very different. A recent investigation of Lau[31] shows that the two velocities are within 11% of each other.

Thus the composite resistance coefficient f_0 and Chézy coefficient C_0 can be derived in forms of

$$f_0 = (f_i + f_b)/2 \tag{32}$$

$$C_0 = \sqrt{\frac{2}{\left(\frac{1}{C_i^2} \right)^2 + \left(\frac{1}{C_b^2} \right)^2}} \tag{33}$$

and

$$n_0 = \left(\frac{n_i^{3/2} + n_b^{3/2}}{2} \right)^{2/3} \tag{34}$$

Laboratory data by Tatinclaux and Gogus[56] supported Nezhikhov-skiĭ's and Calkins's result that the resistance and roughness coefficients increase with the thickness of ice.

In field observations reductions of discharge capacity of as much as 20–30% due to ice cover have been frequently recorded.

Analysis of the data from the Beuharnois canal[57] shows that the ratio of the discharge capacities may vary during the winter season and the corrective coefficient to Chézy's C follows a well defined trend during the ice season (Fig. 9). A small amount of frazil ice can reduce the flow by 50%.

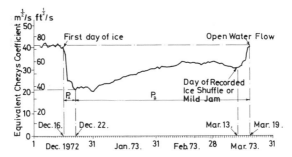

FIG. 9. Trend of the variation of the C velocity coefficient.

Ackermann *et al.*[1] derived an approximate equation for the ice discharge Q_i

$$\frac{Q_i}{b} = K \frac{h}{D^{0.33}} b^{0.13} S_0^{0.32} q^{0.36} \tag{35}$$

where b is the bottom width of the channel, D is the ice floe diameter, S_0 is the bed slope, q is the specific water discharge (Q/b), h is the ice thickness and K is a constant.

7   ICE JAMS

Ice jams may occur when the ice transport capacity of river, at a given reach is less than the actual ice drift. Thus ice jams can accumulate at the time of appearance of ice or at the time of break-up. An ice jam may produce very high stages relative to the open water stage for the same discharge.

Jams may be caused by: morphological features such as constrictions, shallows, bends; islands; reductions in slope and velocity; undisturbed ice cover where the continuous advance of ice run is stopped and man-made obstacles, bridge piers, dams, barrages, intakes.

Often jams form because of the existence of two or more features simultaneously and at the same location, e.g. serious cases may occur at bends upstream of a bridge, or at reaches just upstream of a river mouth at a lake or a large, slow recipient.

The earliest quantitative comprehensive description of ice jams on a river was reported by Pariset *et al.*[42] They made several assumptions in order to derive equations: jam thickness is independent of the distance and the resistance to shear at the sides consists of a cohesive and a frictional term. Pariset *et al.*[42] distinguished narrow and wide channels. In narrow channels the thickness of the jam is governed by the mean velocity v_u under the jam

$$v_u = \sqrt{2g\left(1 - \frac{\rho_i}{\rho}\right)h} \tag{36}$$

where ρ_i is the density of the ice and h its thickness. The theory of narrow channels was recently advanced by the laboratory studies of Tatinclaux and Gogus[56] and Calkins and Ashton.[15]

For a relatively smooth ice cover and bed and for the range

$0.05 < h_i/L < 0.5$ Tatinclaux and Gogus[56] recommended that the equation

$$\frac{v_e}{\sqrt{\frac{\Delta\rho}{\rho}gh_i}} = Fr_e = \left[-2.26\left(\frac{h_i}{L}\right)^2 + 2.14\left(\frac{h_i}{L}\right) + 0.015 \right]^{-1/2} \tag{37}$$

be adopted for the calculation of the critical value of Fr_e beyond which a jam will not thicken because of floe entrainment (L is the length of the ice floe, v_e is the flow velocity under the ice cover).

In wide channels the stress in the jam increases with the distance and the jam thickness is governed by structural considerations. The

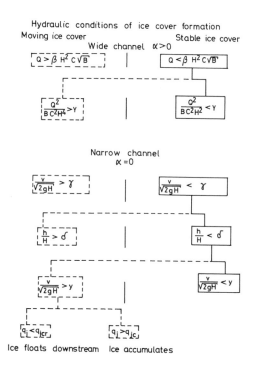

FIG. 10. Ice cover stability criteria, α, β, γ, δ, y, Y are constants depending on the parameters of the river reach. Under average conditions $\gamma \sim 0.11$, $\delta \sim 0.33$ and $y = f(h, H, \rho_i, \rho)$, α, β and Y are also functions of friction coefficients. q_{icr} is the critical specific ice discharge depending also on the slope.

comprehensive strength of the jam is calculated assuming that the full passive resistance is mobilised.

Pariset et al.'s[42] method is comprehensively summarised in Fig. 10 by Starosolszky[51] where alternatives are given on how to investigate stability of ice cover. In Fig. 10 α, β, γ, δ, y and Y are constants depending on the parameters of the river reach. Under average conditions $\gamma \cong 0\cdot11$, $\delta \cong 0\cdot33$ and $y = f(h, H, \rho_i, \rho)$. α, β and Y are functions of friction coefficients. q_{icr} is the critical specific ice discharge depending also on the slope.

Kennedy[25] formulated the time-dependent differential equations describing the flow under the jam and the equilibrium therein. The quasi-steady condition is characterised by an upstream advance of the jam head. The jam thickness increases to an equilibrium value which remains constant thereafter. It can be concluded that Uzuner and Kennedy's equation coincides with that of Pariset et al.[42] for wide channels for a certain friction value.

$$\frac{B}{H} < (2\mu\rho_i/\rho f_0)(h/H)\left[1 - \frac{\rho_i h}{\rho H}\right]\bigg/\left[\frac{f_i}{2f_0} + \frac{\rho_i h}{\rho H}\left(1 - \frac{f_i}{2f_0}\right)\right] \qquad (38)$$

in which H is the overall depth ($H = H_w + \rho_i h/\rho$) and μ is a coefficient depending on the internal friction of the ice jam. Substituting realistic values into this equation, it becomes clear that narrow channel jams should be rare in nature and for natural rivers the wide channel concept should be accepted.

Assuming that $\rho_i g = 9200\,\text{N/m}^3$, and the depth of flow, H, under the jam is

$$H = \left[\frac{q}{(4gS/f_0)^{1/2}}\right]^{2/3} \qquad (39)$$

in which $q = Q/B$, a non-dimensional equation was derived by Beltaos[8]

$$\eta = \frac{H}{BS} = 0\cdot63 f_0^{1/3}\zeta + \frac{5\cdot75}{\mu}\left[1 + \sqrt{1 + 0\cdot11\mu f_0^{1/3}(f_i/f_0)\xi}\right] \qquad (40)$$

where $\xi = \dfrac{q^{2/3}}{(gS)^{1/3}}\bigg/BS = y_{cr}/BS^{4/3}$ (y_{cr} is the critical depth).

The dimensionless jam stage (η) depends on the dimensionless discharge (ξ), on the frictional resistance of the jam and on the flow boundaries.

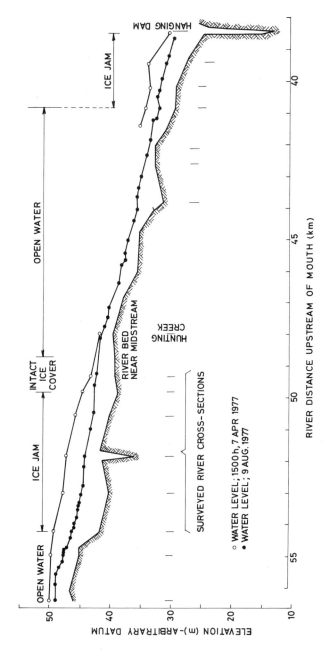

FIG. 11. Water level profile along ice jams.

For testing the theory the National Water Research Institute of Canada (Burlington) executed a field research program which consisted of documenting water level profiles along jams (Fig. 11). From the surveys reach-averaged hydraulic characteristics have been determined. Despite considerable scatter, the data points on Fig. 12 show a trend for qualitative support of the relation between η and ξ (see above definitions).

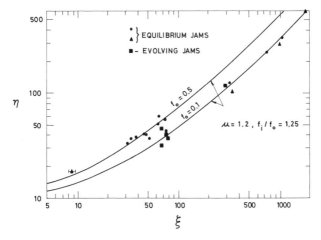

FIG. 12. Theoretical and observed values on the relation of η and ξ.

The theory assumes a wide rectangular prismatic channel, a floating jam in equilibrium, and that the theoretically derived jam stage discharge relationship provides an upper envelope of actual events, excluding grounded jams. The accuracy of prediction depends on the hydraulic resistance of the jam's underside. Effects of special constraints (flood plains, bridges, etc.) should be studied carefully. The method can be useful to supply information on break-up stages and on critical conditions for jamming. Formation and break-up of ice cover was comprehensively discussed by Billfalk.[13]

8   IMPACT OF RIVER ICE

Structures constructed in the river bed or on the shoreline are also affected by the ice. Ice can cause serious damage due to the forces transmitted from the ice to the structure. The computation of the potential forces is based on the equilibrium of action and reaction. An ice sheet cannot impose on a structure a force bigger than that necessary for crushing of the ice. When designing a structure capable of resisting ice, one may assume that ice should fail before the structure could be damaged. Thus, the basic principle of the calculations is that the design forces due to the ice impact can be the crushing forces of the ice. The method of failure of ice determines which strength of ice should be considered (compression, tensile, shear, buckling, etc.; see Table 1).[38]

The governing design ice force will be the lower of the limit-stress load and the limit-force load. The limit-stress load is determined by the force generated in the ice at the structure $F = \sigma h d$, where σ is the strength of the ice, h is the ice thickness and d is the width of the structure.

The response of ice depends on the behaviour of the structure and the ice loading. The deformation of ice (Fig. 13) can be divided into three

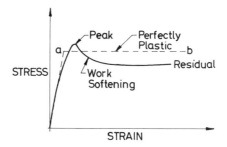

FIG. 13. Deformation of ice.

parts: elastic deformation, elastic lag and viscous deformation (creep). The loading is followed first by an instantaneous elastic deformation, which is recovered when the sample is unloaded. This is followed by a transient creep, which also includes the elastic lag; the rest is permanent viscous deformation. Elastic lag needs a certain time to be recovered. Such behaviour can be described by a rheological model similar to a spring, representing the elastic deformation, with a member representing the permanent viscous deformation and a special unit representing the elastic lag.

The magnitude of the *thermal ice pressure* in an ice cover depends on the rate of change of temperature in the ice, the coefficient of thermal expansion, the rheology of ice and the restriction on the shores. The process of thermal ice pressure depends on the type of the cracks of the ice; dry, narrow, wet or wide cracks can be found on the ice sheet.

When the ice cover is contracted due to low temperature it cracks till it becomes free from tension. When the ice cover expands due to increasing temperature there is complete restriction from the shores. Often the ice moves up on beaches or on gently sloping shores. The maximum pressure may be limited also by buckling, or wide cracks. In the analysis of thermal ice pressure elastic buckling is considered, and a linear rise of temperature (sometimes sinusoidal rise) is assumed.

For practical calculations the method of the latest USSR norm (USSR-SN-T 6/66) is suggested, which includes a wind speed function for the thermal transfer.[60]

The level of maximum pressure depends on a special combination of maximum ice thickness and change of weather (in particular temperature rise). Bergdahl[12] suggested the calculation of the recurrence of extreme pressure from time series of the calculated ice pressure over a recorded period. Starosolszky[54] suggested selecting the days of maximum ice thickness and the days of maximum temperature rise from the recorded data and time series of the calculated values of simulated ice pressures. The distribution functions of the simulated time series may enable the user to extrapolate the ice pressures of different occurrence. It has been concluded by several authors that the measured maximum thermal ice pressure can be in the range of 50–400 kN/m.

Wind and water flow drag on ice cover can be calculated by

$$\tau = C_{\tau 1}\, \rho_a\, U(Z)^2, \quad \tau = C_{\tau 2}\, \rho_w\, V(Z), \text{ respectively,} \tag{41}$$

where $U(Z)$ and $V(Z)$ are wind and flow velocity at a certain distance from the surface.

For a wind speed measurement at 10 m elevation $C_{\tau 1} = 2 \times 10^{-3}$. From calculations it was concluded, that in the case of 100 mm ice thickness for crushing to occur in a wind velocity of 33 m/s a fetch of about 10 km is necessary. The underside of an ice cover is usually rougher than its surface, and the boundary layer is thinner in water than in air. Michel[36] observed $C_{\tau 2} = 5 \times 10^{-3}$ for river ice referring to 0·5 m water depth under ice cover.

In the last decade formulae for the computation of *ice pressure on vertical and inclined structures* have been derived using the theories of elasticity and plasticity.[17] The most considerable contributions using the limit theorem were made by Croasdale *et al.,*[19] Michel,[36] Ralston,[44] Mellor[34] and Ashton.[5] However, for practical application empirical formulae are still suggested; e.g. Korzhavin[28] and USSR-SN-T 6/66 Code

$$F_h = m\,Abh\,\sigma_c \qquad (42)$$

where the shape coefficient (m) for wedge 45° is 0·54 and for a flat 180° is 1·0. A is a regional climatic coefficient for spring break-up $0.75 < A < 2.25$, and for winter break-up $2 < A$. The crushing strength σ_c in winter is $0.75\ \text{N/m}^2$ and for spring time $0.45\ \text{N/m}^2$.

The Canadian Bridge Code[16] gives the formula

$$F_h = \sigma_c bh \qquad (43)$$

where the ice strength $0.69\ \text{N/m}^2 < \sigma_c < 2.76\ \text{N/m}^2$. In the equation h is the design ice thickness and b is the width of the structure where ice is impacted.

On sloping structures local crushing occurs on the underside of the ice sheet. A normal interaction force and tangential frictional force are generated. For approximate, quick calculations the following formula is suggested

$$F = K\sigma_0\,bln \qquad (44)$$

where K is a function of mechanical properties of ice and geometrical properties of structure; at slender structures (piles) for $b/h = 0.5$, $K = 3$, and for $b/h > 10$, $K = 1.0$.

At inclined planes K should be taken from Fig. 14 where

$$f = \frac{1 - \mu\,\tan\beta}{\mu + \tan\beta} \qquad (45)$$

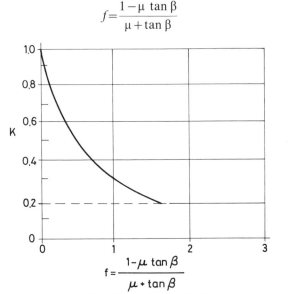

FIG. 14. K coefficient for inclined plates.

where β is the slope angle and μ is the slope friction. The smallest value for K is 0·2.

At inclined wedges the ice force should be reduced to 10–30% of the force on a vertical pile.

If the ice floe is too small or has low velocity, the kinetic energy is small and flow is arrested before full penetration is reached. In this case the force exerted by ice can be calculated from

$$F = V \cdot h \sqrt{2\rho_i \sigma_c A \tan \alpha} \qquad (46)$$

where

$$A < \frac{\sigma_c h^2}{2\rho_i V^2 \tan \alpha} \qquad (47)$$

(A is the area of the flow and V its velocity, ρ_i is the ice density and 2α the wedge angle).

Sörensen[50] made a detailed experimental and theoretical study on interaction between floating ice sheets and sloping structures. He gave formulae for sloping planes with compression or bending failure and for sloping pier structures with dynamic bending failure.

Ice sheet impinging on a vertical structure can be studied by using the differential equation describing the buckling of the beam resting on elastic foundations and subjected to an axial compressive force. Floating ice may *freeze* to piers, piles and walls. When the water level changes the ice cover tends to rise or fall. The fixed structure will, thus, be loaded by the hanging ice cover. Analysis of the vertical forces on a cylinder was performed by Kerr.[26]

The force due to frozen ice mass can be calculated from the equation

$$P = 0 \cdot 2 B \frac{\Delta H}{\Delta t} t_1 \sqrt[4]{\frac{h_i^3}{\phi}} \text{ [MN]} \qquad (48)$$

where B is the length of the structure affected by ice, $\Delta H / \Delta t$ is the rate of the water level change in m/h, t_1 is the period of the change to be considered in hours and ϕ is a non-dimensional parameter according to

$$\phi = 1 + \frac{3 \times 10^5}{\mu} [t_1 + 50(1 - e^{0 \cdot 4 t_1})] \qquad (49)$$

where μ is the viscosity of ice in kN.h/m^2 (when $T_i = -20°C$, then $\mu = (3 \cdot 3 - 0 \cdot 28 T_i + 0 \cdot 083 T_i^2) \times 10^5$) and T_i is the temperature of ice.

The equation can be used up to the change of water level ΔH equal to the ice thickness h_i.

A single pile can be loaded by a force due to frozen ice mass approximately on the basis of the tensile strength limit of the surrounding ice cover

$$P = k_s \sigma_t h_i^2 \, [\text{kN}] \tag{50}$$

where the parameter k_s is given as a function of d/h with d the diameter of the pile.

d/h	0·1	0·2	0·5	1·0	2·0	5	10
k_s	0·16	0·18	0·22	0·26	0·31	0·43	0·63

The momentum (M), due to water level variations, of the ice cover frozen to the shore or the bank lining can be calculated from

$$M = \sigma_t \frac{h^2 \times w}{6} \tag{51}$$

and the reaction force (F_M)

$$F_M = \frac{1 \cdot 37 \, M}{\sqrt[4]{\dfrac{EI}{w \rho g}}} \tag{52}$$

where w is the width of the frozen ice floe, E is the modulus of elasticity, I is the moment of inertia of the ice cross-section.

Interactions between drifting ice and a fixed structure may cause *vibrations*. The starting point of the vibration analysis is an appropriate oscillator mode. Määttänen[32] suggested a method for resonant vibrations of flexible structures which describes the periodic forcing due to ice floe impact.

In many cases the minimum ice thickness required to carry a particular load is of vital interest. It should be noted that *load* is supported by the water not by the ice sheet. To distribute the load the ice sheet must deform and the exact calculations are, therefore, based on the theory of an elastic plate on an elastic foundation. The so-called characteristic length (l) of an ice sheet was found by Gold[22] for short-term loads as

$$l = 16 \, h^{3/4} \tag{53}$$

where the ice thickness (h) is measured in metres.

For an infinite ice sheet the maximum deflection is

$$w_{max} = \frac{P}{8 \rho g l^2} \tag{54}$$

and stresses can be neglected for the range over the distance $5l$. Gold[22] concluded that sound ice cover should not fail under a slowly moving load, if $P < 1 \cdot 4 \, h^2 \, MN$.

As a load moves across an ice sheet the deflection bowl moves with it. The deflection bowl generates water waves and if their celerity is the same as the velocity of the vehicle a resonance phenomenon may occur and deflections and stresses are amplified.

Long term loads may generate plastic strain or creep; the critical stress depends on the duration of loading. The failure depends on the work done by the applied load. Beltaos[7] gave an inter-relationship between critical work (W_1) and ice thickness (h) in metres for ice sheets of good quality.

$$W_1 = 300 \, h^{5/2} \, kN.m \tag{55}$$

9 ICE CONTROL

The prevention of ice damage, in particular to river structures,[49] is an important role of river engineering.

Frazil ice can clog the water intakes during the period of ice formation, it can accumulate somewhere on the riverbed or under an ice jam where velocity is slow. Dangerous (active) frazil formation is generally of short duration, so that frazil clogging occurs for a few hours at the beginning of the winter, when strong cooling coincides with cold winds generating high waves.

Frazil formation is particularly dangerous for the safe operation of river structures. One basic solution is to create a reservoir to accumulate frazil slush before the deposits get close to the intake or to divert all ice from the intake to allow only clear water to enter.

Frazil particles adhere strongly to metals in supercooled water $(T_w < 0°C)$. Inactive frazil forms deposit in separated, low velocity flow areas. Frazil slush may easily pass through intakes where openings are large enough. Heating is not effective against inactive frazil, but mechanical cleaning can be applied when frazil formation is not too heavy. Structures can be protected against active frazil ice by using a protective coating (plastic resins, polyethylene and silicone grease) to prevent adhesion, or by heating the surfaces and trash racks.

Safe *release of ice* needs proper sizes of openings at barrages, dams and bridges. The total width of the openings according to experiences in the USSR should be at least (0·3–0·45) B, where B is the width of the pool upstream of a dam. Each opening should be 15–30 m, but for northern rivers 50 m can be advantageous. For the ice release over a dam a head not less than $1·7 h$ is necessary, where h is the maximum thickness of the ice.

Korzhavin[28] gave the following relation for the minimum total opening size, B_0

$$1 \geqslant \frac{7·3\, F_{H\,max}\, L}{hpv_0^2\, B_0} \tag{56}$$

where L is the length of the ice floe, v_0 is the velocity of the approaching flow, p is the density of ice flow (the ratio of ice covered water surface to the whole river surface) — about 0·6–0·85 — $F_{H\,max}$ is the maximum horizontal force from the crushing of ice floe, $F_{H\,max} = \sigma b_0 h$, σ is the strength of ice characteristic for crushing, and b_0 is the width of a pier. The buckling tensile strength should be chosen as the constant because its value is the lowest among the different strengths.

Special ice skimming walls should also be designed on the same principle.

A special ice control structure is the *ice boom* (Fig. 15) usually applied upstream of structures. Booms can also be used to retain ice cover on lakes away from intakes, or at the border of ice free channels kept open by ice-breakers. The largest floating ice retention boom was applied on Lake Erie at the outflow of the Niagara River in order to retain the ice cover in the Lake and to minimise frazil ice formation. The floating boom yields and submerges if the ice thrust becomes too excessive, and thus the ice can pass over it.

Thermic methods are used to prevent supercooling and frazil ice production, or the freezing of ice cover to the structures. Steam or hot water heating, air bubbling and electrical heating mainly at trash racks have been effectively used. Air bubble systems can only be effective if deeper warmer water layers can be found in the vicinity which can be forced to rise by the rising bubbles thus preventing local ice formation. For heating systems to be effective heating must start before the ice forms.

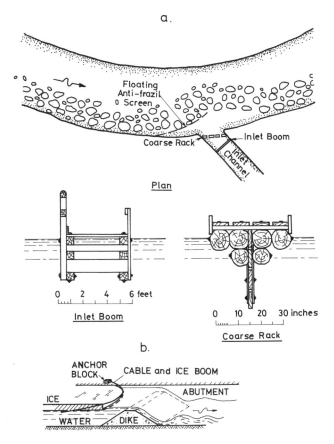

FIG. 15. Ice boom.

Electrical heating of racks, steel sluices and the concrete parts of locks is frequently used. For the power N required for the rack heating Pekhovich[43] found that

$$N = \alpha_1 v^r (T_r - T_w) \qquad (57)$$

where T_r is the temperature desired at the rack, T_w is the water supercooled temperature, r is a coefficient depending on rack form ($r \sim 0.6$–0.8), and α_1 is a parameter depending on the heat transfer coefficient and the conversion units.

Suggestions for selection of the appropriate *de-icing method* are given in Table 2.[2]

TABLE 2
RECOMMENDATIONS FOR SELECTION OF DE-ICING SYSTEMS

Part of the hydraulic structure	Method of protection
Screens	Heating by resistance; coating
	Electric pulse
	Pneumatic
	Induction heating
Gate seals	Physico-chemical (liquid or petroleum jelly)
	Infra-red radiation
Small size movable parts	Induction or infra-red heating
	Liquid or petroleum jellies
	Thermal curtain
Lock mechanisms	Induction or infra-red heating
	Thermal curtain
	Petroleum jellies
Intakes of thermal power stations	Return flow of waste (heated) water
Concrete surfaces	Mobile devices for the infra-red radiation or mechanical fracturing
	Polymer coats

Attempts have been undertaken to *accelerate ice melting* by dusting the ice surface. A dust layer of suitable dark hue increases solar radiation and, in turn, the heat available for ice melting. Successful applications have been reported by using slag or powdered coal, ash, soil and sand.

Mechanical control may consist of ice cutting, use of ice-breaker vessels, ice blasting or aerial bombing.[48]

Ice jam removal can be accelerated by using *ice blasting*. This technique needs suitable explosives, convenient size of rivers and experienced manpower. Explosives are usually selected from those used either by the army or for mining operations. One should, however, consider the different nature and behaviour of ice. A desirable explosive has a high energy release, small susceptibility to shock and flame, is relatively cheap and can be prepacked in a convenient form. The US Army Corps of Engineers have found, for example, ANFO (a mixture of ammonium nitrate and fuel oil) to be an effective explosive for ice blasting.

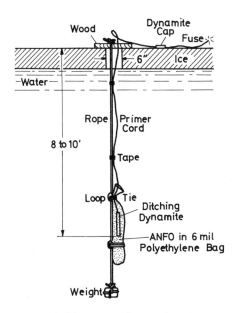

FIG. 16. Placement of explosive charge.

The effectiveness of blasting depends also on the location of the charges. The charges should be properly sized and placed on, in or under the ice jam. The Hungarian Water Services developed different charges for penetrating ice in order to place the blasting charges.[45]

The size of the crater caused by blasting depends on the weight of the explosives, the hole diameter usually being linearly proportional to the cube root of the charge weight. Figure 16 shows the arrangement for the placement of explosive charges and Fig. 17 the suggested location of charges at different sites and under differing conditions.[35]

When using blasting, special care should be taken not to endanger buildings and personnel by shock waves and debris. In remote, unpopulated areas bombing by airplanes can also be used if bombs can be properly located. Bombing or blasting usually starts at the downstream side of the ice jam, where free water can transport ice blocks away. The combined operation of blasting and ice breakers can be particularly effective to start the ice to move.

Icebreaker vessels can be used to keep open water surfaces free of ice, to open navigational waterways, to prevent the formation of jams, and to assist in the moving of ice jams (Fig. 18).[29]

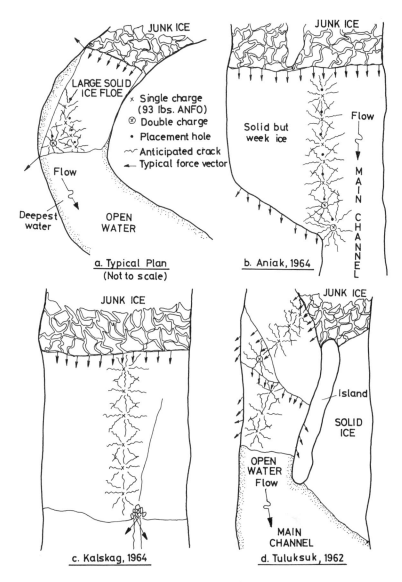

FIG. 17. Ice blasting.

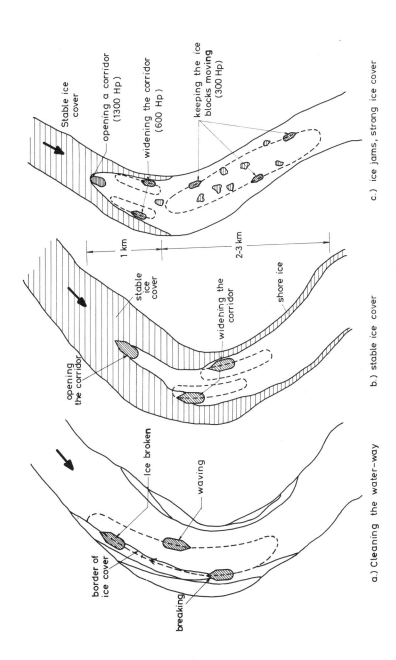

Fig. 18. Ice breakers in operation.

a.) Cleaning the water-way

b.) stable ice cover

c.) ice jams, strong ice cover

Their application is particularly useful in the vicinity of hydraulic structures. In many cases winter operation of dams, barrages, intakes and hydropower stations cannot be ensured without a small icebreaker fleet.

When dismantling ice jams or clearing a waterway, icebreakers work best in groups. Usually, they move upstream in the central part of the jam, cutting out ice that can drift downstream with the current. The breaking of side ice can be carried out by small icebreakers, while the opening of a way needs very powerful vessels. There are different types of icebreakers designed for river operations. Good experiences have been gained in connection with winter navigation on the Saint Lawrence sea water way.

Particular problems of storage reservoirs and downstream sections of hydropower stations are described by Gotlib et al.[23]

10 MODELLING ICE PHENOMENA IN RIVERS

Model experiments related to ice may be divided into two groups, namely those using actual ice in a cooled environment and those performed with ice substitutes. In both cases difficulties are bound to arise in the determination of scales.[40]

An ice laboratory where natural thermal conditions can be simulated needs a cooling system. The recirculation of ice water and ice floes presents special difficulties. For this reason, where the objective is to study ice-run conditions or to design structures for passing ice, artificial ice is used. Floating simulated ice particles can be regarded as suspended sediment, while ice floes floating on the surface as bedload, having a negative submerged density.

Basically the following types of models are used:[40]

ice-run: ice can be replaced on the basis of $\rho_{mi}/\rho_{pi} = 1$ (ρ_{mi} and ρ_{pi} are model and prototype ice densities, respectively);
ice-impact: ice can be modelled also by strain–stress similarity;
thermal processes: cooling should also be modelled.

When the ice cover is studied for stability and jamming, the basic stability criteria should also be modelled.[51] Considering an inter-relationship between relative ice thickness and relative discharge and assuming a stable and an unstable zone, the identity of Bv^2/C^2H^2 must be ensured in the model and prototype. This implies that the scale factors

(λ) are required to meet the condition

$$\frac{\lambda_B \lambda_v^2}{\lambda_C^2 \lambda_H^2} = 1 \tag{58}$$

As from the Chézy eqn

$$\lambda_v = \lambda_C \lambda_R^{1/2} \lambda_y^{1/2} \lambda_x^{-1/2} \tag{59}$$

and

$$\lambda_B = \lambda_x \text{ and } \lambda_H = \lambda_y,$$

where λ_x is the horizontal and λ_y is the vertical scale it follows that

$$\frac{\lambda_R}{\lambda_y} = 1 \tag{60}$$

The condition $\lambda_R = \lambda_y$ is satisfied, only if the condition $\lambda_x = \lambda_y$ is also met, i.e. the model is an undistorted one. Thus where ice jamming and stability of ice cover are to be reproduced, distorted models do not yield quantitatively correct values. Under certain conditions a distortion of not more than 3 can be permitted.

Due to the difference in surface tension between the ice–water and plastic–water interface, when submergence of plastic blocks is concerned, the thickness of the model floes should be adjusted so that their submergence, velocity, and the surface tension effects are properly scaled.

When modelling stresses and the various moduli the derivation of scaling ratios, in particular at ice impact models, needs special considerations. In the case of distorted models the properties of the material used to simulate ice would be rather unusual if complete similarity were to be achieved. Fortunately, in most cases one physical property may be dominant and thus this should be scaled correctly, neglecting the other properties. If, however, both buckling and flexure are equally important it is difficult to design model–ice material.

Various authors pointed out that the strength and elasticity of ice should be reduced by the same scale ratio.[27,40] The Cauchy number (Ca) of the ice should be, thus, the same in the model and the prototype. Atkins[6] introduced an 'ice number' as a new dimensionless group

$$I = \text{Ca}^4 \frac{E_{\text{ice}} L}{R_1}, \text{ where } \text{Ca} = \frac{v}{\sqrt{E_{\text{ice}}/\rho}} \tag{61}$$

and R_1 is the breaking viscosity, that is the resistance to the spreading of cracks.[27]

Lack of attention to Cauchy law falsifies the results of model experiments. Reynolds law can be ignored in ice-breaking experiments if the viscous forces are small compared to the resultant of other resistance components.

Hydraulic modelling is usually a compromise according to the factors involved and the addition of ice and further imposition of thermal factors may cause serious difficulties. A satisfactory degree of similarity can be achieved by considering the following thermodynamic dimensionless numbers: Densimetric Froude, Reynolds, Nusselt (N), Peclet (P), Prandtl and Grashof (Gr). P and Gr are essentially the same for model and prototype, but $N = CRe^n$ and for an undistorted model $\lambda_N = (\lambda_l^{3/2})^n$ assuming that in an ice-hydraulic model the main driving force is gravity and thus the basic similarity criterion is the Froude number.

REFERENCES

1. ACKERMANN, N. L. *et al.* Transportation of ice in rivers. *IAHR International Symposium on Ice*, Quebec, 1981.
2. ALEINIKOV, S. M. *et al.* Protection of hydraulic structures from icing. *IAHR International Symposium on Ice*, Quebec, 1981.
3. ASHTON, G. D. River ice. *Ann. Rev. Fluid Mech.*, **10** (1978).
4. ASHTON, G. D. Suppression of river ice by thermal effluents. CRREL Report 79–30, Hanover, 1979.
5. ASHTON, G. (ed.) IAHR Committee on Ice Problems: River and Lake Ice Engineering. International Association for Hydraulic Research, 1984.
6. ATKINS, A. G. Ice breaking modeling. *J. Ship, Res.*, **19** (1) (1975).
7. BELTAOS, S. Field studies on the response of floating ice sheets to moving loads. National Research Council Canada Technical Memorandum. No. 123, 1978.
8. BELTAOS, S. Ice freeze up and break up in the Lower Thames River, Canada Centre for Inland Waters, Burlington, 1981.
9. BELTAOS, S. River ice jams: theory, case studies and applications. Canada Centre for Inland Waters, Burlington, 1982 and *J. Hydraul. Eng. ASCE*, **109** (10) (1983).
10. BELTAOS, S. Notes on ice hydraulics. Canada Centre for Inland Waters, Burlington, Nov. 1982.
11. BELTAOS, S. Transverse mixing tests in natural streams. *J. Hydraul. Div. ASCE*, **15** (1980) 731.
12. BERGDAHL, L. Thermal ice pressure in lake ice covers. Report Series A2. Dept. of Hydraulics, Chalmers University of Technology, Göteborg, 1978.
13. BILLFALK, L. Ice cover formation and break-up of solid ice covers on rivers. Royal Institute of Technology, Sweden, Stockholm, 1982.

14. BOGOROUSKIĬ, V. V. and GABRILO, V. P. Led (Ice). Gidrometeoizdat, Leningrad, 1980.
15. CALKINS, D. J. and ASHTON, G. D. Arching of fragmented ice covers. *Can. J. Civil Eng.*, 2 (4)(1975).
16. CANADIAN STANDARDS ASSOCIATION Standard S-6. Design of Highway Bridges, 1974.
17. CARSTENS, T. (ed.) Ice forces on structures. State-of-art report, IAHR WGr, Hanover (USA)–Trondheim (Norway), 1980.
18. CHAUDHRY, M. H., CASS, D. E. and EDINGER, J. E. Modelling of unsteady flow water temperatures. *J. Hydraul. Eng. ASCE*, 109 (5) (1983).
19. CROASDALE, K. R. and MARCELLUS, R. W. Ice forces on large marine structures. *IAHR International Symposium on Ice*, Quebec, 1981.
20. DEVIK, O. Über Wasserstandsänderung eines Flusses bei Eisbildung auf Götaälv angewandt. VI. Baltische Hydrologische Konferenz, Bericht 36 Berlin, 1938.
21. GINSBURG, B. M. Methods of forecasts on ice phenomena on rivers and reservoirs. WMO Interim report, Geneva, 1979.
22. GOLD, L. W. Use of ice covers for transportation, *Can. Geotech. J.* 8 (1971).
23. GOTLIB, YA L., DONCHENKO, R. V., PEKHOVICH, A. J. and SOKOLOV, I. N. *Led v vodohranilishchah i nizhnih befah.* Gidrometeoïzdat, Leningrad, 1983.
24. HIRLING, GY. and KÁROLYI, Z. Ice forecasting on the Danube and Tisza Rivers. (in Hungarian.) VIZDOK, Budapest, 1980.
25. KENNEDY, J. F. Ice jam mechanics. *Proc. Third Int. Symp. on Ice.* Hanover, 1975.
26. KERR, A. D. Ice forces on structures due to change of the water level. *Proc. Third Int. Symp. on Ice.* Hanover, 1975.
27. KOBUS, H. (ed.) Hydraulic Modelling. German Association for Water Resources and Land Improvement in cooperation with IAHR, Bulletin 7. (14.1. Ice models by J. Schwarz), Verlag Paul Parey, Hamburg, 1980.
28. KORZHAVIN, K. N. Vozdeystvie lda na inzhenernue sooruzheniya, Moscow, 1962.
29. KOVÁCS, D. et al. Results of protection against icy floods in Hungary, (In Hungarian.) Hidrológiai Közlöny, 1980/3.
30. LASZLÓFFY, W. Ice regime of rivers with particular reference to the Danube. (In Hungarian.) Vizügyi Közlemények, 1934/4.
31. LAU, Y. L. Velocity distributions under floating ice covers. *Can. J. Civil Eng.* 9 (1) (1982).
32. MÄÄTTÄNEN, M. Ice forces and vibrational behaviour of bottom founded steel lighthouses. *Proc. Third. Int. Symp. on Ice*, Hanover, 1975.
33. MATOUSEK, V. A mathematical model of the discharge of frazil in rivers. *IAHR Int. Symp. on Ice*, Quebec, 1981.
34. MELLOR, R. Mechanical Properties of ice. *Proc. IUTAM Symp. Physics and Mechanics of Ice.* Copenhagen, 1980.
35. MICHEL, B. Winter regime of rivers and lakes. Corps of Engineers, Hanover, New Hampshire, 1971.
36. MICHEL, B. Ice mechanics. Les Presses de l'Université Laval. Québec, 1978.
37. MÜLLER, A. Frazil ice formation in turbulent flow. Iowa Institute of Hydraulic Research, Report No 214, Iowa, 1978.

38. NEIL, C. R. Dynamic ice forces on piers and piles. *Can. J. Civil Eng.* **3** (2) (1976).
39. NEZHIKHOVSKIĬ, R. A. Coefficients of roughness of bottom surface on slushice cover. Soviet Hydrology. Am. Geoph. Union, Washington, 1964.
40. NOVAK, P. and ČÁBELKA, J. *Models in Hydraulic Engineering — Physical Principles and Design Applications*, Pitman, London, 1981.
41. OSTERKAMP, T. E. Frazil ice formation — a review. *J. Hydraul. Div. ASCE*, **104** (HY9) (1978), 1239–55.
42. PARISET, E., HAUSSER, R. and GAGNON, A. Formation of ice covers and ice jams in rivers. *J. Hydraul. Div. ASCE*, **92** (HY6) (1966).
43. PEKHOVICH, A. J. Thermal calculations in prediction of action on hydraulic structures. *IAHR Symposium on Ice*, Leningrad, 1972.
44. RALSTON, T. D. Ice force design considerations for offshore structures. *Fourth POAC Conference*, St John's, Newfoundland, 1977.
45. ROZSNYÓY, P. (ed.) Guidelines for ice control. (In Hungarian.) VIZDOK, Budapest, 1981.
46. SCHWARZ, J. *et al.* Standardization of testing methods for ice properties. *J. Hydraul. Res.*, **18** (2) (1980), 153–65.
47. SHULYAKOVSKIĬ, L. G. K modeli processaraskrutyia rek. Trudü Gidrometcentra, Moscow, 1972.
48. SIPOS, B. (ed.) Manual of ice control. (In Hungarian.) VIZDOK, Budapest, 1973.
49. SKLADNEV, M. F. and LYAPIN, V. E. Ice engineering investigations in the USSR — Present state of the art. *Proc. IAHR XX. Congress*. Vol. II, Moscow, 1983.
50. SÖRENSEN, C. Interaction between floating ice sheets and sloping structures. Inst. Hydrodynamics and Hydraulic Eng. Techn. University of Denmark. Series Paper No. 19 Lyngby, 1978.
51. STAROSOLSZKY, Ö. Ice in hydraulic engineering. Institutt for Vassbygging. NTH, Report No 70-1. Trondheim, 1970.
52. STAROSOLSZKY, Ö. The application of heat-transfer relationships to watercourses. *IAHR Symposium on Ice*, Leningrad, 1972.
53. STAROSOLSZKY, Ö. Thermal regime and ice forecasting for fresh-water bodies. *IAHR International Symposium on Ice*, Quebec, 1981.
54. STAROSOLSZKY, Ö., KAMARÁSNÉ SZABÓ, Cs. Analysis of the parameters controlling the design ice thrust in a lake. *Proc. IAHR XX. Congress*, Vol. II. Moscow, 1983.
55. STAROSOLSZKY, Ö. (ed.) IAHR: Multilingual Ice Terminology, VITUKI, Budapest, 1977 and 1980.
56. TATINCLAUX, J. C. and GOGUS, M. Stability of floes below a floating cover. *IAHR International Symposium on Ice*, Quebec, 1981.
57. TSANG, G. Resistance of Beauharnois canal in winter. *J. Hydraul. Div. ASCE*, **108** (2) (1982), 167–86.
58. VMS 251/7–81: Primary data processing of hydrological measurements (in Hungarian). *Data on Ice Phenomena*, Budapest, 1981.
59. VMS 231/7–78: Hydrological measurements (in Hungarian). *Ice Phenomena*, Budapest, 1978.
60. VNIIG Rukovodstvo po opredeleniyu nagruzok i vozdeystoiyna gidro-

tehnicheskie sooruzheniya volnovih, ledovih i of sudov. P-58–76 Leningrad, 1977.
61. WMO: Hydrological forecasting practices. Operational Hydrology Report No. 6. WMO No 425, Geneva, 1975.
62. WMO: Guide to Hydrological Practices. Volume I. Data acquisition and processing, WMO No. 168, Geneva, 1981.

Chapter 6

INLAND WATERWAYS

J. ČÁBELKA

Czechoslovak Academy of Sciences, Prague, Czechoslovakia

and

P. GABRIEL

Technical University of Prague, Prague, Czechoslovakia

1 RENAISSANCE OF INLAND WATERWAYS AND NAVIGATION

Inland navigation is the oldest type of continental transport. In the course of its historical development over a number of centuries it has passed through prosperity, stagnation and depression. At present, however, it forms an important part of the transport infrastructure of the majority of industrially developed, as well as developing, countries.

Modern waterway development was brought about by industrialisation. In the course of the 18th and 19th centuries a relatively dense network of navigable rivers, interconnected by artificial canals, was established in England and was subsequently developed in France, Belgium and the Netherlands. These waterways connected the principal centres of production and consumption. In the course of their development a number of navigation structures (locks, lifts, aqueducts and tunnels) were constructed, which were of remarkable design for their time. At that time inland navigation was the transport mode with the largest capacity. Many waterways built in that period have been subsequently modernised and are still in use.

The second stage of waterway development dates from the beginning of our century, already in the railway era.

Thanks to the introduction of high capacity steel boats, steam traction and mechanisation of reloading in ports, water transport gradually developed into a modern transport branch with a high productivity. At that time a number of waterways were rendered navigable in Europe and a number of navigation canals, capable of accommodating ships of up to 1000 t built. The density of the waterway network could, however, no longer compete with the unified railway network and the rapidly developing motorway network. Nevertheless, it became a highly effective means of transport, especially of materials transported in bulk.

In recent decades the importance of inland navigation as an integral component of a transport system of industrially developed countries has steadily increased.[4,18,25,27,29] In a number of European countries further stretches of rivers are being made navigable, older waterways modernised to conform to uniform larger specifications and new canals or multipurpose canal systems being built. This new development of inland waterways is often called the renaissance of waterways and inland navigation.

The advantages of transport by inland navigation are determined by a number of universally valid factors. The most important are:

— low energy requirements, navigation transport has less than 80% of specific energy consumption requirements of rail transport and less than 30% of road transport;

— low labour requirements and consequent high productivity of labour per unit of transport output;

— the lowest material requirements per unit of transport volume; the values for railway and highway transport being two and four times higher, respectively;

— the lowest interference with the environment, navigation transport is associated with the lowest noise generation, the lowest exhaust fume generation per tonne of transported material and the lowest accident incidence in comparison with other modes of transport. In the case of navigable rivers, the number of these advantages is increased by negligible land requirements; on the contrary, water transport increases the value of the land adjacent to waterways;

— practical impossibility (or great difficulties) of replacement by other modes of transport for the conveyance of cargo of large bulk and dimensions, such as metallurgical products, principal components of nuclear power plants, etc.

2 INTEGRATION OF EUROPEAN WATERWAY NETWORK

The fundamental prerequisite for making full use of all technical, operational and economic advantages of water transport is not only an adequate integration of newly built and reconstructed waterways into the uniform transport network of every country, but also their mutual interconnection and a gradual generation of an international waterway network on a European or eventually world-wide scale.

The contemporary European waterways, which are of differing technical standards and not of entirely identical parameters in the individual countries, form approximately four self-contained groups (Fig. 1):

— French waterways;
— Central European waterways between the Rhine in the west and the Vistula in the east, consisting of navigable rivers flowing to the north and the canals interconnecting them in the east–west direction;
— South European waterways, comprising the Danube, the navigable sections of its tributaries and accompanying canals;
— Soviet waterways, consisting of the navigable rivers in the European part of the Soviet Union, and the Volga–Moskva canal, Volga–Don canal, Volga–Baltic Sea canal, Baltic Sea–White Sea canal, etc.

Apart from that there is a large number of isolated waterways in the boundary regions of Europe, connected with the sea, especially in Italy, Portugal, Spain, England, Sweden and Finland.

From the four above mentioned European waterway groups satisfactory navigation interconnection exists only between the French and the Central European waterways. The generation of an integrated network of European waterways necessitates primarily the link between the South and Central European waterways by means of two canal systems: the Rhine–Main–Danube canal, which is nearing completion, and the Danube–Oder–Labe (Elbe) canal, whose phased construction has already started. Of considerable importance would be also the connection of Soviet waterways by means of the planned Oder–Vistula–Bug–Dniepr canal.

In the endeavour to ensure gradual unification of European waterways

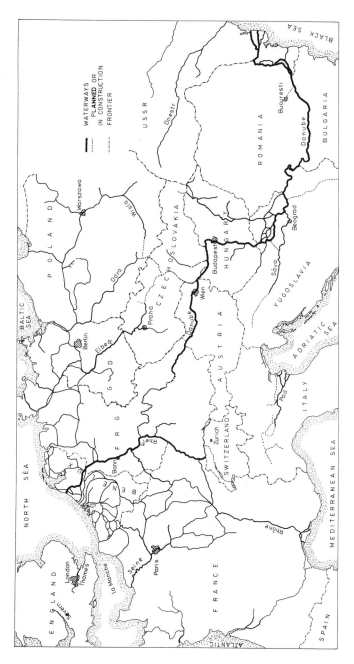

FIG. 1. European waterways.

and the standardisation of their parameters, the Economic Commission for Europe (ECE) adopted, in 1961, a uniform classification of inland waterways. This classification is based on the dimensions and the tonnage of traditional standard vessels and classifies the waterways into six classes.[7,25,35]

For every class the necessary parameters of the waterway and its structures were deduced from the parameters of standard vessels, i.e. the depth of water in the fairway of the canal or navigable river, the widths of a one-way and two-way fairway, the minimum radius of curvature of the fairway axis, the widening of the fairway in curves, minimum clearances, the clear navigation spans of bridges, useful dimensions of locks, etc.[2,3]

Simultaneously with the adoption of the above classification it was agreed that the European waterways of international importance would be so built or reconstructed as to ensure that their specifications would correspond with the requirements of at least the IVth class and enable continuous passage to vessels of a tonnage between 1350 and 1500 t. Classes I to III waterways have a regional character.

Big European rivers, such as the Rhine, the Danube and others, are being made navigable at present mostly to the specifications of the Vth class (1500–3000 t). The VIth class includes primarily the Soviet navigable rivers and canals or the lowland stretches of the biggest European rivers. Similar or even larger dimensions are found in navigable rivers of other continents, notably in North and South America.

The above mentioned international classification of inland waterways was adopted in the period when — with the exception of motorboats — towing by tug boats was used almost exclusively. In the past two decades, however, this traditional navigation technology was almost completely replaced by the economically and operationally more advantageous pushing of the barges by push-boats.[5,20] In this case the barges are grouped and firmly fixed next or behind each other so as to form a continuous body pushed and controlled by a push-boat (Fig. 2). In plan the barges and the push-boat have a rectangular form and a driving bow and stern.

The speedy development of the push-boat navigation technique has been determined above all by the following positive factors:[18]

— the resistance of the pushed barge train is lower than that of the towed barge train of the same tonnage; the pushed train can thus

FIG. 2. Push-train.

either increase the navigation velocity or reduce fuel consumption
by as much as 30%;
— the control and manoeuvrability of the whole train and its
  navigation safety are improved;
— the overall freight transport period by pushed trains is shorter;
— minimum number of crew, concentrated on the push-boat only,
  leading to better organisation of labour and better working and
  living conditions of the crew;
— the investment costs of construction of push-barges are about
  40% lower than those of comparable tug-barges because of their
  simple shape and minimum equipment;
— the operating costs of freight transport are 20–25% lower than
  those for the towing technique.

The longer push-trains can navigate through waterways and their locks without having to be disconnected the greater are the advantages of push-boat technology.

The introduction of the progressive push-boat technology resulted logically in repeated proposals for amendment of the approved waterway classification in order that it may reflect better the mode of transport used.

Originally the Europe I pushed barge was considered, with the dimensions of $70.0 \times 9.5 \times 2.5$ m and a maximum tonnage of 1240 t for class IV waterways. Since it did not fully utilise the dimensions of existing locks, a more economic Europe II type was introduced with the dimensions of $76.5 \times 11.4 \times 2.5$ m and a tonnage of 1660 t. This standard barge is built also for Class V waterways (draft 3.5 m, tonnage 2520 t) and Class VI waterways (draft 4.0 m and tonnage 2940 t). Therefore, Seiler[35] recommended that the type Europe II barge be used as standard barge for waterways of international importance, together with the recommendation that Class IV to Class VI waterways should be designated according to the number and arrangement of these barges in pushed trains (Fig. 3). For Class IV waterways he assumes the use of

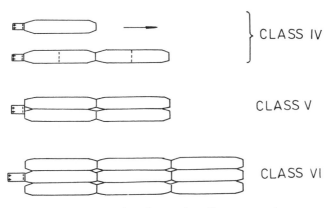

FIG. 3. Standard push-trains used on European waterways.

$1 + 1$ pushed trains and the necessary lock dimensions of (95–105) $\times 12 \times 3.5$ m, or $1 + 2$ pushed trains of the tonnage of 3320 t and the corresponding lock dimensions of $190 \times 12 \times 3.5$ m. For Class V waterways he suggests a $1 + 4$ pushed train as standard, which has a tonnage of 10 080 t for the draft of 3.5 m and the corresponding lock dimensions of $190 \times 24 \times 4.5$ m. For Class VI waterways he recommends a $1 + 9$ pushed train as standard, which has a tonnage of 26 460 t for the draft of 4·0 m and requires the construction of locks of the dimensions $(260–300) \times 36$ m.

More wide ranging changes are contained in the proposal of waterway classification prepared in Czechoslovakia,[25] which is based on the endeavour to maximally homogenise the European navigation network and to achieve its operational integrity. This proposal differentiates two waterway categories:

— waterways of international importance, whose fundamental specifications are determined by the type I pushed barge with the dimensions of $82.0 \times 11.4 \times (2.2 - 4.0)$ m;
— waterways of local importance, whose fundamental specifications are determined by the type L pushed barge with the dimensions of $41.0 \times 5.7 \times (1.8 - 3.0)$ m.

The pushed barges and their push-boats can be arranged next to one another or in series, in accordance with the character of the waterway. The possible composition of pushed trains is illustrated in Fig. 4. On their dimensions all the waterway parameters and the dimensions of their locks are based.

The afore-mentioned proposals for the revision of waterways classification differentiate more sharply the waterway classes, defining more accurately their fundamental parameters, and are strictly based on the progressive push-boat technology of navigation. However, no international agreement on this amendment of waterway classification has been concluded so far, even though it is urgently required.

With the development of international trade, inter-continental freight transport acquires an ever increasing importance on the principal European waterways.[21] After an extraordinarily speedy development of container transport and the establishment of the container transport system with an internationally unified ISO container series the very progressive method of international transport by means of floating containers, called lighters, has begun to assert itself. This system is intended above all for the transport of goods, whose consigner and recipient are situated on navigable waterways of different continents. Lighters, grouped on inland waterways into pushed trains, are transported across the sea in special marine carriers provided with loading and unloading equipment of their own. Apart from all the advantages of container transport the system does not require any

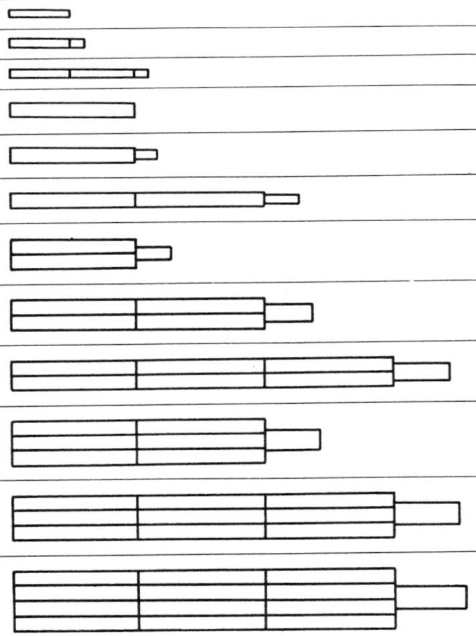

	CLASS	PUSH-TOW UNIT	PUSH-TOW UNIT DIMENSIONS (m)		LOCK CHAMBER DIMENSIONS (m)	
			LENGTH	WIDTH	LENGTH	WIDTH
LOCAL WATERWAYS	L 10		41	5,7	45	6
	L 11		41,0+9,0	5,7	55	6
	L 12		2×41,0+9,5	5,7	95	6
INTERNATIONAL WATERWAYS	I 10		82,0	11,4	85	12
	I 11		82,0+15,0	11,4	100	12
	I 12		2×82,0+23,0	11,4	190	12
	I 21		82,0+23,0	2×11,4	110	24
	I 22		2×82,0+32,0	2×11,4	200	24
	I 23		3×82,0+36,0	2×11,4	285	24
	I 32		2×82,0+36,0	3×11,4	205	36
	I 33		3×82,0+42,0	3×11,4	295	36
	I 43		3×82,0+46,0	4×11,4	300	48

FIG. 4. Proposal for the new waterway classification.

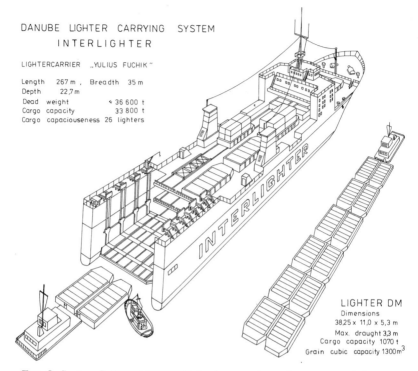

DANUBE LIGHTER CARRYING SYSTEM
INTERLIGHTER

LIGHTERCARRIER „YULIUS FUCHIK"

Length   267 m ,   Breadth   35 m
Depth   22,7 m
Dead weight   ⁓ 36 600 t
Cargo capacity   33 800 t
Cargo capaciousness 26 lighters

LIGHTER DM
Dimensions
38,25 x 11,0 x 5,3 m
Max. draught 3,3 m
Cargo capacity 1070 t
Grain cubic capacity 1300m^3

FIG. 5. System INTERLIGHTER for intercontinental transport of lighters.

harbour structures, so that the marine carriers can re-load the lighters
outside the harbour area. While a conventional sea-going ship can load
and unload in an hour some 100 t of freight, a pallet ship about 350 t and
a container ship about 600 t, a marine lighter carrier can handle 1500–
2000 t of freight per hour.

At present there are four systems of this transport: the BACAT system
with lighters of 140 t, suitable for navigation on British small waterways,
the LASH system with lighters of 375 t, the SEA BEE system with
lighters of 850 t, and the INTERLIGHTER system with lighters of up to
1100 t (Fig. 5) used by the Danubian states.

All systems are characterised by three fundamental components: big
sea-going carrier of floating containers — lighters; lighters, i.e. inland
waterway barges for the transport of package or bulk freight; and special
mechanisation equipment for loading and unloading of lighters, their
placing on the carrier and safe fastening.

The sea-going carriers are mostly designed to accommodate in their hold not only lighters, but also the ISO series standard containers.

3 MULTIPURPOSE UTILISATION OF WATERWAYS

The principal characteristic feature of inland waterways, particularly the newly designed and built waterways, is their multipurpose utilisation. Waterways fulfil not only their function of high capacity transport routes with low operational costs, but also serve a number of other branches of national economy.

The training of rivers for navigation purposes simultaneously improves also the run-off conditions and the flood protection of the adjoining territory, which ensures its better economic exploitation. The canalisation of the river makes it possible also to solve effectively:

— the utilisation of water power in hydraulic power plants, built next to the navigation locks or lifts;
— off-take of service and cooling water for thermal or nuclear power plants and industrial works;
— off-take of water for irrigation of adjoining agricultural land or drainage of water from drained land;
— waste water disposal from urban and industrial agglomeration and improvement of water quality in the waterway;
— new possibilities of recreation for the population and improvement of the environment.

At present, practically all waterways are being designed, built and utilised integrally with the endeavour to utilise optimally their water resources. The qualitatively new approach to the solution of waterway problems applies most markedly to the design and construction of canals and canal systems which gradually interconnect the navigable rivers into an integrated waterway network, as is the case of the Rhine–Main–Danube canal system (Fig. 1) and the Danube–Oder–Elbe canal system. The Danube–Oder–Elbe canal (Fig. 6), especially, is being designed as a multipurpose transport and water system, intended for the conveyance of the Danube water to the water-poor regions in the river basins of the Morava, the Oder and the Elbe. It is even expected that the water resources function of this system may gradually prevail over the transport function.

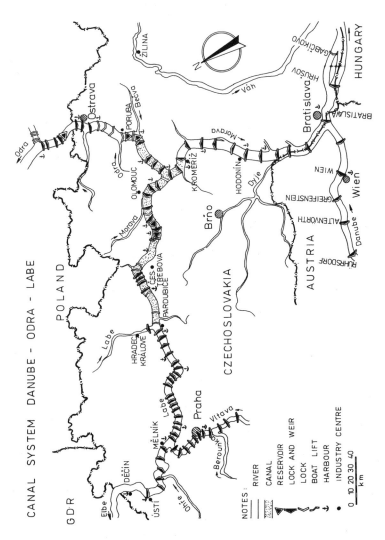

FIG. 6. Canal connection of the rivers Danube–Odra–Labe.

The power generating industry is the most frequent co-user of canalised rivers. In the places of head concentration the construction of weirs, dams and locks is usually accompanied by the construction of hydroelectric power plants, operating either continuously, or as peak-load stations and mostly influencing negatively the navigation on the river. Above all, the peak-load operations produce an unsteady flow regime in the reservoirs, with relatively fast changes of water level and flow velocities. Even more marked changes of these specifications are produced if the power plant participates in the frequency regulation of a power system.[14] However, the most unfavourable effect on navigation is produced by surge waves formed at sudden failure of the power plant or in the case of a very fast rise to its full capacity.

The unfavourable effect of power plant operation on navigation in general must, in the majority of cases, be reduced by suitably technical measures applied as close as possible to the place of its origin. According to this principle the following technical measures may be considered.[19]

(a) In the electrical part of the hydroelectric power plant — by switching the generator outlets to water resistance.

(b) In the mechanical part of the plant — by disconnecting the linkage between guide and runner vanes of the Kaplan turbines or turbines of analogous type. In this case the output of the turbine drops to a minimum, but the discharge hardly changes. The turbine is then gradually stopped without producing surge waves in the adjoining reservoirs. This measure has been used on the Aschach and the Jochenstein schemes on the Danube for example.

A similar effect can be achieved if the turbine spiral casings are directly connected to short auxiliary outlets provided with gates. The gate control is interlocked with the turbine regulator so that in case of a sudden turbine failure the auxiliary outlet gates are automatically opened.

(c) In the structural part of the plant — by constructing special auxiliary outlets, designed as by-passes in the turbine blocks or in separate blocks outside of the proper power plant; in both cases the turbine regulators have to be interlocked with the gate/valve control of the auxiliary outlets.

To reduce the unfavourable effect of surge waves on navigations it is not necessary to design the auxiliary outlets for the same capacity as that of the turbines. However, in general, flow under pressure of excess water is to be preferred to overflow which is not very effective.

In the case of river power plants situated next to weirs it is possible to reduce the unfavourable effect of surge waves by adequate operation of the weir gates.

(d) In the civil engineering part of the power development — by a suitable layout, e.g. by the widening of the head/tail races, by the separation of the navigation channel from the power plant, by a more suitable alignment of dykes and the navigation fairway, etc.

The resulting effect, i.e. the required reduction of the unfavourable effect of the surge wave on barges and the navigation, can be achieved by a combination of two or more above mentioned measures. However, none of them is capable of eliminating this effect completely.

The design of the Gabčíkovo scheme on the Danube[12,19] which was based on scale and mathematical modelling of the flow regime represents a typical example of the solution of mutual interference of navigation and power generation. This scheme consists of a reservoir from which water is passed through a canal to the power station and locks. The upstream canal is about 18 km long and the downstream canal about 7 km long. The maximum power plant output is 700 MW and its total capacity $Q = 4800 \text{ m}^3/\text{s}$.

After a detailed analysis and experiments on existing schemes of a similar type, attention was directed to the investigation of three measures for the reduction of surge waves effects: adjustment of the layout; design of auxiliary outlets of a suitable type and capacity; and disconnecting the linkage between the guide and runner vanes of the turbines.

In the study of the optimum layout 12 variations of the design have been investigated differing in the size and shape of the upstream canal and the location of the individual parts of the structure. The resulting layout differs considerably from the original design (Fig. 7) and is characterised by a considerable width of the power plant fore-bay up to the entrance to the upper approach basin of the locks. It represents an optimum solution not only for power generation but also for navigation.

The necessary capacity of outlets, the effect of turbine vane linkage disconnection and their joint effect on the reduction of surge wave parameters was investigated on a hydraulic model scale 1:70.

If a complete power plant breakdown occurs reducing Q from 4800 to 0 m³/s a positive surge wave with a maximum height of about 80 cm occurs in the upstream canal and a negative wave 125 cm high in the outlet downstream canal. Auxiliary outlets with a capacity of $Q_J = 1600 \text{ m}^3/\text{s}$ and fast opening in time $t_j = 10 \text{ s}$ reduce these waves by about one-third; greater outlet capacity was found to be ineffective. Still more striking was the effect of disconnecting the turbine vane linkage. In

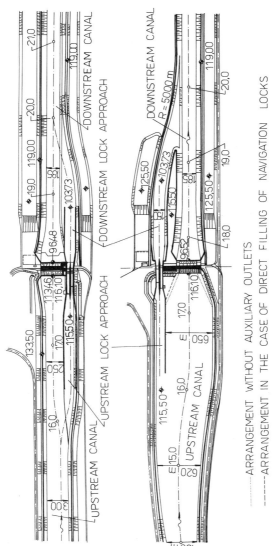

FIG. 7. Investigation of an optimum layout of the Gabčíkovo scheme on the Danube, Czechoslovakia. Above, initial design; below, final design.

this case the wave heights in the inlet and outlet canals were only about 20–30 cm. The results of the experiments have shown that each of the two investigated measures is sufficient in itself to reduce the unfavourable effect of power plant breakdown to a permissible magnitude. This was confirmed also by the last experiments in which the simultaneous effect of both types of measures was investigated. However, bearing in mind the importance of the international navigation on the Danube, it was decided on safety grounds to use both measures.

The optimum control of cascades for safe and continuous navigation on canalised rivers, mainly used for navigation and power generation purposes, e.g. the Rhône in France, the Labe in Czechoslovakia, etc., is usually solved by mathematical modelling combined with field measurements.[16,17]

In the case of the Labe cascade (Fig. 6) consisting of 25 'steps' — weirs and power plants — two methods of control were investigated:[15,18] local automatic control of all weirs and central control system for the whole cascade.

The originally considered local automatic control of all weirs of the cascade assumed that by maintaining a constant water level above each lock and weir the necessary navigation depths along the whole length of the canalised waterway would be ensured. That being the case, this automated operation would evidently represent the optimal and final solution.

However, research and practical experience have shown that the basic condition of ensuring minimum navigation depths along the canalised waterway has not been met. In the period of low discharges the amplitudes of waves, often generated by power plant operations in the upper reaches of the canalised waterway, increase during their transformation. This can result in a complete discharge failure through the weir or the power plant and lead to an extreme lowering of the tailwater level which is inadmissible for navigation. It was further shown[16] that fixed movable weir gates have a significant dampening effect and that is is suitable to augment the minimum discharges in the river in case of negative waves by making use of the permissible level variations in the headwater.

The most suitable manner of manipulation is, therefore, one where the power plant simulates the function of fixed weir gates whilst at the same time the discharge is regulated within the range of admissible variations of the headwater levels. This regulation principle can be applied, in turn, also to the discharge regulation on the weirs.

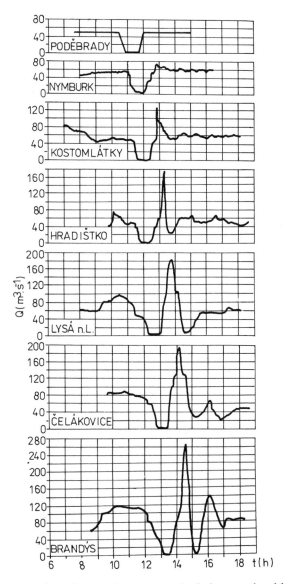

FIG. 8. Transformation of a negative wave on the Labe cascade with a constant level regulation.

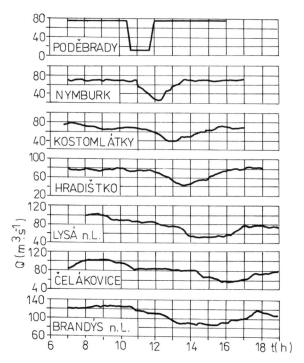

FIG. 9. Transformation of a negative wave on the Labe cascade with discharge regulation.

This system of power plant and weir manipulation ensures effective dampening of discharge waves during their transformation through the cascade. Its efficiency has been verified by a series of experiments on a selected section of the Labe cascade. A comparison of the results of measurements of a negative wave transformation with the original constant level regulation and the newly proposed principle of discharge regulation is given by Figs 8 and 9. However, the complete solution of the problem of ensuring optimal navigation conditions along the whole Labe waterway can be obtained only by a central control system with remote control of all weirs and power plants of the cascade.[15]

To ensure winter navigation on the Labe waterway a number of technical as well as operational measures have been adopted, e.g. the selection of suitable weir gates and upper gates of the locks, the protection of steel structures against ice accumulation by means of compressed air bubbles and spraying with hot water, the discharge of

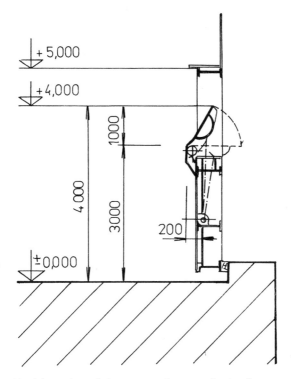

FIG. 10. Adaptation of the upper mitre gate for ice flow transfer.

warm water from the cooling systems of thermal power plants into the river, ice removal from the navigation route by tow-tugs with an icebreaker device, suitable manipulations of the weir gates, etc.[17,34]

Certain problems connected with the maintenance of a free navigation route have remained at the old locks provided with mitre gates. To ensure continuous flow of non-freezing water and ice through these locks simple hydraulically controlled flaps were installed in the upper part of the gate recess (Fig. 10).[18]

The complex utilisation of waterways and the increasing speed and new modes of navigation require also numerous hydraulic studies and considerations, particularly for navigation on canals.[4,18] These include, among others, new methodology of model studies of inland waterways,[33] studies of hydraulic effects of navigation on constrained waterways,[13,31] computation of unsteady flow conditions on navigable waters,[11] etc.

4   DESIGN OF LOCKS

Locks are the most widely used structures intended to overcome the concentrated heads on canalised rivers and on canals. The lock parameters (length L, width B and particularly its head H) together with the selected system of lock filling and emptying, determine the design of the lock as well as the type and function of its gates. In the course of the filling and emptying of the lock a complicated unsteady flow occurs not only in the lock itself but also in its approach basins. This flow exerts considerable forces on the barges; these forces must not exceed a permissible limit and their effect must be eliminated by the tying of the vessels with mooring ropes in the lock or in its approach basin.[7,26]

Experimental and theoretical studies[7,28,30] yield the following conclusions for the selection of the most suitable type of the lock filling and emptying system.

(a) For head locks of small and medium dimensions direct filling and emptying through their gates is most suitable.

(b) For locks of $B = 12$ m and heads of $H > 12$ m indirect filling by means of long culverts situated either in the lateral lock walls or in its bottom and connected with the lock chamber by means of suitable designed outlets is most favourable.

(c) For locks of large dimensions in plan and high heads more complex filling and emptying systems must be used, designed on the basis of hydraulic research so as to ensure regular distribution of water during the filling and emptying along the whole area of its bottom.

(d) Special filling and emptying systems must be provided for the locks with thrift basins intended for high lifts and used, as a rule, on canals with a water shortage.

During the emptying of the locks the vessels are usually affected by smaller forces than during filling because of the greater initial depth of water in the lock.

4.1   Direct Filling of Low and Medium Head Locks of Small and Medium Dimensions in Plan

In the case of low and medium head locks ($H \leqslant 12$ m), of small to medium dimensions in plan ($B = 12$–24 m, $L = 190$–230 m) the locks have the shape of a prismatic trough with vertical walls and a solid bottom, constructed for example of suitable reinforced concrete (RC) pre-cast

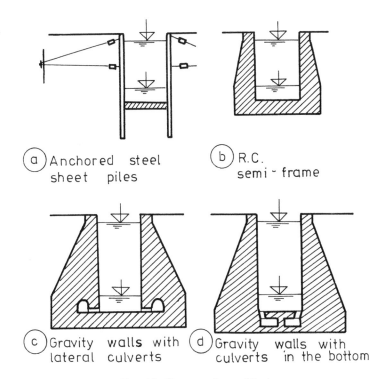

(a) Anchored steel sheet piles

(b) R.C. semi - frame

(c) Gravity walls with lateral culverts

(d) Gravity walls with culverts in the bottom

FIG. 11. Cross-sections of locks.

components or as an *in situ* RC open frame (Fig. 11b), or of anchored steel sheet piles (Fig. 11a) or concreted walls braced at the lock bottom level.[7]

The gates of these locks (Fig. 12) serve as their direct filling mechanism,[23,28] which considerably reduces the costs of the construction as well as the maintenance of the locks. Apart from that it accelerates the speedy passage of the vessels through the locks.

In the Labe–Vltava waterway in Czechoslovakia the direct filling of a number of locks of small and medium dimensions ($B = 12$ m, $L = 85$ m and 190 m) has been ensured by the falling gates of Čábelka type (Figs 13 and 14). The design of the stilling basin below the standard falling gate according to Fig. 13 is suitable for low-head locks of up to $H = 6$ m. The lower edge of the upright falling gate is sufficiently submerged at the beginning of the lock filling below the lowest tailwater level so that the inflowing water is not aerated. In the case of medium head locks

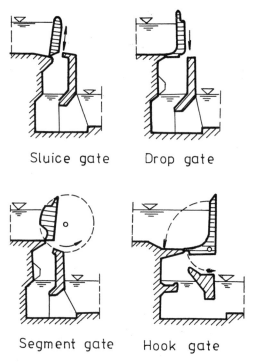

Sluice gate   Drop gate

Segment gate   Hook gate

FIG. 12. Lock gates for direct lock filling.

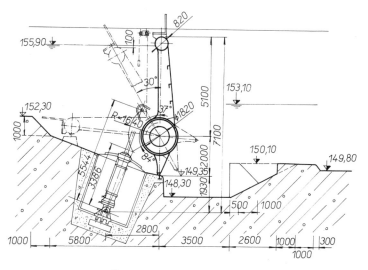

FIG. 13. Rotating gate of Čábelka type for direct filling of modernised locks 22 m wide on the lower Labe.

LONGITUDINAL SECTION

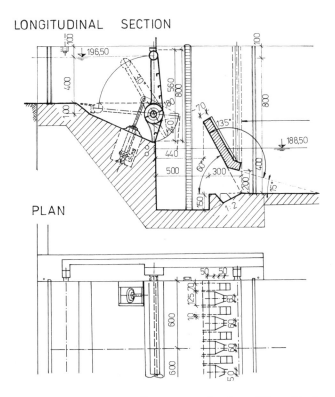

PLAN

FIG. 14. Rotating gate of Čábelka type for direct filling of lock.

$(6 \text{ m} \leqslant H \leqslant 12 \text{ m})$ it is necessary to provide a stilling basin below the gate, separated from the lock chamber by a concrete sill (Fig. 14).

The same principle as that used for the gate 12 m wide was applied to the design of a gate 22 m wide and a smaller height (Fig. 13) for the direct filling of five modernised locks on the Labe. This gate, which is suitable also for the locks of the standard 24 m width, was installed in 1984 by floating it into the first of the modernised locks.

The floating of the gate in the horizontal position is made possible by the two horizontal tubes forming an integral part of its structure, which are hermetically sealed and act as floats. The motion of the falling gate is ensured by a hydraulic motor mounted at the bottom of the upper gate recess in a protective casing with sliding cover.

For direct filling of locks 12 m wide, with an initial water depth of 3·5–4·0 m, an increment inflow below the gate at the beginning of its filling

$dQ/dt = 0.2 \, \text{m}^3/\text{s}^2$ is permissible without the forces in the mooring ropes of the handled ships exceeding their permissible values.[22,36] The rate of rise of the water level varies within the limits of $0.8 \leqslant v_m \leqslant 1.2 \, \text{m/min}$.

Directly filled locks may be emptied either by means of short culverts or directly below the downstream lifting gates or even through the openings in mitre, plate or sliding gates, closed with sluice, butterfly or flap valves.[17]

4.2 Indirect Filling and Emptying of Locks

Indirect filling and emptying of high-head locks ($H \geqslant 12 \, \text{m}$) and minor dimensions in plan ($B = 12 \, \text{m}$) is best achieved by means of long culverts, situated either in the lateral walls (Fig. 11c) or in the bottom (Fig. 11d). In the upper and lower heads they are provided with sluice or segment gates, which must be situated below the lowest possible water level. To reduce outlet losses the overall cross-sectional area of all outlet ports of a culvert must be 1.3–1.5 times as large as the cross-sectional area of the fully opened gate.

The outlet ports of culverts are distributed to ensure, as far as possible, equal outflow along the culvert length and are usually staggered and positioned and shaped to ensure that the water would flow into the lock below the bottom of the vessels in order not to exert bilateral forces on them. For the same reason the outlet ports of long culverts situated in the lock bottom are directed towards its walls (Fig. 11d).

The permissible rate of increase of the inflow of water into the locks filled by a long culvert should not exceed $dQ/dt < 0.6 \, \text{m}^3/\text{s}^2$ at the beginning of the filling. At the same time the mean rate of rise of the water level in these locks varies within the limits of $1.5 \, \text{m/min} \leqslant v_m \leqslant 2.0 \, \text{m/min}$.

The relatively complex filling and emptying system of locks of large dimensions in plan and high heads designed on the basis of model studies must ensure uniformly distributed inflow (outflow) of water into the lock over the whole area of its bottom. Surface flow and translation waves with variable water level inclination which would generate unallowable forces in the mooring ropes of the handled vessels must be eliminated as far as possible. The filling velocity is limited by the possibility of cavitation in the filling system.

This type of complex filling and emptying system can be found in a number of recent large locks on the waterways in the USA, e.g. as shown in Fig. 15. The mean rate of rise of the water level during the filling of these locks varies within the limits of 2–3 m/min.

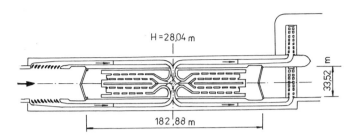

FIG. 15. Filling and emptying system of the lock at Bay Springs on the Tennessee–Tombigbee waterway in the USA.

On the basis of detailed hydraulic research[8] a two-stage filling and emptying system of coupled locks of the Gabčíkovo scheme on the Danube was designed in Czechoslovakia. The locks have $L = 275$ m, $B = 34$ m, $H = 23.6$ m and a minimum depth of water above their bottom level of 4.5 m (Fig. 16). The complex filling and emptying system (although slightly asymmetrical) permits speedy and safe handling of even the biggest push-trains consisting of a push-boat and 3×3 barges. With the asymmetric opening of the filling gates (due to the asymmetry of the filling system) the filling of the single locks lasts less than 16 min and the filling of the coupled locks less than 18 min with a 46% economy of handling water. Safe emptying of single locks lasts less than 14 min. The intake of water for the filling of coupled locks or the outlet for their emptying is placed in the upper and the lower reservoirs of the power plant, i.e. outside their approach basins, lest the push-trains awaiting their handling be affected by translation waves (Fig. 17).

4.3 Approach Basins of Locks

The approach basins represent an indispensable part of locks. Their principal purpose is to ensure a continuous, safe and sufficiently speedy entry of the vessel (push-train) from the waterway into the approach basin and the lock and vice versa. If the lock is not ready to receive it the vessel must reduce speed during the entry into the approach basin, stop there and be moored in the mooring area situated outside the fairway, which proceeds directly into the lock and which must remain free to let vessels move out of the lock. These requirements, the number of locks side by side and the number of push-trains waiting for handling, are the factors determining the necessary approach basin width.

On a waterway with flowing water the approach basin is divided into

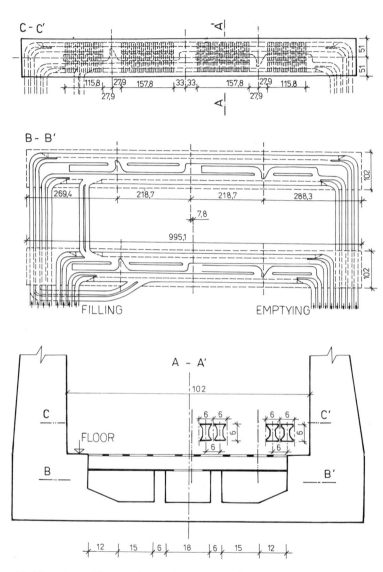

FIG. 16. Two-stage filling and emptying system of coupled locks at Gabčíkovo on the Danube (dimensions in cm apply to the lock model scale of $M_x = 33·3$).

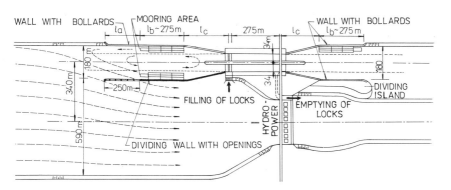

FIG. 17. Design of approach basins of coupled locks at Gabčíkovo on the Danube.

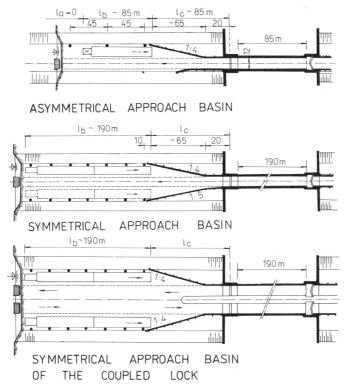

FIG. 18. Forms of lock approach basins on still water canals.

three parts along its length (Fig. 17). The first part (l_a) is intended for the braking of the vessels entering the lock[10] or for their accelerating at departure. The next part (l_b) is intended for passing and overtaking of vessels or push-trains, possibly for their mooring. The third part (l_c) with jetties or guide walls (at inclination of 1:4–1:5) represents a transitory part between the wider approach basin and the narrower lock head.[9]

The design of approach basins of the locks on canalised rivers, situated either in the channel next to a weir, or on derivation and navigation canals next to a power plant is highly exacting (Fig. 17). The approach basins of these locks are usually separated from the power plant or weir by a long dividing wall or an island. A sudden change of the width and cross-section at their head results in critical flow regions with lateral contraction, transverse and reverse flow, very unfavourable for navigation and causing frequent accidents. To reduce the transverse velocity in the critical area below the permissible value of about 0·35 m/s, it is advisable to afford a passage to water in the part of the dividing wall near its head (Fig. 17).

The approach basins of navigation locks on still water canals are relatively short, since no braking length is required (Fig. 18), as vessels can reduce their speed before entering the approach basin. The same applies to the downstream approach basins of the locks on waterways with flowing water (Fig. 17), since the vessels enter them against the flow direction.

5 HIGH-HEAD NAVIGATION STRUCTURES

5.1 Locks
Of all the structures enabling the vessels to overcome the high-heads on waterways, locks can be considered as technically the simplest and operationally most reliable. However, their applicability is limited to heads within which it is still possible to solve rationally their filling and emptying system. The biggest heads in the world, overcome by simple locks are $H = 42·5$ m on the Ust–Kamenogorsk scheme on the Irtysh river, USSR (lock dimensions 100×18 m, minimum water depth 2·5 m), then $H = 35$ m at the Carrapatelo dam on the Duero river, Portugal and $H = 34·5$ m at the John Day Dam on the Columbia River, USA.

On canalised rivers used for power generating purposes as well, where water requirements for navigation must be minimised, high heads are overcome by means of coupled locks (e.g. on the Gabčíkovo scheme on

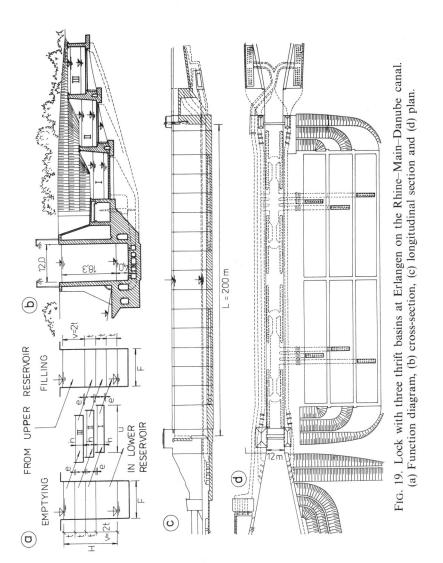

FIG. 19. Lock with three thrift basins at Erlangen on the Rhine–Main–Danube canal. (a) Function diagram, (b) cross-section, (c) longitudinal section and (d) plan.

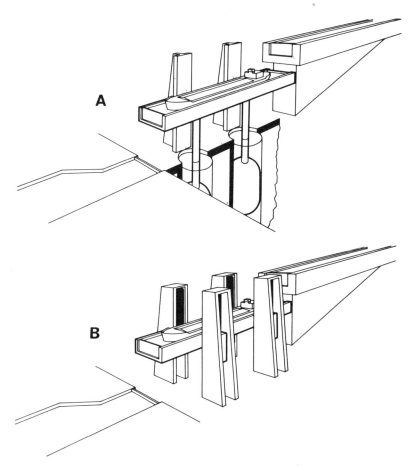

FIG. 20. Vertical boat lifts with floats (A) or counterweights (B).

the Danube, Fig. 16), two-step locks (e.g. on the Djerdab scheme on the Danube), three-step locks (e.g. in the Dnieprogess scheme on the Dniepr river, USSR) or a whole cascade of locks with intermediate reservoirs. The economy of handling water is achieved at the cost of increased capital outlay and longer time of the passage of vessels through the given step.

In canals with a water shortage, the high-head is overcome either by means of locks with thrift basins (Fig. 19) or by boat lifts (Figs 20–22). In comparison with boat lifts the locks with thrift basins have the

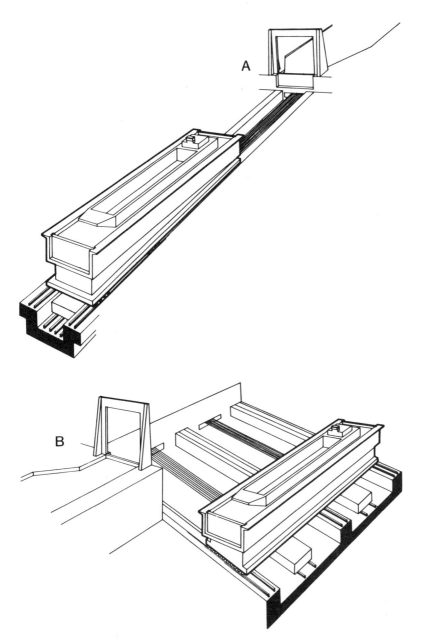

FIG. 21. Inclined boat lifts.

LONGITUDINAL   SECTION

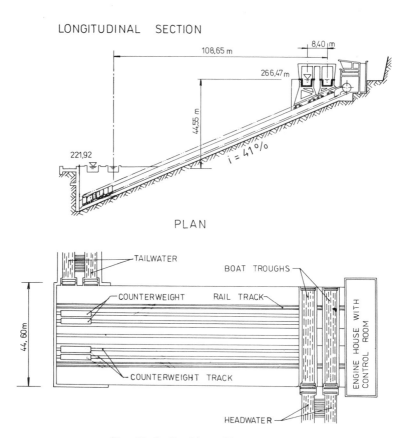

PLAN

FIG. 22. Inclined boat lift at Arzviller.

advantage of the possibility of large layout dimensions, enabling simultaneous handling of large push-trains. Considerable reduction of water use is achieved by the fact that during the lock emptying a part of the water is conveyed by gravity to thrift basins and returned to the lock during its subsequent filling (Fig. 19a). Thrift basins are usually constructed next to the lateral lock wall, either as open (Fig. 19) or as superimposed closed reservoirs. Every basin is connected with the lock by its own conduit provided with two-way gates (Fig. 19b, d). The filling and emptying system is symmetrical and balanced and should be checked by detailed model studies.[28] By increasing the number of basins to more than four, only a very small additional reduction of water consumption can be achieved and the handling time increases disproportionately in comparison with simple locks. Locks with thrift basins are used for heads of up to 30 m. For these heads they can still be designed so that their efficiency is comparable with standard types of boat lifts.

5.2 Boat Lifts

If the provision of water for the operation of high head locks causes major problems, it is possible to use boat lifts for the operation of which the water requirements are almost zero. To overcome very great heads (as much as 100 m) only these structures are used.

Boat lifts consist, as a rule, of a horizontal water filled trough provided at both ends with gates. When overcoming the navigation step, the vessel enters this trough and is conveyed in it from one reservoir to another. The troughs of the boat lifts have a maximum length of about 100 m. Therefore they are suitable for the handling of motor vessels and short 1 + 1 push-trains; major push-trains must be disconnected. Because of the great travelling speed of the trough, however, the capacity of the boat lifts is relatively high.

According to the direction of motion of the trough it is possible to distinguish[7] vertical and inclined boat lifts.

A vertical boat lift consists, apart from the steel boat trough filled with water, of the equipment required for balancing and moving the trough. According to the principle used for balancing it is possible to discern piston boat lifts, boat lifts with floats (Fig. 20a), boat lifts with mechanical counterweight balances (Fig. 20b) and special types.

Inclined boat lifts usually have the boat trough mounted on a special undercarriage travelling on a track on an inclined plane, either in the direction of the longitudinal trough axis (Fig. 21a) or normal to it (Fig. 21b). The boat trough is, as a rule, counterbalanced by a weight suspended on the other end of the driving rope and travelling on an inclined track below the undercarriage level of the boat trough. The acceleration of the trough during starting and the deceleration during braking must be small enough to maintain the variations of the water level in the trough within permissible limits and thus to reduce also the forces in the mooring ropes of the boat to permissible magnitude. To reduce these forces, part of the water is sometimes let out of the trough before its lifting to settle the boat at the bottom of the trough and thus stabilise it.

The boat lifts are more sensitive in operation than the locks and more prone to damage. Where a new boat lift replaces an obsolete series of locks, the locks can be left in operation as a reserve. However, if a boat lift is built on a new navigation canal, it is advisable to provide it with two separately operating boat troughs.

A special type of inclined boat lift is an inclined trough with a mobile water retaining wall ('pente d'eau') forming a water wedge for the handled boat (Fig. 23). The 'wall' is moved by two coupled electric

INCLINED   TROUGH   AT   MONTECH

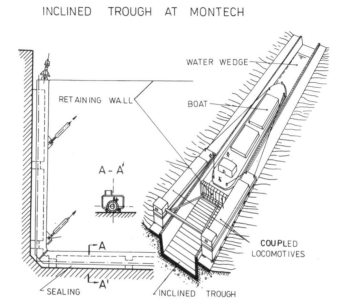

FIG. 23. Inclined trough with mobile water retaining wall.

locomotives with the floating boat moored to the locomotives. The design is very simple, requiring merely that a gate must be provided on the upper end of the inclined trough. This type of boat lift has been built in Montech on the Garonne River, France.[1] It may be used to overcome even very large heads. Difficulties in operation can be caused by the circumferential sealing of the travelling water retaining wall (Fig. 23).

The selection of an optimum type of equipment to overcome a great head always represents a very difficult technical as well as economic problem. The construction of an inclined boat lift at Arzviller (Fig. 22) on the Rhine–Marne canal, which replaced 17 old locks, the inclined boat lift at Ronquières on the Bruxelles–Charleroi canal, of the boat lift at the 100 m high dam at Krasnoyarsk in the USSR, and of the current highest vertical boat lift at Lüneburg on the Elbe–Seiten canal, testify to the fact that this type of navigation arrangement cannot be by far considered as obsolete in spite of its high structural demands. When deciding between a suitable boat lift type and the locks of some of the afore-mentioned types it is always necessary to consider all the prevailing technical and economic conditions.

The subject of energy recuperation during the operation of the locks overcoming large heads still awaits solution. It involves the exploitation of water power and utilising it for return pumping of water from the lower reservoirs into the lock. This problem has not yet been solved in practice because of the great costs and low efficiency of energy conversion caused by considerable discharge and head fluctuations. However, the proposal by Záruba[38] to use a combination of a rotary hydraulic motor and a pump on a common shaft, in which the effective piston area of the hydraulic motor and pump is continuously adjusted in accordance with the variations of the head is promising. A successful application of this idea could result in a new design of locks with large heads.

6 INLAND PORTS AND TRANSFER CENTRES

Inland ports serve for loading and unloading of vessels, transfer of goods and their further handling, i.e. storage, classification, packing and despatch. Ports are connected not only by water with their hinterland but also by railway, highway and pipeline transport routes. The ports can have specialised zones or basins intended for the transfer of certain cargoes (ore, coal, aggregates, sand, etc.), individual shipments or containers only.

The extent, location and layout of an inland port are determined by its transfer capacity.[6,32] For a small handling capacity a port or an industrial transfer centre can be built directly on the bank of a navigable river or canal by widening it outside the navigation channel at least by two or three standard boat widths or by the width required for barge turning (Fig. 24).

For a medium transfer capacity it is more advantageous to build one or two port basins outside the waterway, 200–1200 m long and 60–100 m wide, connected with the fairway by a suitably designed entry (Fig. 24c, d).

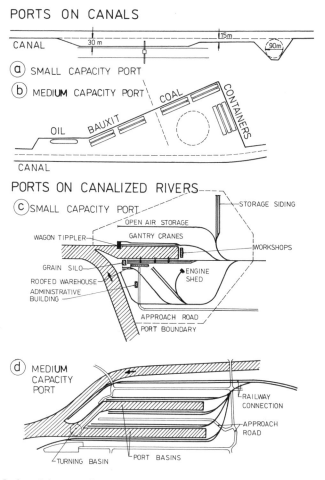

FIG. 24. Industrial ports of a small and medium capacity on canals and canalised rivers.

A commercial large transfer capacity port, which should be as compact as possible, has several basins connected with the waterway by means of an approach canal, extending beyond the entry into a port approach basin intended for the formation of push-trains or for vessels waiting for unloading. A turning basin is usually situated in the proximity of the port approach basin (Fig. 25).

The port layout depends above all on local conditions and the purpose

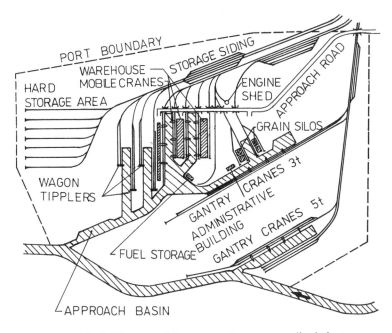

FIG. 25. Public port of large capacity on a canalised river.

which the port should serve. On wide navigable waterways a combined layout is often used with port quays and transfer berths situated in basins and along the river bank.

Manual or semi-mechanical transfer of freight in ports has been almost fully replaced with speedier, more economic and productive mechanised transfer. Mechanical handling can be discontinuous (e.g. when using cranes of different types) or continuous (e.g. when using various types of transfer mechanisms for bulk, such a bucket, chain and screw unloaders and transloaders, bucket elevators, exhausters, conveyor belts, pneumatic conveyors, etc., or pumps for the conveyance of liquid substances).

Automated continuous transfer suitable for large quantities of freight, above all for bulk and liquid cargo, is the most productive form. Some substances may be liquefied for transport as it is the case for asphalt, sulphur, gases, etc. By this method a high transfer output per 1 metre run of the port waterfront can be achieved.

The equipment for automated continuous transfer is usually installed in fixed position in the port; on the other hand, the multipurpose cranes of various types (gantry, rotary, overhead cranes, etc.) are usually mobile, travelling along their tracks on the port embankment. To increase the output of packaged goods handling there is a tendency to concentrate them in large bundles, boxes or large standard containers.

In commercial ports in which goods of the most varied assortment are handled, mobile slewing cranes represent the most important and universal transfer equipment. They can be used for the transfer of packaged goods, (cranes with a hook), bulk (cranes with a grab) or coarse materials, such as quarried stone or tree trunks (erectors) or steel scrap (magnet crane). Gantry cranes have their rail tracks laid along the waterfront, as close to the water as possible, to ensure that at least two barges are within reach of their jibs. In the interest of efficiency the cranes should not travel over too long distances but they must have a large action radius.

Between the rails of a gantry crane two rails of the port railway are usually laid. Their rail heads are usually flush with the embankment level to permit safe driving of lorries. The port highway intended for intensive lorry traffic runs parallel with the port railway.

For goods sensitive to moisture, roofed berths are used, provided with overhead travelling cranes. Apart from that ports are provided with modern storage capacities for packaged goods, dumps for temporary storage of bulk and grain silos. Separate from the remaining port territory are large capacity tanks for the storage of inflammable substances, situated in the proximity of tanker berths.

Every major inland commercial port has a container terminal, connected with the railway and highway network, with specialised container berths adjoined by hard storage and handling areas of sufficient dimensions connected with the port marshalling yard and the highway network. The containers are handled by wide-gauge gantry cranes (rail distance of 40 m and over) travelling along the waterfront. Their bridge with overhanging ends is provided with a spreader for automatic gripping of containers (Fig. 26).

Heavy and bulky goods weighing up to 40–45 t are handled in special berths for container handling. For the handling of goods of even greater weight (up to 200 t) truck mounted or railway cranes can be used.

Some ports have large capacity stationary gantry cranes with travelling trolleys intended for the transfer of very heavy and bulky goods. In their vicinity concrete assembly surfaces are provided, intended for the assembly of large size products which could not be transported to the port on the highway or railway owing to their large dimensions.

CONTAINER LOADING

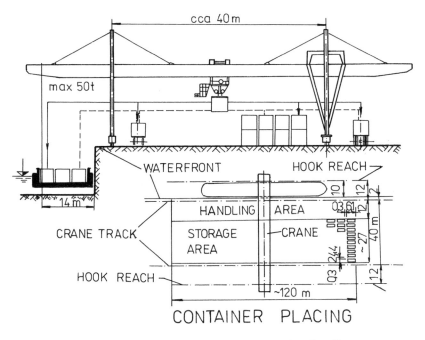

FIG. 26. Wide gauge gantry crane for container handling.

For products of excessive weight and dimensions, which cannot be handled by any of the afore-mentioned methods, the roll-on/roll-off transfer system has been devised. Its principle lies in the fact that a special highway trailer carrying the bulky object, rolls on a special vessel lying longitudinally in a small port basin (sized 12 × 120 m). The vessel must be specially modified for this purpose and at the time of the transfer it must be perfectly fixed and connected to the ramp at the head of the basin.

At present the volume of goods transported in bulk is gradually decreasing. At the same time, however, there is a tendency to use waterways for the transport of very valuable goods. The waterway transport of containers and of heavy bulky goods, above all transport based on the roll-on/roll-off system, is increasing.

The ever increasing intensity of utilisation of inland waterways and the mechanisation of transfer operations necessitates automated control of ports and transfer operations. This is particularly so in the rapidly developing container transport system.[37]

Contemporary systems[24] of automatic container terminal control are based on a suitable combination of computer data processing and remote control of man-operated transfer mechanisms. As a rule such a system comprises:

— a planning computer, preparing — on the basis of the data on ship movements, reservations and orders — an optimum plan of container handling and storage, which is passed on to a control computer;

— a control computer, issuing commands for the location of containers and receiving information about their arrival and departure;

— remote transfer of commands and information between the control computer and the operators of transfer and transport mechanisms, using most often wireless communication. The movements of transfer mechanisms can be automatically signalled back to the control computer.

REFERENCES

1. AUBERT, J. et al. La pente d'eau à Montech. Navigation, ports et industries, Paris, 1973, pp. 291–6.
2. BLAAUW, H. G., KOEMAN, J. W. and STRATING, J. Nautical studies in port and channel design. Dock and Harbour Authority, **63** (1982).
3. BLAAUW, H. G. and VERHEY, H. J. Design of inland navigation fairways. J. Waterway, Port, Coastal and Ocean Eng. ASCE, **109**, (1) (1983) 18–30.
4. BINEK, H. Einzelfahrten von Schubverbanden in Schiffahrtskanälen, HANSA, **8**(1976) 673–80.
5. BOUWMEESTER, J., VAN DE KAA, E. J., NUHOFF, H. A. and VAN ORDEN, R. G. J. Recent studies on push towing as a base for dimensioning waterways. 24th International Navigation Congress PIANC, Leningrad, 1977, subject 3, pp. 139–158.
6. BOURRIERES, P. and CHAMEROY, J. Ports et Navigation Modernes, Eyrolles, Paris, 1977.
7. ČÁBELKA, J. Inland Waterways and Inland Navigation (in Czech). SNTL Praha — Alfa Bratislava, 1976.
8. ČÁBELKA, J. et al. Rational design of locks and weirs on waterways in Czechoslovakia. 26th International Navigation Congress PIANC, Bruxelles, 1985.
9. ČÁBELKA, J. et al. Modern equipment of locks raising the traffic capacity and

security of navigation on inland waterways in ČSSR. *24th International Navigation Congress PIANC*, Leningrad, 1977.

10. ČÁBELKA, J. and KUBEC, J. Construction et modernisation des écluses sur l'Elbe en Tchécoslovaquie. *22nd International Navigation Congress PIANC*, Paris, 1969.

11. CUNGE, J., HOLLY, F. and VERWEY, A. *Practical Aspects of Computational River Hydraulics*. Pitman, London, 1980.

12. DANIŠOVIČ, P., SIKORA, A. and GABRIEL, P. Construction of multipurpose water schemes for improving conditions within the section of fords on the Danube. *23rd International Navigation Congress PIANC*, Quebec, 1973.

13. DELFT HYDRAULIC LABORATORY: Aspects of navigability of constrained waterways. *Inter. Symposium 1978*, Waterloopkundig Laboratorium, Delft, 1978.

14. GABRIEL, P. Regelung von Frequenz und Übergabeleistung in Kanalkraftwerken, *Österreichische Zeitschrift für Elektrizitätswirtschaft*, **2** (1969).

15. GABRIEL, P. Optimisation de la gestion de la cascade des ouvrages hydrauliques à chute basse. *XX. IAHR Congress*, Moscow, 1983.

16. GABRIEL, P. *et al.* Improvement of the conditions of navigation on the canalised rivers in Czechoslovakia. *24th International Navigation Congress PIANC*, Leningrad, 1977.

17. GABRIEL, P. *et al.* Means of increasing the capacity and safety of navigation transport of the Labe waterway. *25th International Navigation Congress PIANC*, Edinburgh, 1981.

18. GABRIEL, P. *et al.* Technical and economical aspects of upgraded utilisation of the Labe–Vltava waterway. *26th International Navigation Congress PIANC*, Bruxelles, 1985.

19. GABRIEL, P., GRUND, I. and SIKORA, A. Barrage on the Danube at Gabčíkovo (in Slovak), *Technical Report*, VÚVH, Bratislava, 1967.

20. HAGER, M. *et al.* Methods of increasing the capacity and safety of waterways. *24th International Navigation Congress PIANC*, Leningrad, 1977.

21. HILLING, D. *Barge Carrier Systems — Inventory and Prospects*, Benn Publications, London, 1977.

22. JONG, R. J. and DE VRIJER, A. Mathematical and hydraulic model investigation of longitudinal forces on ships in locks with door filling systems. *XIX IAHR Congress*, New Delhi, 1981.

23. KOLKMAN, P. A. Low Head Navigation Lock Door Filling and Emptying Systems. Developed by Hydraulic Investigations, Delft Hydraulics Laboratory, Publication No. 111, Delft, 1973.

24. KOUDSTAAL, R. and VAN DER WEIDE, J. Systems approach in integrated harbour planning. *Seatech III Conference on Asian Ports Development and Dredging*, Singapore, 1981.

25. KUBEC, J. Improvement of the integration of ocean and inland navigation by means of a unified system of dimensions of barges and lighters. *25th International Navigation Congress PIANC*, Edinburgh, 1981.

26. KUHN, R. *Binnenverkehrswasserbau*. Verlag Ernst & Sohn, Berlin, 1985.

27. MICHAJLOV, A. V. *Vnutrennie Vodnye Puti* (inland waterways — in Russian), Stroizdat, Moskva, 1973.

28. NOVAK, P. and ČÁBELKA, J. *Models in Hydraulic Engineering, Physical Principles and Design Application.* Pitman, London, 1981.
29. L'OFFICE NATIONAL DE LA NAVIGATION. La voie navigable — une voie d'avenir, Paris, 1980.
30. PARTENSCKY, H. W. Grenzen der Leistungsfähigkeit von Binnenschiffschleusen. *Jahrbuch der Hafenbautechnischen Gesellschaft*, Hamburg 39. Band, 1982.
31. Principles governing the design and construction of economic revetments for protecting the banks of rivers and canals. *22nd International Navigation Congress PIANC*, Paris, 1969, S.I.-S.6.
32. PORTEOUS, J. D. *Canal Ports*, Academic Press, London, 1977.
33. RENNER, D. Schiffahrtstechnische Modellversuche für Binnenwasserstrassenein neues Messsystem und neue Auswertungs-möglichkeiten. *Bericht Nr. 48*, Versuchsanstalt für Wasserbau der Technischen Universität München, 1984.
34. ROEHLE, W., ADOLF, E. and FRÜHWIRT, K. Measures against damage to locks and ships and measures during winter operations on the Austrian Danube. *24th International Navigation Congress PIANC*, Leningrad, 1977.
35. SEILER, E. Die Schubschiffahrt als Integrationsfaktor zwischen Rhein und Donau. *Zeitschrift für Binnenschiffahrt und Wassterstrassen*, **8** (1972).
36. VRIJER, A. Fender forces caused by ship impacts. *8th International Harbour Congress*, Antwerp, June, 1983.
37. WHITTAKER, J. R. *Containerization.* John Wiley, New York, 1975.
38. ZÁRUBA, L. Means and device for lock chambers operation (in Czech), Czechoslovak patent No. 80928, Praha.

Chapter 7

PORTS AND HARBOURS

M. W. Owen

Hydraulics Research Ltd, Wallingford, Oxon, UK

NOTATION

A	cross-sectional area of beach
C	wave celerity
C_f	Chézy friction coefficient
C_g	group velocity of waves
D	typical dimension of armour unit
d	water depth
E	wave energy
f	wave frequency
f_w	Jonsson's wave friction factor
g	acceleration due to gravity
H	wave height
H_s	significant wave height
K	factor in longshore transport equation
K_D	Hudson's breakwater damage coefficient
L	wave length
Q	alongshore sediment transport rate
R_2	two-per-cent run up
R_s	significant wave run-up
s	alongshore distance
S	sand flux
S_r	specific gravity of armour units relative to the local fluid
S_{cw}	sediment transport rate due to waves and currents
S_c	sediment transport due to currents alone

t	time
T	wave period
$\bar{u}$	depth-mean tidal velocity
v_0	peak value of orbital velocity at the sea bed
$\bar{v}'$	rms value of orbital velocity at the sea bed
v_c	critical value of orbital velocity
V	current velocity
W	weight of rocks in rock-armoured breakwaters

α	angle between wave crests and sea bed contours
α_1	angle between wave crests and channel edge
α_b	angle between breaker line and beach contours
β	slope of beach or breakwater face, above horizontal
γ_s	specific weight of sediment or armour material
θ	wave direction
ξ	factor correcting for effect of waves on shear stress
τ_{cw}	shear stress due to waves and currents
τ_c	shear stress due to currents alone
Δs	grid size
Δt	time-step

1 INTRODUCTION

Whenever a new engineering project is being designed, or an existing structure assessed, two fundamental questions have to be asked, namely how well does the project fulfil its design function, and how long will it last (or, alternatively, how much maintenance will be required to make sure that it continues to function)? The sole purpose of ports and harbours (Fig. 1) is to provide an area of water which is sufficiently sheltered from wave activity, and has adequate water depth, to allow vessels of given types either to anchor safely, or to moor and discharge their cargoes. For port and harbour projects, the main questions from the hydraulic engineering viewpoint are therefore:

(1) How well is the harbour designed so as to minimise the wave disturbance and ship movements inside the harbour for a range of likely storm conditions outside?

(2) How long will the harbour exist before repairs or maintenance are necessary?

In order to be able to answer these questions, a whole range of interrelated items have to be considered. Firstly, it is necessary to know

FIG. 1. Typical coastal harbour (Napier Harbour, New Zealand).

the wave climate outside the harbour in order to know what degree of protection is likely to be required. A good knowledge of the wave conditions is also necessary in order to be able to predict the ferocity of the extreme storms which the various component structures of the harbour must be designed to withstand. Secondly, the basic shape of the harbour must be designed to achieve the necessary degree of protection for particular types of ships as efficiently as possible. This relates mainly to the layout in plan of the breakwaters, the location of the berths, the provision of spending beaches, etc. It is also important at this stage to consider the mooring arrangements for the ships, because the movement of the ships at their berths is a function of both the wave activity at the berth and the mooring system employed. Thirdly, the various structures around the harbour must be designed to withstand the extreme storms without catastrophic damage. This item relates mainly to the stability of the protective breakwaters, and to a lesser extent to the selection of the deck levels of jetties and quays. Fourthly, the harbour must be designed so that vessels can safely navigate in and out of the harbour under all but the worst storm conditions. This means that the approaches to the harbour must be as straightforward as possible, with adequate space and water depth for manoeuvring. Finally, the whole question of sediment movement both inside and outside the harbour must be considered. In particular, attempts must be made to estimate how much siltation will occur in the harbour and its approaches, because the amount of maintenance dredging which is required may make the port

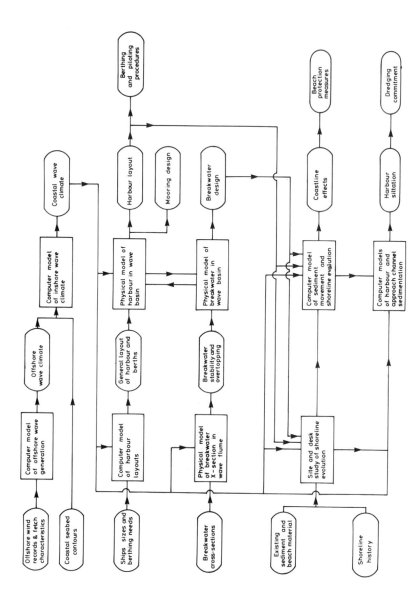

FIG. 2. Typical range of hydraulic studies for a major port.

uneconomical. At the same time the effect of the harbour on sediment transport in the channels and on the beaches outside the harbour must not be forgotten.

Almost all the above items apply equally whatever the size of harbour or type of port being proposed. In principle the problems of designing a small marina for pleasure boats or a large commercial port for bulk carriers are the same. The financial resources available to tackle the problems are, however, vastly different. In many ways it is more difficult to design a small marina than a large port: there are usually insufficient funds to investigate all aspects thoroughly and so the design engineer has to rely heavily on his wide experience and intuition. For the major port it is possible to justify the considerable expense involved in carrying out the full range of design studies, which should lead to greater confidence in the final port scheme. For several decades, a central part of these design studies has been the use of relatively large scale models of the particular port under consideration. These models have been used, for example, to measure the attenuation of regular waves as they penetrate the harbour, or to study navigation into the port using radio-controlled models of the actual ships using the port. Today such models still perform a very important part of harbour design studies, but the increasingly powerful computers which have become available in the past 10–15 years have enabled a whole new range of techniques to be developed. These include the use of mathematical models, for example, to hindcast storm waves from given wind conditions or to predict the theoretical attenuation of the waves inside the harbour. Computer-controlled ship simulators have largely replaced radio-controlled models for studying navigation into harbours. Also the scale models themselves have benefitted from computer technology, with complex wave generators able to produce totally realistic wave conditions for the model tests. Figure 2 shows in schematic form the range of studies which nowadays would be considered necessary for designing a major port. In the remainder of this chapter the intention is to describe the hydraulic engineering aspects of the main components of this package of design studies.

2   WAVE CLIMATE

A good knowledge of the wave climate is required for almost all aspects of maritime engineering, whether it is the design of an offshore oil rig, the planning of a new harbour or an examination of the adequacy of coastal defences. It is not the intention in this chapter to describe in detail the many methods which are available nowadays for either measuring or calculating the wave climate, but to concentrate instead on describing the type of information which is required for planning coastal ports and harbours. However some reference will have to be made to recent, major developments which enable this information to be acquired more easily.

For a particular harbour, good wave information is required for two main reasons. Firstly, to define the normal operating conditions for the harbour, since for economic viability it is important that the harbour should be designed to give good shelter for most of the storms which occur in an average year. Secondly, the various harbour structures, such as the breakwaters or jetties, must be designed to withstand extreme storms without serious damage, and therefore good information is necessary to estimate the severity of these extreme waves. Because the harbour and the various structures will respond to waves of widely varying periods, the wave information has to be available in sufficient detail to define not only the significant wave height, mean period and prevailing direction, but also the complete wave energy/frequency/direction spectrum for any given sea state. In other words we require the time history of the expression $E = F(f, \theta)$ where E is the wave energy, a function F of the wave frequency f and of θ the wave direction.

By far the most reliable method of obtaining all this wave data is actually to carry out measurements at the harbour site for as long as possible.[1] Modern field instruments such as the Datawell Waverider Buoy (Fig. 3) enable wind waves to be measured on a routine basis both reliably and relatively inexpensively. Instruments based on various remote-reading pressure transducers allow the same measurements for swell waves and long waves. Unfortunately these instruments only give the part function $E = F_1(f)$: routine measurement of wave direction in coastal waters is still not possible, although several new instruments are being developed which might enable this to be done in the near future. In the meantime we have to rely on visual observations of the mean wave direction, or on aerial or radar photographs, or on the assumption that the direction of wind-waves is the same as the wind direction. With any wave measurements it is vital that they are continued for at least 12 months in order to be able to assesss, for example, the number of days during a year when given wave conditions will apply at the harbour entrance. Of course there is no guarantee that the year of measurements

FIG. 3. Datawell Waverider Buoy.

will represent a 'typical' year, and ideally measurements should be continued for several years. Such extended measurement periods are also very important if, for example, a prediction has to be made for the wave conditions occurring only once during the 50 or 60 year design lifetime of the harbour. Unfortunately there is very rarely enough time allowed during the planning of a new harbour to allow measurements for much longer than 12 months, and sometimes not even that much data is obtainable. However, information on wind conditions in the vicinity is usually available for quite long timespans. By comparing the wind conditions during the measurement period with the 'average' annual wind conditions it is possible by various methods to correct the measured wave conditions to give estimated average wave conditions.[2] With much more careful analysis it is also possible to estimate extreme wave conditions, but this will be discussed a little later.

Although there are often no wave data available at the actual harbour site, occasionally there may be data obtained for another purpose at some other site not too distant. Recently most of the reliable wave data around the world has been catalogued by the major meteorological and/or oceanographic institutions,[3] making it much easier to check the availability of wave information near a particular site. If such information does exist at a location not too far away then some method has to be used to 'translate' the data from one site to another. Frequently the data exist far offshore: in order to bring the wave conditions closer to the shoreline wave refraction calculations have to be carried out. If the wave information is at another inshore site, then it is often possible to back-calculate the wave conditions offshore and then refract those conditions inshore again to the required harbour site. Traditionally these refraction calculations have been performed by graphically constructing the wave rays or paths as the waves traverse the sea bed from deep water offshore to shallow water inshore. These rays have to be drawn for a given wave period and offshore direction, and then re-drawn for each different period or direction. Understandably enough only a few wave periods or directions were considered: however the wave rays are quite sensitive to even small changes of period or direction, and quite misleading results could occur on anything except the simplest of sea bed bathymetries. With the advent of computers these wave ray diagrams could be produced more easily, but a much larger number of diagrams only led to difficulties in interpretation. In order to overcome these difficulties Abernethy and Gilbert[4] in 1975 developed a method of refracting the complete wave spectrum, not just a few wave periods and directions within that spectrum. Their method now forms the basis of many modern refraction computer programs,[5] and is based on the fact that if linear wave theory is assumed then the track of a wave of given period and inshore direction when propagating out to sea is identical to the track of a wave of the given period and corresponding offshore direction being propagated inshore.

Starting from the point of interest near the coastline, the method relies on a very efficient computational routine to track the paths of a very large number of rays, of closely spaced frequencies and directions, as they propagate out towards the seaward boundary of the refraction area. By logging the wave period, the inshore and offshore direction of each ray, and summing the results into given bands of offshore direction and frequency, an accurate 'transfer matrix' is derived for that site. Each matrix column represents a frequency band, each row an offshore direction band, and the value stored at each matrix location indicates the ratio between the offshore wave energy and inshore wave energy in that component of the wave energy/frequency/direction spectrum. Once the matrix is derived many different offshore spectra, assembled in a similar matrix form, can be quickly multiplied by the transfer matrix, to give the equivalent inshore spectra. For harbour design, this method of wave refraction is very valuable because it enables a large number of offshore wave spectra to be examined, to determine which is most likely to give the worst conditions inshore. Frequently it is not possible to make this assessment without such refraction studies.

Because this refraction method is based on linear theory, it excludes consideration of wave dissipation processes such as bed friction and breaking. However, harbour entrances are usually well seaward of the breaker line, and are also at a depth where friction loss is usually insignificant.[6] When friction and breaking are required a more complicated (and more expensive) finite difference wave refraction model is required.[7,8] This model has to be re-run completely for each different offshore wave spectrum, so the simpler refraction model is usually run first to identify the important offshore spectra, in terms of giving the likely worst conditions inshore.

Occasionally there are no wave records in existence at any location within a reasonable distance of the proposed harbour site. In these cases, total reliance has to be placed on wave hindcasting/forecasting techniques. Simple formulae for calculating wave heights and periods from wind speeds and duration have of course been available for many years.[9,10] Once again, the advent of computers has enabled much more detailed predictions to be made,[11] either by using well established simple formulae for a very large number of wind conditions (for example, to give wave heights at every hour in a typical year), or by using more sophisticated wave models incorporating the growth and decay of each of the component parts of the wave energy/frequency/direction spectrum for the wind-waves, together with the creation and propagation of the swell-sea spectrum.[12] These various models will not be described in detail here, but it is important to point out that these models should ideally present information both on the wave climate (i.e. the variation in wave conditions during a normal year) and on the likely extreme wave conditions. For the former requirement, a fairly simple model which is cheap to run for a very large number of wind conditions will probably be sufficiently accurate (Fig. 4). For predicting extreme conditions, however,

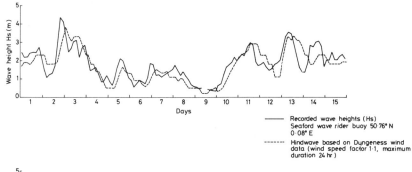

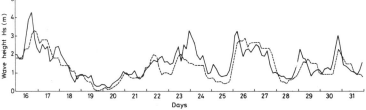

FIG. 4. Comparison between measured and hindcast wave heights (Seaford, Sussex, UK).

the most accurate model possible should be assembled: this will probably be fairly expensive to run, but need only be used to examine the wave conditions produced by relatively few known storms classified according to the severity of the winds.

Whichever of the above types of wave hindcasting models is used, the reliability of the results will of course be greatly enhanced by comparison with recorded wave data, preferably at the harbour site. Earlier, reference was made to the frequent requirement to predict say the 50 or 100 year return period storms from very short lengths of wave records. Using some form of hindcasting model coupled with any available long-term wind records is the only way in which it can satisfactorily be achieved.[2]

Finally it should be emphasised that such hindcasting techniques as are presently available can only predict wind waves and swell waves (in sophisticated models only). They cannot predict the very long waves (periods from about 30 s upwards), and for these waves the only possible way of obtaining the data is by direct measurement at the harbour site. As we shall see in the next part of this chapter, these very long waves can be very significant in determining the performance of the harbour.

3   HARBOUR LAYOUT

In designing the harbour the layout of the harbour entrance, dredged channels, berth locations, quay walls, etc., have to be chosen to give the most efficient scheme for reducing the ship movements at their moorings. It is worth recalling at this stage the various wave processes which have to be taken into account.[13]

3.1   Diffraction

The ability of waves to bend or diffract around obstacles is well known, and this process usually makes the largest contribution to wave activity on the sheltered side of breakwaters. Accurate predictions of the wave diffractions are therefore essential. Diffraction is clearly illustrated by waves arriving at a harbour whose entrance is formed by a gap between the breakwater arms. The wave crests inside the harbour consist of almost concentric arcs spreading out from the harbour entrance with wave height decreasing with increasing distance from the entrance. For small gaps of less than a wavelength the wave height is fairly uniform all the way along circular crests. Such a pattern can be shown to be consistent with the idea of a point source of energy which is radiating waves into the harbour from the entrance. As the size of the gap increases relative to the wavelength the wave height starts to vary along each crest inside the harbour with a maximum height tending to occur at a point opposite the entrance that is in line with the incident wave direction. Height then decreases on both sides of this maximum as one moves along a wave crest into the shelter of one of the breakwater arms.

3.2   Wave Refraction and Shoaling

In the absence of dissipation due to effects like bottom friction and wave breaking the flux of energy of waves propagating over a varying bed level remains constant. However, as a wave propagates inshore into depths of less than half the wavelength the velocity of propagation, known as the group velocity, decreases. Therefore, even when waves approach the coastline with crests parallel with the sea bed contours, there will be an increase in wave height, known as *shoaling*.

If, however, a wave approaches with its crest making an angle with the sea bed contours the crest will propagate with a varying speed along its length, with portions in deeper water travelling faster than portions in shallower water. The result is that the wave refracts such that its crest tends to line up with the local sea bed contours. Wave *refraction* can cause significant changes in wave height in coastal waters, independent of the effects of shoaling.

For harbours with a varying bed level both wave refraction and shoaling will cause changes in wave height within the harbour. Deeply dredged entrance channels to the harbour can also cause strong refraction effects. For example, Fig. 5 shows regular waves approaching

FIG. 5. Waves reflecting off a dredged channel in a harbour model (Mina Jebel Ali, Dubai).

the deeply dredged entrance channel in a physical model of the harbour of Mina Jebel Ali, Dubai. As they approach the deep water of the channel, the waves undergo such strong refraction that they are 'reflected' at the side of the channel. This leads to increased wave disturbance alongside the channel, but wave heights within the channel are reduced. This total reflection occurs[14] whenever the wave period, wave direction and the depths of water inside and outside the channel satisfy the equation

$$\sin \alpha_1 > C_1/C_2$$

where α_1 is the angle between the wave crests and the channel edge, and C_1 and C_2 are the wave celerities at water depths d_1 and d_2, respectively, with wave celerity being defined as

$$C = gT/2\pi \ \tanh 2\pi d/L$$

where L is the wavelength and T its period. Thus 10 s waves travelling in a water depth of 5 m will totally reflect from the edge of a 10 m deep channel whenever they approach the channel at an angle greater than about 47°.

3.3 Wave Reflections
Reflections from interior harbour boundaries will cause additional disturbance within the harbour. It is good practice, therefore, to build breakwaters, quay faces and reclamation areas with rubble slopes where possible as these can be made into good dissipators of wave energy. In particular the more gentle the slope and the larger the size of rubble, the more efficient the slope becomes in dissipating wave energy. These energy losses are thought to occur through a combination of frictional losses on the rough surface and wave breaking on the slope. Natural beaches inside the harbour are also very good wave absorbers.

3.4 Harbour Resonance
If the interior harbour boundaries are highly reflective the internally reflected waves will undergo many re-reflections: for certain wavelengths these multiple reflections can reinforce one another giving rise to harbour resonance. For the pumping or Helmholtz mode, which is the longest resonant wavelength, a vertical rise and fall of water occurs over the harbour area and large horizontal oscillating currents are formed in the harbour entrance. The next longest resonant wavelength is one where the water rises vertically along one boundary when it is falling vertically along an opposite boundary with a region between the two boundaries where oscillatory horizontal flows occur. This oscillation, for which half a wavelength fits between the two boundaries, is sometimes called the sloshing mode. A whole range of shorter resonant wavelengths can occur but they become increasingly complex for harbours with irregularly shaped boundaries. Since resonance occurs for wavelengths that are dependent on the dimensions of the harbour, the resonant period, which is a function of water depth as well as wavelength, will vary with the state of the tide.

3.5 Random Waves

At any one time, or for a given 'sea state', the harbour is being subjected to waves which have a random distribution of wave heights, periods and directions, with each wave behaving differently according to the processes described above. In addition, there will be occasions when groups of several large waves in succession arrive at the harbour entrance. It is believed that these groups are the main source of energy for generating the very long waves which are noticeable in the real sea. These long waves, with periods ranging from 30 s to many minutes are very important for harbour studies[15] because of their ability to excite resonance in the harbour, and also because they have approximately the same periods as the natural periods of horizontal oscillation of vessels on their moorings. The occurrence of these groups of large waves, and the resulting high velocities, causes a local set-down in the sea surface, which is tied to the groups of waves as they propagate shorewards. The set-down propagates at the group velocity and grows as the waves reach shallow water because the velocity of wave propagation tends to the group velocity, and consequently a resonant build-up occurs in the amplitude of set-down. A set-down amplitude of 1 m or more is thought to be possible in severe storm òr swell conditions. When the waves and the set-down reach the shoreline most of the wave energy is dissipated by wave breaking and friction, but the set-down energy is not entirely destroyed because of its long wave character. Instead long waves of similar period are produced, and these can either propagate back out to sea as surf beats, or the energy can be trapped by the coastline in the form of edge waves.

3.6 Scale Models of Harbours

If all the waves at a harbour site had the same height, period and direction then it would be relatively easy to design a suitable harbour layout, taking account of all the wave processes described earlier. However, all harbours have to operate over a range of mean wave heights and periods and usually for many wave directions as well. In each case the waves are also random in occurrence. The harbour layout therefore has to be optimised over all these conditions. For several decades this optimisation has been carried out with the use of scale models. In these models the harbour area together with part of the offshore area and the coastline adjacent to the harbour are accurately reproduced to a scale usually between about 1:60 for small harbours to 1:120 for very large ports. The earlier models were equipped with a

FIG. 6. Model of Peterhead Harbour, Scotland (scale 1:80).

simple wavemaker to generate waves in the offshore part of the model, and the wave heights at various locations inside the model harbour were measured for regular waves with a range of wave heights, periods and directions. Scale models are still extensively used for harbour design (Fig. 6) but modelling techniques have advanced substantially. Compared to the very simple early models, present day models differ mainly in two respects. Firstly, all the major laboratories are now equipped to test harbour designs using waves which are at least random in height and period, and occasionally in wave direction as well. The simple wave generator consisting of a paddle driven by a constant speed motor has now been replaced by a servo-controlled paddle which is programmed to respond to a rapidly fluctuating electronic signal which represents the wave energy/frequency spectrum. Where random directions are also required then many such paddles are placed in line. For example, Fig. 7 shows the multi-directional wave basin at Hydraulics Research, Wallingford, where 80 paddles are controlled by a fairly large computer to produce the full wave energy/frequency/direction spectrum. That particular basin is used mostly for offshore engineering applications: for harbour modelling it is usual to employ a single long wavemaker, because most harbour entrances are in comparatively shallow water where wave refraction considerably reduces the range of wave directions occurring at a given sea state.

There is still considerable discussion about the best method of generating the randomly varying electrical signal which drives these servo-controlled wavemakers. Based on the assumption that waves in the real sea can be fully described by the wave energy/frequency spectrum, Gilbert, Thompson and Brewer[16] developed a method of driving wave generators in which the required spectrum is obtained by trimming and filtering the signal produced by a digital white noise generator. This method produces waves which have the correct statistical distribution of wave heights within the spectrum, with phases which are random in relation to each other. However, this method became seriously questioned when it was realised that the frequently occurring groups of several larger-than-average waves were very important in harbour design, and their correct reproduction was therefore vital. It has been maintained by some researchers that the occurrence of these wave groups suggests that real sea waves not only have a well defined wave energy/frequency spectrum, but also have a definite wave phase spectrum.[17] Because there is no known way of predicting this phase spectrum, these researchers use actual wave measurements recorded at the harbour site

FIG. 7. Multidirectional wave basin.

to generate exactly the same sequence of waves in the model. This method has several disadvantages. In particular it is very rarely that wave records are available for a storm equal to the design condition for the harbour, so that extrapolation is necessary for design testing. If the phase spectrum is incompletely understood, then this extrapolation becomes rather subjective. Also what wave records do exist are usually of short duration, typically 20 min, and reproduction and repetition of a 20 min sequence of waves is rarely truly representative of the full wave height/wave groups statistics for a given sea state. In fact, recent research[18] has now shown that over a very large number of waves the frequency of occurrence of wave groups is purely a function of the random phases of the individual waves in a given spectrum. More and more laboratories are therefore adopting the method proposed by Gilbert et al.[16]

With the generation of random waves in models, the methods of measuring and recording the wave heights and periods have had to be correspondingly improved. Model wave measuring instruments have changed very little over the years, but whereas a simple graphical output was sufficient for recording regular waves, in random wave models the wave measurements are now converted to digital form, and input to a computer, where sophisticated analysis techniques can be performed. Thus the model measurements can be presented in a variety of ways, such as histograms of wave heights, or the full wave energy/frequency spectrum. However, remembering that the main purpose of most harbours is to minimise the movement of ships at their berths, it is now quite common to include scale ships in the model, especially if the harbour is to cater for vessels with a displacement greater than about 5000 t.[19] The movements of these model ships are then measured as well as wave heights inside the harbour for given wave conditions and harbour configurations. In order to make sure that these movements are realistic, the ship must be accurately modelled in terms of its shape, mass, displacement and moments of inertia about the three principal axes. In addition the mooring lines and fenders must be correctly scaled for stiffness or elasticity. The ship must then be instrumented to allow its movement in the six degrees of freedom to be measured. Figure 8 shows a model boat which is equipped to enable measurements to be made of the translational movements (surge, sway and heave) and the rotational motions (pitch, roll and yaw). At the same time the tension in the mooring lines and the thrust on the fenders can be measured: this is done by measuring the extension of the mooring lines or the compression of

FIG. 8. Model of a moored vessel.

the fenders using strain gauges, and then calculating the forces from known stress/strain relationships.

Because the ship in the model is being subjected to random waves, the output signals from all these measurement devices are again input to a computer. Various analysis programs can then be used to process the data, perhaps presenting them in exactly the same way as the wave data (histograms of forces, force/frequency spectra, etc.), or as maximum forces in a given time. Figure 9 shows the spectra for the six degrees of freedom for a moored vessel as measured in a model, compared with the same information for an actual vessel tied up alongside at the Port of Acajutla, San Salvador. By measuring the movements of ships in model harbours, and looking at the entire system of harbour layout/ship design/mooring arrangements, it is sometimes possible to identify ways in which the ship movements can be reduced to a tolerable level by redesigning the mooring/fendering arrangements rather than the much more expensive solution of reconstructing the harbour entrance. For example, a recent model study for the ship repair yard in the Port of

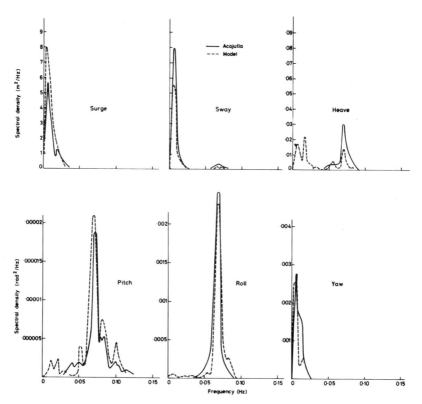

FIG. 9. Comparison of model and prototype motions of a moored vessel.

Dammam, Saudi Arabia, established that with compliant dock moorings a 900 m long island breakwater and a 300 m long east dock breakwater provided sufficient shelter with minimum downtime for 22 000 t floating dry docks. Without compliant moorings the breakwaters would need an extension of about 300 m to keep mooring loads within prescribed limits under extreme conditions.

3.7 Mathematical Models of Harbours

Mathematical models of wave disturbance are becoming increasingly important in harbour engineering, where they can give a relatively quick and inexpensive means of comparing the shelter provided by various harbour designs. However, there are many non-linear processes in the propagation of waves in harbours which are still not clearly understood, and can therefore not be incorporated accurately into mathematical models. For this reason the most common use of mathematical wave disturbance models is to compare several different designs of harbour, and then select the most promising design for detailed testing in a physical model where non-linear effects are automatically reproduced.

Mathematical modelling of wave disturbance within harbours has only been possible within the last decade or so, coinciding with the arrival of powerful computers, and the models currently available fall into two broad groups — finite difference/finite element models, and ray models. Most work has been devoted to the development of finite difference models, but these are best suited to studying long waves in harbours because they have two important drawbacks which can become especially noticeable at shorter wave periods.[20]

These disadvantages are:

(1) Difficulties in representing wave conditions at the harbour boundaries, especially partial reflections inside the harbour, and radiated and reflected waves at the harbour entrance.

(2) Although applicable to harbours of almost any size, shape and bed topography, the computing time and storage become excessive for large harbours and/or short wavelengths. Typically this stage is reached when the harbour dimensions are greater than about 5–10 wavelengths.

In contrast, ray methods are best suited to modelling short waves, but not long waves, for the following reasons:

(1) Ray methods are initial value problems, not boundary value problems, and so none of the difficulties with boundary conditions are encountered.

(2) Although the computing time in a ray model does increase with the harbour size, the increase is far less rapid than for the finite difference models.

(3) The greatest difficulty in ray models is the representation of diffraction effects at harbour entrances. The methods usually adopted are inaccurate within about one wavelength of the diffraction source, but for short waves this is only a small distance.

Taken together, finite difference and ray models can therefore be used to provide a mathematical description of harbour response to the full range of wave conditions, with finite difference models being used to study resonant wave periods (typically several minutes) and ray models for storm and swell wave periods (typically 6–30 s). Both types of models give information on wave heights inside the harbour, but as yet there are no proven mathematical models available to predict the resulting ship movement at a berth.

Because of the increasing use of both finite difference and ray models of wave disturbance in the circumstances outlined above, a brief description of each is appropriate. The *ray model*[21] is based closely on the methods used to describe the refraction of waves as they propagate inshore over a varying sea bed level. To allow for waves diffracting around the breakwaters the rays from the harbour entrance are given a distribution of energy which is consistent with the diffraction process. For narrow harbour entrances (less than one wavelength) the diffraction process is consistent with the idea of a point source of energy at the entrance, radiating waves into the harbour, which can easily be incorporated into the ray model. For wider entrances, or single breakwater designs, rays describing the diffracted wave field are plotted into the harbour from points located on the geometric shadow line for that particular wave direction. The harbour area is digitised as an array of water depths at each vertex of a square grid. Harbour boundaries and breakwaters are represented by straight line segments in the grid squares, allowing a fine description of the harbour geometry. The models incorporate wave diffraction, refraction and reflection (partial or total), and the results are obtained in the form of wave heights at the centres of the grid squares over the whole harbour area, based on averaging the effects of all the rays which cross each grid element. Each run of the model gives wave heights for a single incident wave period and direction, and a wave spectrum can be built up from a series of such runs (assuming that linear superposition is valid in this situation). The results can of course be presented in a variety of ways, and Fig. 10 shows wave height contours for a single wave period and direction, where the wave heights are expressed as a proportion of the incident wave height.

In *finite difference* models, the equations of motion of water waves are solved numerically to give the water surface elevations and velocities at grid points within the harbour area being studied. The full equations of conservation and momentum governing the propagation of arbitrary, long wave disturbances of small to moderate amplitude over a slowly varying bathymetry were derived by Peregrine in 1967[22] and these form the basis of the finite difference models.[23] Additional terms are necessary to describe the loss of wave energy inside the harbour. For long waves of typical harbour resonance periods the most important mechanisms of

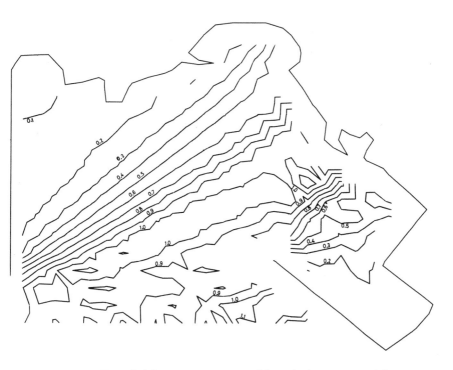

FIG. 10. Wave height contours generated by a harbour ray model.

energy loss are bed friction, flow separation at harbour walls, recirculation near openings (e.g. harbour mouths) and obstacles (e.g. jetties), and radiation from the harbour mouth. The exact definition of many of these non-linear processes is still very difficult, and the mathematical models are therefore often calibrated against a physical model if possible, before making predictions for other schemes.

The method of solution is to prescribe the water surface elevation at the outer boundary of the model (outside the harbour entrance) at consecutive time steps, and then solve the equations of motion to give the water surface elevations at selected grid points within the harbour at each time step. If a random wave spectrum is used as the model input, then spectral analysis of the water levels at the positions inside the harbour will give the wave heights at these positions, as well as highlighting the problematic resonant periods.

The numerical techniques for solving the equations of wave motion place fairly stringent requirements on the grid size and time step which may be used. The grid size Δs typically has to be no larger than 1/6th of the wave length of the shortest waves to be studied, and the time step Δt has to be less than $\Delta s/\sqrt{2gd_0}$, where d_0 is the maximum water depth. For normal storm waves a typical grid size of no more than 10 m, and a time step of about 1 s will be necessary, requiring considerable computing power for a large harbour. For studying harbour resonance problems, however, where wave periods are much longer, a grid size of about 50 m and a time step of 3–4 s will usually be sufficiently accurate. For those very long waves it may also sometimes be possible to simplify or to ignore the non-linear or higher order terms in the equations of motion without significant loss of accuracy, hence leading to a further reduction in computing time required to obtain the solution.

4 BREAKWATERS

The breakwaters constructed to protect harbours are usually one of three main types, or sometimes a composite of the three. Figure 11 shows the three main forms and also an example of one form of composite breakwater. Until about the middle of the twentieth century the blockwork breakwater was very common. Labour was plentiful and cheap enough to contemplate quarrying large blocks of stone, dressing them into very precise shapes, and then fitting the blocks together to form either a solid stone breakwater, or more often solid stone facings and crest, with rubble infill. Obviously such a method of construction was very difficult in deep water, and when it was necessary rough quarried stone was placed on the sea bed until the water depths were sufficiently shallow to commence construction using blockwork. Alderney breakwater in the Channel Islands is an example of such a breakwater — a composite between a blockwork and rubble–mound breakwater. Blockwork breakwaters are occasionally constructed today, although with pre-cast concrete blocks rather than dressed stone. Caisson breakwaters have been designed since about the 1930's, and consist of pre-cast concrete caissons which are cast remote from the harbour site. They are designed to be floated to the harbour, where they are sunk into position onto prepared foundations on the sea bed. The Mulberry Harbour constructed for the D-day landings in Normandy in 1944 was a classic example of caisson breakwaters, and they are

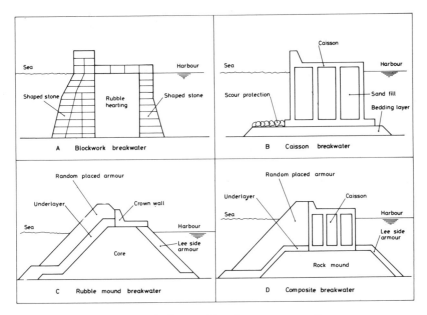

FIG. 11. Main forms of breakwater construction.

constructed today in many parts of the world, especially in Japan and along the northern coasts of the Mediterranean Sea.

Again, caisson breakwaters are frequently founded on large underwater mounds of rock, and are thus composite structures. However by far the most common breakwater design in present times is the full rubble–mound breakwater, consisting of a large mound of quarried rubble, protected by an armour layer of either large rocks or specially designed concrete blocks, with various intermediate 'filter' layers to prevent the quarried rubble leaching out through the armour layer.

Whichever type of breakwater is adopted, the structure must be able to withstand severe storms without serious damage. For blockwork breakwaters the three possible models of failure are due to (a) loosening of the joints between adjacent blocks (which depends entirely on how the blocks are fitted together), (b) erosion of the sea bed causing an undermining of the foundations, and (c) movement of the whole breakwater either backwards or by overturning as the result of the wave forces acting on the face of the breakwater. A recorded instance of this type of failure was that of the blockwork breakwater at Wick Harbour,

Scotland. This breakwater was designed by a very experienced engineer in the mid-19th century, but was destroyed soon afterwards. Because of its location and alignment the breakwater was parallel to the dominant wave front, and Stevenson[24] described how a succession of large waves slewed round a block of masonry estimated at 2600 tons. Caisson breakwaters are also liable to fail either by undermining of the foundations causing the caisson to fall seawards, or by backwards movement or overturning due to wave forces. Because it is a much more loosely constructed structure, a rubble–mound breakwater fails in a totally different manner. As the wave height increases, the individual rocks of the armour layer gradually move more and more until they either fracture, or are plucked out of the assembly, usually to roll down the rubble slope. As the wave height increases further, more and more rocks or blocks are removed, allowing the rubble core to be washed away. At some stage in this process the whole armour layer may also become fluidised and slide down the rubble slope *en masse*. For a rubble–mound breakwater therefore, its stability (or its resistance to damage) depends on a long list of parameters,[25] including such items as:

— armour block shape, weight, density and strength;
— inter-block friction and interlocking;
— armour layer packing density and permeability;
— height and slope of breakwater.

Despite intensive research over many years the importance of most of these parameters is still not fully understood, and the most widely used formula for the initial design of the breakwater armour groups all but three of these parameters into an empirically derived damage coefficient K_D. This Hudson formula[26] for the minimum stable weight (W) of rocks

$$W = \frac{\gamma_s H^3}{K_D (S_r - 1)^3 \cot \beta}$$

(where γ_s is the specific weight of armour material, H the wave height, S_r the specific gravity of armour units relative to the local fluid and β the slope of the breakwater face) also takes no account of a wide range of wave parameters except wave height. Thus the wave period, the shape of the wave energy/frequency spectrum, the direction of the waves relative to the breakwater, etc., are not represented. It is clear therefore that rubble–mound breakwaters have to be designed very much on the basis of past performance and/or scale model studies. It is also apparent that any model should reproduce as closely as possible the details of breakwater construction and of the wave climate to which it will be subjected.

The Hudson equation was developed originally for rock-armoured breakwaters. However rock is very scarce in many parts of the world and is also very difficult to obtain in sizes much greater than about 10t. To overcome these difficulties, coastal engineers in the second half of the 19th and first half of the 20th century turned to large concrete cubes or rectangular blocks, in some cases weighing up to about 100 tons. In 1950, however, a French company (Neyrpic Hydraulic Laboratory) invented the 'Tetrapod' breakwater armour unit (Fig. 12). Rock and

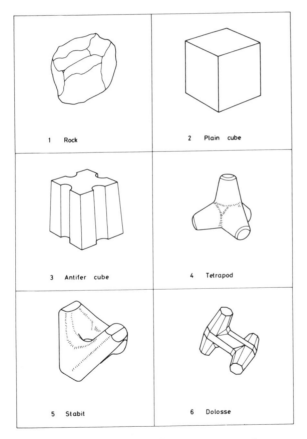

FIG. 12. Common breakwater armour units.

concrete cubes rely for their resistance to movement under wave attack mainly on weight, and to a lesser extent on friction with adjacent blocks. The protruding arms of tetrapods, however, cause the armour units to partially interlock with each other, thus increasing their resistance to wave attack. For a given wave height, therefore, tetrapods can be significantly lighter than rock or cube armouring, being typically about half their weight. Following the example of the tetrapod, many engineers since have attempted to design more and more efficient armour units, in terms of reducing the weight required to resist a given wave height. There are probably about 40 such designs in existence, but Fig. 12 shows the most commonly used designs, numbered in approximate order of increasing interlocking properties, and hence reducing weight requirements. However it can be seen that this reduction in weight was achieved at the expense of greater fragility.

Most engineers did not appreciate the full significance of fragility until the major failure of the breakwater at Sines, Portugal.[27] This breakwater was armoured with 42 t dolosse units on a slope of 1:1·5. Laboratory tests around the world for many different projects had shown that the dolosse was very effective in resisting wave attack, with some researchers claiming that it need be as little as one-sixth of the weight of the equivalent rock armour. However all those tests had been carried out with unbreakable model dolosse. Although the exact cause of the Sines breakwater failure has never been established, it was found that almost every one of the dolosse had fractured. In so doing they had lost their interlocking capabilities, and because they were so much lighter than rock their weight alone was totally inadequate to resist the wave attack.

Since the failure of the Sines breakwater many aspects of breakwater design have been seriously questioned. In particular much more attention has been paid to unit fragility, to look at the impact forces which different units can withstand before fracture, to examine ways of reducing thermal cracking during the manufacture of these concrete units, and to make an assessment of why very large units appeared to fracture much more easily than smaller units. For example, dolosse units had previously been used on many different breakwaters before Sines, with considerable success, but in smaller sizes. As a result of these activities the fashion in breakwater design has now reversed almost back to 'square one', with the use of very much bulkier and hence less fragile units, such as the 'antifer' cube. Even for units as bulky as this, however, the possibility of breakage is being assessed, and a recent suggestion is to insert a cylindrical hole down the centre of the cube to assist concrete curing and reduce the likelihood of internal cracking during manufacture. However, provided this question of armour unit fragility is continually borne in mind, there is no reason to shun completely the use of the more efficient armour units, because in many situations they offer considerable advantages over bulkier units, and there are many breakwaters where they have been completely successful.

Despite the discussion above of the different types of armour units, the overall design of the breakwater requires many other aspects to be considered. As with the harbour itself, they relate to the operational performance of the breakwater, as well as the ability to withstand severe storms without serious damage. As far as operational performance is concerned, the items to be considered include wave run-up and run-down on the seaward face, wave overtopping, wave transmission through the breakwater, and wave reflections from it. Data on wave run-up and run-down are required to give some idea of the crest height for the breakwater, and also to indicate the extent of the area which requires the greatest armour protection. Surprisingly, there is very little data available on the run-up and run-down of random waves on breakwaters protected with different types of armour, although recent work is now beginning to remedy this situation. Information on wave overtopping is required for two reasons — firstly there may well be reclaimed areas behind the breakwater, which will need well-designed drains to remove the overtopping water, whose quantity must therefore be estimated. Secondly, this water can damage the lee side of the breakwater, and also generate waves inside the harbour. Again there is very little information readily available which enables overtopping quantities to be assessed. For wave transmission through the breakwater, mathematical models are available for estimating purposes, but for wave reflection very little information has been published. Wave reflection is important because of the increased wave heights which may be caused at the entrance to the harbour.

For the breakwater to withstand severe storms without serious damage, each portion of the breakwater must be closely examined. Firstly the toe of the seaward face, which supports the bottom row of armour units, must be designed to stay in place during the storm. Those armour units on the seaward face must also be chosen to move as little as possible, and the underlayers must be large enough not to migrate through the gaps in the armour layer, while at the same time preventing the core from leaching out. Similarly the backface of the breakwater must withstand wave forces without movement. The details of the crest of the breakwater can also have an important bearing on the breakwater stability. If it includes a wave return wall then the wave forces on that wall will tend to slide it backwards, and at the same time the reflected waves will tend to make the armour units at the top of the seaward slope less stable. On the other hand, a well designed crest wall detail can be used to throw the overtopping water back away from the backface of the breakwater, to fall relatively harmlessly into the water, instead of impinging directly onto the backface armour. As well as examining each portion of the breakwater, the geotechnical stability of the complete rubble–mound ought also to be considered. At present this is only done on the basis of very approximate steady state calculations, although recently much more sophisticated calculations have been carried out for the reconstruction of the Sines breakwater referred to earlier.

From the foregoing it can be seen that there are many aspects of breakwater design where there is very little information readily available to assist the engineer. As a result, scale models have been used for decades as an aid in designing breakwaters (Fig. 13). Apart from a tendency

FIG. 13. Flume studies on Douglas Harbour Breakwater, Isle of Man (scale 1:40).

towards the use of much larger models, the two major developments in the last few years have been the use of random wave generators in place of regular wavemakers, and a much greater attention to the assessment of damage occurring to the breakwater. The use of random waves in breakwater testing developed in parallel with harbour models, but for different reasons. In applying the Hudson formula it is not at all clear whether it should refer to the maximum wave height, mean wave height or significant wave height (which is the normal interpretation). Since the weight of armour unit required to resist movement is proportional to the cube of wave height, in a random train of waves reproduction of the magnitude and frequency of occurrence of the highest waves are important. It has also been observed that groups of moderate waves sometimes cause more damage than a single large wave, so it is also important that the occurrence of wave groups should be correctly reproduced. For rock-armoured breakwaters all the test results have shown that wave period is not important (hence its omission from the Hudson equation, which was originally developed for rock breakwaters). However, wave period is believed to be important for some concrete armour units, and therefore the amount of wave energy present at each wave period is essential. Similarly, the correct reproduction of the wave directional energy spectrum may be important, although little is known of this as yet. All these requirements for the wave climate are achieved using the method of Gilbert et al.[16] referred to earlier. The model waves which are generated are pseudo-random to the extent that a sequence of waves can be generated having random distribution of wave heights, periods and phases, but the particular wave sequence can be repeated. This has the significant advantage that comparative tests can be run for different breakwater (or harbour) designs using exactly the same sequence of waves. Most of the major laboratories of the world have now realised the importance of using random waves for breakwater testing, and have installed random wave generators in their channels and wave basins.

Apart from random waves, the other major development in breakwater testing has been the assessment of damage. Although this was already receiving more detailed attention, the massive failure of the breakwater at Sines, Portugal in February 1978 triggered an explosion of research efforts in this field. To explain the background to this effort, it is necessary to explain how model breakwaters are normally constructed. Referring back to Fig. 11 for a typical cross-section of a rubble–mound breakwater, normally the rock forming the core and underlayers is modelled according to the basic geometric scale, and it is laid in the model to the correct porosity. The specific gravity of the rock is unchanged if both the actual breakwater and the model breakwater are both either in salt water or freshwater. Usually, however, the real breakwater is in the sea, and the model breakwater is in freshwater. Since the submerged weight is important, the specific gravity has to be adjusted accordingly. The crown wall is modelled geometrically and also to the correct specific gravity. Modelling of the armour layer is probably the most important part of the breakwater, involving both the reproduction of the armour units themselves, and of the methods and patterns of placing them. Ideally the units should have the correct shape, size, specific gravity, surface roughness and strength. The first four are easily reproduced, but it is extremely difficult to scale down the strength of the concrete while still retaining the correct specific gravity. Considerable attempts have been made to achieve this ideal, notably in Canada,[28] but in the vast majority of models either micro-concrete or compounded plastics are used in armour unit manufacture, resulting in units with grossly exaggerated strength compared to full sized armour. In traditional model tests of breakwater stability, damage to a breakwater for given model storm conditions was expressed in terms of the number of armour units which were totally dislodged from the armour layer in a given time. However, this assumes that the armour unit remains intact at all times (which of course it does in the model). With the original rock-armoured breakwaters this was probably a reasonable assumption, but with the more fragile concrete units it is now known that breakage can occur at wave heights lower than those required to pluck the units out of the armour layer. Because this breakage cannot be reproduced in the model, very much greater attention has to be paid to the movements of the armour units before they reach the stage where they are totally dislodged. For example, the movement of each individual unit could be categorised[25] as:

0—no discernible movement
R—unit seen to be rocking, but not permanently displaced
1—unit displaced by up to $0.5 D$
2—unit displaced by between 0.5 and $1.0 D$
3—unit displaced by more than $1.0 D$

where D is a typical dimension of the armour unit (possibly its height, or the height of its equivalent weight cube), and category 3 corresponds closely with the traditional 'extraction' of the unit from the armour layer. Category R can be determined visually either by observation during the test run, or by analysis of video records or cine film. The other damage categories can be determined easily by close examination of photographs of the breakwater face taken immediately before and after the test run. For example, if these photographs are taken from exactly the same viewpoint, then they can be printed to the same scale on translucent paper and the prints overlaid. The units which have moved then appear to be óut of focus, and the amount of movement can be scaled off. The number of units falling into each category is counted and the result expressed as a percentage of the number of units present in the armour layer (Fig. 14). Unfortunately there is not as yet any uniform standard

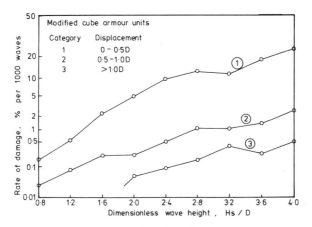

FIG. 14. Example of model results of armour layer damage.

for categorising the damage in this way, and at present the choice of movement limits for each category is arrived at by discussion between the design engineer, the concrete technologist and the modeller. These limits depend on the amount of movement which a particular type of armour unit is expected to be able to withstand before fracture. The example categories listed above were for tetrapods and antifer cubes, and different categories might well be needed for more slender armour units.

As well as checking the stability of the breakwater, the model tests can also provide data on the general performance of the breakwater. Run-up and draw-down in the breakwater can be measured by special gauges fitted to the armoured face (if possible), or can be determined by analysing a video record of the test to determine the percentage number of waves which exceed certain specified levels. Either of these methods

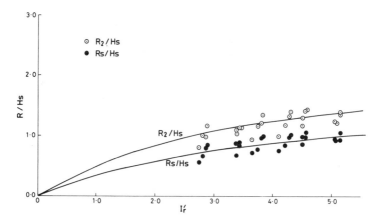

FIG. 15. Wave run-up on a tetrapod-armoured slope.

enables the run-up or draw-down statistics to be presented — for example to give the 'significant' run-up (R_s, defined in the same way as significant wave height) or the 'two-per-cent' run-up (R_2) (Fig. 15).[29] (In Fig. 15 the I_r' denotes the Irribarren number modified for random waves

$$I_r' = \tan \beta / \sqrt{H_s/L_0}$$

where L_0 is the deepwater wavelength $g \, T_p^2/2\pi$ and T_p is the wave period at the peak of the wave energy spectrum.) Wave reflections from the breakwater, and wave transmission through it can be measured with a series of three or four wave probes. If the probes are placed in front of the breakwater at a specified distance apart then using the method suggested by Kajima[30] both the incident wave spectrum and the reflected wave spectrum can be identified. Dividing the various components of the reflected spectrum by the equivalent components of the incident wave spectrum then gives the spectrum of wave reflection coefficient over all wave periods. Similarly, dividing the transmitted wave spectrum by the incident spectrum gives the spectrum of transmission coefficient.

For the determination of wave overtopping, two options are generally available. Firstly, as an extension of the wave run-up measurements, the number of waves which run up and over the crest can be determined. Alternatively, the water which overtops the crest can be collected over a fixed time, and its volume measured to determine the mean rate of overtopping.

Taking account of the various uses to which model testing can be put, a typical series of model studies is likely to encompass:

(a) Outline test in a wave flume to obtain a rough estimate of the performance of a typical cross-section of the breakwater under design storm conditions and to identify critical features of the design. Various modifications can be examined to determine which is the most promising design.

(b) Detailed tests in a wave flume to refine the most promising design and to subject it to a range of wave heights, water levels, spectral shapes, etc.

(c) Detailed tests in a wave basin to examine the performance of the breakwater roundhead, the performance of the breakwater trunk under angled wave attack and any other three-dimensional problems.

(d) Construction stage tests to examine possible damage if the contractor is unlucky enough to experience a moderate or severe storm during the course of construction.

Obviously all these model studies of breakwater stability and performance are not cheap, because they require fairly expensive equipment, and are at the same time fairly labour-intensive. However, the failure of a full-size breakwater would cost incomparably more than the model study, and also there is very little information available on the detailed design of breakwaters without resorting to model testing.

Recent developments in modelling techniques now give greater confidence in the applicability of model results to full sized breakwaters.

5 NAVIGATION ASPECTS

Whenever a new harbour is being designed or an existing one is being modified, consideration must always be given to the navigation of the various vessels which are due to use that harbour. Vessels will wish to enter and leave the harbour under all possible wind, tide and wave conditions, but the harbour authorities must define the range of conditions within which navigation can proceed with complete safety. In defining these conditions they must also take account of the possibility of human error.

As it approaches the harbour, a vessel is subjected to translational forces due to tidal currents acting on the hull and due to windage on the superstructure, and to translational and both vertical and horizontal oscillatory forces due to the waves. In addition, the vessel can be subject to movements caused by other ships passing nearby. To resist these forces the ship's master can only control engine speed and rudder angle, although in some cases he can also call on the assistance of tugs, or perhaps a bow-thruster propellor. The effectiveness of these controls in maintaining the correct route of the vessel will depend partly on the ship's design, but also on the depth of water, and the width and alignment of any approach channel. Clearly with this in mind it is difficult for a harbour designer or even for an experienced shipping pilot to fully appreciate the possible difficulties of navigation into and out of a new harbour. For many years, therefore, it has been the practice to use scale models to assist in predicting navigational difficulties[31,32] or for training pilots assigned to a new port. The techniques used for scale model studies of navigation at harbours fall essentially into two categories — unmanned and manned models. For the unmanned models, a model of the harbour and its approaches is constructed to a relatively small scale, typically between about 1:60 and 1:100. Frequently this would be the same model on which the wave conditions inside the harbour are studied. In any case the model would be equipped with both wave and tidal current generators to reproduce conditions in and around the harbour. Details of the vessels which will use the harbour are then obtained, and a model of a typical vessel is built to the same scale as the harbour model. The ship is modelled carefully so that its mass distribution is correctly reproduced, and is equipped with motor and propellor which together give the correct forward thrust for a specified engine speed. The ship's rudder is also correctly scaled to give the required turning circle at given forward speeds. In order to reproduce any tug forces or windage forces the model ship would usually also be equipped with deck-mounted ducted air fans. Three such fans would be typical, one each at the bow and stern of the vessel mounted across the beam to reproduce lateral tug or wind forces, and one fan usually mounted midships lying along the bow/stern line to reproduce longitudinal forces. For the navigation of this model ship, five controls are therefore available: engine speed, rudder angle, speed and direction of bow, stern and midships fans. These are operated by radio-control, with the operator or pilot being situated alongside the harbour model, or possibly overhead. Starting from a given offshore position, the task of the operator is to navigate the model ship into the harbour, along a prescribed route, for a range of wind, wave and tide conditions. At each stage of the journey readings are taken of the vessel position and heading, engine speed, rudder angle, tug forces, etc., which the operator is using at that time. Also measurements of the underkeel clearance will continually be taken. These readings can either be transmitted by radio, or can be obtained by frequent photography of the model ship and of various dials mounted on deck (Fig. 16). Because the model ship is under

FIG. 16. Radio-controlled ship for navigation studies.

human control each test has to be repeated several times until a fairly representative navigational pattern arises. This, therefore, is a major disadvantage of this technique: the other disadvantage is that the model operator has a totally different viewpoint from the pilot standing on the ship's bridge. Also, because the model time scale equals the square root of the basic model scale, the operator must in theory react about eight to ten times more quickly than the pilot. The advantages of these model studies of navigation are of course that the harbour configuration can be changed rapidly, and pilots can acquaint themselves with possible navigational risks under certain storm conditions.

In order to get over some of the disadvantages mentioned above manned ship models are used.[33] For this a very much larger model of the harbour and its approaches is specially constructed in a large tank or lake, usually with rather less detail of sea bed bathymetry than in the small scale model. Because of the larger scale, the model ship must now be large enough to carry one person, who will be either sitting or lying down so that his view of the harbour approaches is the same as that of the ship's master (Fig. 17). However the scale of these models usually has

FIG. 17. Manned ship model for navigation studies.

to be about 1:20 to 1:40, so the reaction times still have to be five to six times faster in the model than on the real ship. Nevertheless this method has been used to train many pilots in handling large ships entering new harbours.

The use of scale models of both types described above has declined somewhat in recent years, due to the development of 'ship simulators' of varying degrees of complexity and realism. These simulators depend on the ready availability of computers, and on the derivation of mathematical expressions to describe the response of the vessel to different commands and to various winds, waves and currents.

The simplest of these simulators provide a graphic display giving a plan view of the ship, the buoyed approach channel, the harbour layout, and perhaps the attendant tugs.[32–34] To reproduce the track of a vessel as it navigates into the harbour two sets of data are required. Firstly, the depth contours, current patterns and wave conditions are required. Depth contours for a particular site can be input directly into the simulator computer. Current and wave patterns can also be input directly if they are available in sufficient detail. Usually, however, they are not, and have to be separately determined, either by the use of a scale model or increasingly by the use of numerical tidal flow and wave propagation models. Numerical models are much easier to adapt to different sites, and can sometimes be programmed to run on the same computer as the simulator. The other set of data required is the response of the ship, both in terms of its motion arising from hydrodynamic forces, and also of its reactions to propellor thrust, rudder angle, tug forces, etc., under different circumstances. In many cases these data cannot be predicted for a given vessel: in these situations recourse has to be made to data available for a broadly similar ship, or again a scale model has to be built and tested, and then subjected to a range of conditions to obtain the required data. In particular, for studying navigation into harbours, the response of the ship has to be determined for a range of underkeel clearances, since this has a significant effect on vessel behaviour.

When all the required data are available in the simulator for a specific site, it can then be used in two ways, just as the scale models described earlier. For the design of new ports the simulator can be programmed to run on 'automatic pilot', and the track of a given vessel as it is navigated into the harbour can be recorded for a wide range of wind, wave and tidal conditions. Because no human intervention is required no variability is obtained and the simulator can be run at many times real time. Each condition needs therefore be studied only once, and modifications to the design of the harbour and its approaches can be quickly evaluated for their effect on safe navigation. The other way in which these computer simulators can be used is for training pilots and ship's masters: while undoubtedly assisting pilots in this respect, these graphical simulators do suffer from the fact that the pilot has a completely different perception than he would get from the vessel's bridge. To overcome this substantial disadvantage more sophisticated ship simulators have been developed,[35] bearing a close resemblance to aircraft simulators used for training airline pilots. In these more complex simulators the vital parts of the vessel's bridge are constructed as a mock-up, with all the usual controls. The windows of the bridge are replaced by TV projector screens. The whole bridge structure is mounted on a large vibrating platform, to simulate propellor vibrations which have been found to be a very important sensory clue. The visual scene is generated from a computer software database, and is projected onto several screens giving viewing angles varying from about 120° to 200° depending on the exact simulator. These picture generators can reproduce both day and nighttime views, and can also include passing ships.

Clearly these more complex simulators require all the data on water depths, winds, waves and tides, as well as all the data on the ship's response to different environmental conditions and control commands which are required by the simpler simulators. In addition, however, a considerable amount of data is required to produce the various views which the pilot would observe during the different navigational manoeuvres. This can be a considerable task, working from drawings, photographs and charts and taking perhaps several months to achieve.

These more complex simulators are used predominantly to train pilots, either people relatively new to pilotage, or experienced pilots being introduced to a new port. They are rarely used for assessing different designs of new ports. For this purpose very many runs would be necessary to establish the swept area of a number of slightly varying ship's tracks, and it would be prohibitive in terms of time and expense to use the simulator in real time. The simpler simulators described earlier are therefore used for that purpose, and only when the design is more-or-less finalised is the more complex system brought into use.

6 SEDIMENT MOTION

Whenever a harbour is being designed at a particular location, considerable thought must be given to the sediment movement in and around the harbour. In particular the whole question of siltation must be considered, both in the harbour itself, and also in any of the approach channels. Maintenance dredging may well contribute a significant portion of the running costs of the harbour, and if possible the siltation rates should therefore be quantified. The approach channel configuration should also be examined to see if a slight re-design might reduce the siltation. Apart from the harbour itself, the sediment movement on the adjacent coastline will be affected, possibly resulting in a realignment of the beaches. These beach changes should also be predicted, because possible erosion on the downdrift side may cause problems at the root of the harbour breakwater, as well as threaten the coastal defences. The accretion of beaches on the updrift side may be useful in providing reclaimed land for further port development, but if the accretion is too great then sediment will eventually pass around the breakwater and into the harbour.

6.1 Coastal Changes

Of the two parts of this sediment movement problem (predicting siltation rates and forecasting coastline changes), the second part is considerably easier to solve at present.[36] This is because the transport of sediment along beaches is relatively well understood, in the global sense at least. Waves breaking at an angle to the shoreline cause sediment to move along the coastline, and because there is usually a dominant wave direction then there will normally be a net drift of material in one direction. If any structure, such as a breakwater, is built on the coastline then the physical barrier to the sediment movement will cause accretion updrift, and erosion downdrift of that structure. Assuming that an equation can be found which relates the wave conditions and the sediment transport rate along the beach, a very simple mathematical model can be developed to predict how the plan shape of the beach changes when a breakwater is constructed.[37] Several equations have been proposed, but a typical equation for the alongshore transport rate (Q) is[38]

$$Q = \frac{K}{\gamma_s^1}(EC_g)_b\left(\sin 2\alpha_b - 3 \cdot 24\frac{dH_b}{ds}\cot\beta\cos\alpha_b\right)$$

where E is the energy density of the waves ($\rho g H^2/8$); C_g is the group velocity of the waves; γ_s^1 is the *in situ* submerged weight of the beach material; α is the angle between the wave crests and the beach contours; β is the mean slope of the beach (above the horizontal); s is the alongshore distance; and subscript b refers to breaking wave conditions.

The sediment transport rate Q is in units of volume/time, and the coefficient K is therefore non-dimensional, with a value which varies according to the type of beach. For straight sandy beaches Komar and Inman[39] suggested that $K = 0.385$, based on field measurements of transport rate and wave conditions. It should be pointed out that this equation gives the bulk flow rate of the sediment, that is, it gives the total alongshore transport rate without attempting to describe whether the sediment is transported along the surf zone, along the breaker line, or at any other location. More complicated equations will undoubtedly become available to include this distribution of sediment movement, and these equations will be referred to when discussing harbour siltation. For the time being, however, this relatively simple and fairly reliable equation is used.

The second equation necessary for setting up the mathematical model is that of conservation of mass, namely

$$\frac{\delta Q}{\delta s} + \frac{\delta A}{\delta t} = 0$$

where A is the cross-sectional area of beach and t is time.

These two equations can then be solved to give the rate of change of beach plan shape, assuming that the wave conditions are known. Essentially the beach is divided into lengths. From the beach direction and the wave direction and height the alongshore transport rate is calculated at each end of that particular length of beach. If more sediment enters the updrift end of the length of beach than leaves at the downdrift end, the beach must be accreting. Similarly if more sediment is leaving than entering, beach erosion must occur. In most models the beach is assumed to maintain the same cross-sectional shape, so that as the beach erodes or accretes at different rates, the beach plan shape changes. The angle between the breaking waves and the shoreline is therefore altered, and the alongshore transport rate is recalculated.

In carrying out these calculations it is assumed that the wave conditions can be predicted at frequent intervals along the beach. This is no great problem, relying mainly on wave refraction modelling, but near to a breakwater wave conditions may be quite complicated due to diffraction around the breakwater head, reflections off the breakwater, etc., and these effects have also to be included in the determination of the wave conditions.

Although these mathematical models can be used to predict short term changes in the plan of beaches, they are normally used to predict changes that are likely to occur over periods of several years. The main reason for this is that no attempt is made to quantify the onshore/offshore movements of sediment, which are essentially cyclical, seasonal phenomena. Although this is a major simplification, experience has shown that this very simple model gives reasonable results for most practical purposes. As with any model, the accuracy of the predictions is of course improved if there exists some historical data which quantifies beach changes which have occurred in the past and which can be used to calibrate the model (Fig. 18).

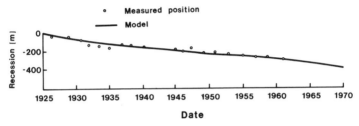

FIG. 18. Measured and calculated positions of the beach east of Port Said, Suez Canal.

6.2 Harbour Siltation

For many coastal harbours it is necessary to provide an approach channel, which often has to be maintained by dredging. This channel has to be sufficiently deep for the draught of vessels using the harbour, it has to be sufficiently wide to allow safe passage and the alignment has to be carefully chosen to balance out the costs of the initial dredging and any future maintenance dredging, as well as providing an easy navigation approach into the harbour. Predicting the siltation rate in such an approach channel is extremely difficult, because the physical processes which determine sediment transport rates in such situations are still far from understood. Several different empirical formulae exist for predicting sediment transport rates under the action of currents alone, and there is a reasonable quantity of measured data available with which to compare these formulae. One or two empirical formulae also exist for predicting transport rates under wave action alone, although there are very few measurements for comparison. However, the most common situation for harbour approach channels is for both waves and currents to be present in varying degrees, with wave heights in particular changing rapidly. During severe storms the amount of sediment in suspension is considerably enhanced, and infilling of the channel can occur at an alarming rate. For these situations various authors have suggested ways in which the empirical formulae for sediment transport due either to waves or to currents acting alone can be modified to take account of their joint action. These attempts have been based mainly on the observation that steady currents generally have to be quite high to bring sediment into suspension, but once material is in suspension it is transported rapidly. However quite low waves can suspend sediment, but that sediment is transported very slowly. When waves and currents act simultaneously it is therefore assumed that waves act mainly to increase the suspended sediment concentration, which the currents then transport. Using this idea, Bijker[40] assumed that the only effect of the waves is to increase the shear stress at the sea bed, and presented a formula for this increased shear stress, based on model tests. Swart[41] later developed this formula for general application, giving the shear stress due to combined current and wave action as

$$\tau_{cw} = \tau_c [1 + \tfrac{1}{2}(\xi v_0/V)^2]^2$$

where τ_c is the shear stress due to currents alone; v_0 is the amplitude of the horizontal orbital velocity at the sea bed and V is the depth-averaged current.

The factor ξ is defined as $\xi = C_f \sqrt{(f_w/2g)}$ where C_f is the well known Chézy friction factor for currents alone, and f_w is the Jonsson friction factor[42] for waves alone.

Swart then substituted this expression into the Ackers–White formula for sediment transport due to currents acting alone, and then compared computed transport rates and those measured in small scale laboratory tests. Although there was considerable scatter, the general agreement was quite good. This so-called SWANBY sediment transport expression implicitly assumes that the waves are weak relative to the currents. Grant and Madsen[43] took the opposite approach by assuming that the current is weak relative to the waves. This was justified by the argument that even when the depth-averaged current is larger than the maximum wave orbital velocity the smaller scale of the wave boundary layer makes the wave velocity dominant near the sea bed. The equations of motion of the combined wave and current flow were solved both outside and inside the bottom boundary layer. The solution is obtained by assuming that the convective acceleration terms were negligible, and using an eddy viscosity which was assumed to vary linearly with height above the sea bed and taken to be constant throughout the wave period. The results of these theoretical calculations showed that the currents above the wave boundary layer will feel a greater resistance due to the presence of the waves, which will result in a steepening of the velocity profile. Since the suspended concentration is greatest close to the bed where the current profile is reduced the most it is clear that this effect can significantly alter the sediment transport rate.

Unfortunately the extreme difficulties of measuring sediment transport in detail during storms mean that there are very little full scale data available with which to calibrate or check the various formulae which have been suggested. However, the few measurements which have been made demonstrate quite clearly the great extent to which waves enhance sediment transport. For example, measurements were carried out in the Thames Estuary, England,[44] at a location where the water depths average about 4 m, and tidal velocities reach a depth-averaged maximum of about 0·8 m/s. The site was fairly well sheltered, and during the period of measurements the wave heights never exceeded 1·0 m. Nevertheless, even with these relatively small waves the sand transport rate increased by factors up to about 400 times greater than the transport rate at the same current strength without waves (Fig. 19). The transport rate with waves and currents S_{cw} seemed to be greater than that with currents alone S_c in the ratio given by

$$S_{cw} = S_c (\bar{v}'/v_c)^2 \text{ for } \bar{v}' > v_c$$

where $\bar{v}'$ is the rms orbital velocity at the sea bed, and v_c is some critical value of the orbital velocity below which wave action seems to have little effect on sediment transport. For the fine sand at the particular site the critical value seemed to be about 0·05 m/s, corresponding with wind-waves with a significant height of about 0·7 m.

Whichever formula is eventually proved to be correct, it is clear to many people that the best way to estimate siltation in a harbour approach channel is by the use of such a formula in a mathematical model. The difficulties of scaling the sea bed materials in a physical model are legion, especially where most of the sediment transport is expected to be material moving in suspension, which will usually be the case when waves and currents are present together. Mathematical models have been in use for some years now to simulate sediment transport in rivers and estuaries, both to estimate changes in water depths following some man-made alteration to the flow, and to calculate

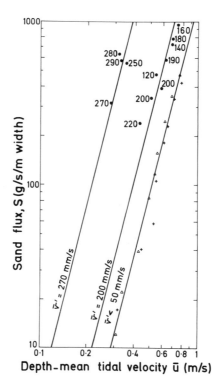

Fig. 19. Effect of waves on sand transport by currents. Sand flux for group A tides.

siltation in dredged channels. In principle these models can be adapted quite simply to the case of waves and currents. For channel siltation calculations they consist of defining the wave and current conditions both in the channel itself and in the shallower areas alongside the channel. Using a sediment transport formula, the sediment transport rate is then calculated at each position, assuming that the flow conditions and the sediment transport rate are in equilibrium. In the simplest models the rate of infill of sediment into the channel is then taken as the difference between the sediment transport rates inside and outside the channel. However in relatively narrow dredged channels the suspended sediment may not have sufficient time, as it traverses the channel, to adjust to the lower equilibrium concentration demanded, especially for finer sediments. The simple model therefore overestimates siltation rates in such cases. More complex models have been developed for current-induced siltation which allow for the rate of change of suspended concentrations as the flow crosses the channel,[45,46] and attempts have been made to use such models for siltation due to waves and currents.[47] However their accuracy in such situations is rather doubtful, and in any case such refinement is perhaps superfluous at present because of the uncertainty over the correct sediment formula to use. Some engineers have adopted the practice of running the mathematical siltation model for a variety of different formulae, and then using the range of siltation rates obtained to make their best estimates of the maintenance dredging required. Although a lot of development has occurred in recent years in the prediction of siltation rates, it is clear from this discussion that much more development is needed, both in gathering data with which to validate existing formulae, and to obtain a better understanding of the physics involved, and hence hopefully a more accurate and better founded expression.

REFERENCES

1. DRIVER, J. S. A guide to sea wave recording *Report No. 103*, Institute of Oceanographic Sciences, Wormley, England, 1980.
2. SHUTTLER, R. M. The wave climate in the Severn Estuary. *Proc. Severn Barrage Symposium.* Inst. Civ. Eng. London, 1981.
3. MARINE INFORMATION AND ADVISORY SERVICE *MIAS Catalogue of wave data*, 2nd edn, Institute of Oceanographic Sciences, Wormley, Surrey, England, 1982.
4. ABERNETHY, C. L. and GILBERT, G. Refraction of wave spectra *Report No. IT 117*, Hydraulics Research Station, Wallingford, England, May, 1975.
5. BRAMPTON, A. H. A computer method for wave refraction *Report No. IT 172*, Hydraulics Research Station, Wallingford, England, September, 1981.
6. BRAMPTON, A. H. and BELLAMY, P. H. Models of wave energy transformation near a coast. *Proc. 2nd Int. Symposium on Wave and Tidal Energy*, BHRA Fluid Engineering, Cambridge, England, September, 1981.
7. WANG, H. and YANG, W. C. Wave spectral transformation measurements at Sylt, North Sea, *Coastal Eng.*, 5 (1) (1981) 1–34.
8. A finite difference wave refraction model *Report No. EX 1163*, Hydraulics Research Ltd, Wallingford, England, April, 1984.
9. US ARMY, *Shore Protection Manual* US Army Coastal Engineering Research Centre, 1984.
10. DARBYSHIRE, M. and DRAPER, L. Forecasting wind generated sea waves. *Engineering*, 195 (1963), pp. 482–4.
11. HASSELMANN, K., ROSS, D. B., MULLER, P. and BELL, W. Parametric wave prediction model. *J. Phys. Ocean*, 6 (2) (1976), pp. 200–28.

12. EWING, J. A., WEARE, T. J. and WORTHINGTON, B. A. A hindcast study of extreme wave conditions in the North Sea. *J. Geophys. Res.*, **84** (C9) (1979), pp. 5739–47.

13. BOWERS, E. C. The modelling of waves and their effects in harbours. Paper 11, *Hydraulic Modelling in Maritime Engineering*. Thomas Telford Ltd, London, 1982.

14. BRAMPTON, A. H. Surface waves over a step *Report No. IT 170*, Hydraulics Research Station, Wallingford, England, November, 1977.

15. BOWERS, E. C. Long period disturbances due to wave groups *Proc. 17th Coastal Eng. Conf.*, Sydney, March, 1980.

16. GILBERT, G., THOMPSON, D. M. and BREWER, A. J. Design curves for regular and random wave generators. *J. Hydraul. Res.*, **9** (2) (1971), pp. 163–93.

17. GRAVESEN, H. and SORENSEN, T. Stability of rubble mound breakwaters. *Proc. 23rd PIANC Conf.*, Leningrad, 1977.

18. BATTJES, J. A. A review of methods to establish the wave climate for breakwater design. *Coastal Eng.*, **8** (2) (1984), pp. 141–60.

19. BOWERS, E. C. *Model simulation of ship movements*. Dock and Harbour Authority, **58**, August, 1977.

20. BOWERS, E. C. and SOUTHGATE, H. N. Wave diffraction, refraction and reflection. A comparison between a physical model and a mathematical model. *Report No. IT 240*, Hydraulics Research Station, Wallingford, England, November, 1982.

21. SOUTHGATE, H. N. Ray methods for combined refraction and diffraction problems. *Report No. IT 214*, Hydraulics Research Station, Wallingford, England, July, 1981.

22. PEREGRINE, D. H. Long waves on a beach. *J.Fluid Mech.*, **27**(4)(1967), pp. 715–827.

23. ABBOTT, M. B., PETERSEN, H. M. and SKOVGAARD, O. On the numerical modelling of short waves in shallow water. *J. Hydraul. Res.*, **16** (3) (1978), pp. 173–204.

24. STEVENSON, T. *Design and construction of harbours and breakwaters*. Adam and Charles Black, Edinburgh, 1874.

25. OWEN, M. W. and ALLSOP, N. W. H. Hydraulic modelling of rubble mound breakwaters. Paper No 6, *Breakwaters — Design and Construction*. Thomas Telford Ltd, London, 1983.

26. HUDSON, R. Y. Concrete armour units for protection against wave attack. *Misc. Paper H-74-2f*, US Army Engineers, Waterways Experiment Station, Vicksburg, Mississippi, January, 1974.

27. BAIRD, W. F., CALDWELL, J. M., EDGE, B. L., MAGOON, O. T. and TREADWELL, D. D. Report on the damages to the Sines breakwater, Portugal. *Proc. 17th Coastal Eng. Conf.*, Sydney, 1980.

28. TIMCO, G. W. The development, properties and production of strength-reduced model armour units. *Report No. LTR-HY-92*. Hyd. Lab., National Res Council, Canada, November, 1981.

29. ALLSOP, N. W. H., FRANCO, L. and HAWKES, P. J. Probability distributions and levels of wave run-up on armoured rubble slopes. *Int. Conf. Numerical and Hyd. Modelling of Ports and Harbours*, Birmingham, England, March, 1985.

30 KAJIMA, R. Estimation of an incident wave spectrum in the sea influenced of reflection *Coastal Eng. in Japan*, **12** (1969), pp. 9–16.

31. DAND, I. W. Model techniques used to study ship behaviour in canals and channels. Paper 3, *Hydraulic Modelling in Maritime Engineering*. Thomas Telford Ltd, London, 1982.

32. BLAAUW, H. G., KOEMAN, J. W. and STRATING, J. *Nautical studies in port and channel design*. Part 1, Dock and Harbour Authority, **63**, May, 1982. Part 2, Dock and Harbour Authority, **63**, August, 1982.

33. DEMENET, P. F., GARRAUD, P. and GRAFF, J. *New computer-aided systems for harbour engineering studies*. Dock and Harbour Authority, **64**, Dec. 1983.

34. TOMLINSON, P. *An aid to port design*. Dock and Harbour Authority, **63**, Dec, 1982.

35. McCALLUM, I. R. *Simulation techniques for harbour design and operation*. Dock and Harbour Authority, **62**, August, 1981.

36. PRICE, W. A., BRAMPTON, A. H. and OWEN, M. W. The prediction of shoreline changes following the construction of coastal harbours — *Proc 25th Congress Permanent International Association of Navigational Congresses*, Edinburgh, 1981.

37. PRICE, W. A., TOMLINSON, K. W. and WILLIS, D. H. Predicting changes in the plan shape of beaches. *Proc. 13th Coastal Eng. Conf.*, Vancouver, 1972.

38. OZASA, H. and BRAMPTON, A. H. Mathematical modelling of beaches backed by sea walls *Coastal Eng.*, **4** (1) (1980), pp. 47–63.

39. KOMAR, P. D. and INMAN, D. L. Longshore transport on beaches. *J. Geophys. Res.* **75** (30) (1970), pp. 5914–27.

40. BIJKER, E. W. The increase of bed shear in a current due to wave motion. *Proc. 10th Coastal Eng. Conf.* Tokyo, 1966.

41. SWART, D. W. Predictive equations regarding coastal transports. *Proc. 15th Coastal Eng. Conf.*, Honolulu, 1976.

42. JONSSON, I. G. Wave boundary layers and friction factors. *Proc. 10th Coastal Eng. Conf.*, Tokyo, 1966.

43. GRANT, W. D. and MADSEN, S. Combined wave and current interaction with a rough bottom *J. Geophys. Res.*, **84** (C4) (1979), pp. 1797–1808.

44. OWEN, M. W. and THORN, M. F. C. Effect of waves on sand transport by currents, Paper No. 76, *Proc. 16th Int. Conf. Coastal Eng.*, Hamburg, 1978.

45. LEAN, G. H. *Estimation of maintenance dredging for navigation channels*. Hydraulics Research Station, Wallingford, England, 1980.

46. KERSSENS, P. J. M. and VAN RIJN, L. V. Model for non-steady suspended sediment transport. *Proc. 17th IAHR Congr.*, Baden-Baden, 1977.

47. BIJKER, E. W. Sedimentation in channels and trenches *Proc. 17th Coastal Eng. Conf.*, Sydney, 1980.

INDEX